ADVANCED POSITIONING, FLOW, AND SENTIMENT ANALYSIS IN COMMODITY MARKETS

Founded in 1807, John Wiley & Sons is the oldest independent publishing company in the United States. With offices in North America, Europe, Australia and Asia, Wiley is globally committed to developing and marketing print and electronic products and services for our customers' professional and personal knowledge and understanding.

The Wiley Trading series features books by traders who have survived the market's ever changing temperament and have prospered – some by reinventing systems, others by getting back to basics. Whether a novice trader, professional or somewhere in-between, these books will provide the advice and strategies needed to prosper today and well into the future.

For more on this series, visit our Web site at www.WileyTrading.com.

ADVANCED POSITIONING, FLOW, AND SENTIMENT ANALYSIS IN COMMODITY MARKETS

Bridging Fundamental and Technical Analysis

SECOND EDITION

Mark J S Keenan

WILEY

This edition first published 2020

© 2020 John Wiley & Sons Ltd

Edition History

Shadwell Publications (for Amazon) (1e, 2018)

Registered office

John Wiley & Sons Ltd, The Atrium, Southern Gate, Chichester, West Sussex, PO19 8SQ, United Kingdom

For details of our global editorial offices, for customer services and for information about how to apply for permission to reuse the copyright material in this book please see our website at www.wiley.com.

Library of Congress Cataloging-in-Publication Data

Names: Keenan, Mark J S, author.

Title: Advanced positioning, flow, and sentiment analysis in commodity
    markets : bridging fundamental and technical analysis / Mark J S Keenan.

Other titles: Positioning analysis in commodity markets

Description: Second edition. | Chichester, West Sussex : Wiley, 2020. |
    First edition published as Positioning analysis in commodity markets by
    Shadewell Publications, 2018. | Includes bibliographical references and
    index.

Identifiers: LCCN 2019027667 (print) | LCCN 2019027668 (ebook) | ISBN
    9781119603825 (cloth) | ISBN 9781119603740 (adobe pdf) | ISBN
    9781119603818 (epub)

Subjects: LCSH: Commodity exchanges—Mathematical models. | Commodity
    futures.

Classification: LCC HG6046 .K43 2020 (print) | LCC HG6046 (ebook) | DDC
    332.64/4—dc23

LC record available at https://lccn.loc.gov/2019027667

LC ebook record available at https://lccn.loc.gov/2019027668

Cover Design: Wiley

Cover Image: © bookzv/Shutterstock

Set in 10/13pts PerpetuaStd by SPi Global, Chennai, India

Printed in Great Britain by Bell & Bain

10 9 8 7 6 5 4 3 2 1

To my wife, Eloïse,
for her continuous support
&
for always being the most incredible person I know.

Mark Keenan is Managing Director, Global Commodities Strategist & Head of Research Asia-Pacific at Société Générale Corporate & Investment Bank (SG CIB) based in Singapore.

With over 20 years of research, trading, and investment experience across all the major energy, metal, agriculture and bulk commodity markets, Mark has worked with corporates, trade houses, investment institutions, and hedge funds to develop, improve, and optimise trading, hedging, and investment solutions. He has specific expertise in quantamental analysis, focusing on supply and demand dynamics in combination with newsflow, sentiment, trading flow, and positioning data to better understand price behaviour and manage risk.

Mark has worked in asset management, risk management, and investment banking in both London and Singapore. He appears regularly on CNBC and Bloomberg television and is quoted widely in global press and media channels.

He has a master's degree in Molecular and Cellular Biochemistry from Oxford University.

Contact details:

mjsk@shadwellresearch.com

ACKNOWLEDGEMENTS

Société Générale, for its support in my writing this book.

Malavika Dinaker and David Schenck, part of the commodity research team in Société Générale and based in Singapore and London respectively, for their input and collaboration on several areas in the book.

Disclaimer

Société Générale (SG) has not, however, endorsed this publication and bears no responsibility in any capacity whatsoever for any of the material in this book. All views, insights, interpretations, and conclusions are the author's own.

Where applicable, all references to any SG research publications are given in the book. This book is based on new material, but also updates and builds on some of the work in the previous book, *Positioning Analysis in Commodity Markets – Bridging Fundamental and Technical Analysis*, by Mark Keenan. Relevant references from the 1st edition are still therefore applicable.

Commodities are real. We did not create them, apart from perhaps corn and electricity, but we have developed ways to find them more effectively and to produce them more efficiently. They are finite and for some perishable, but we have nonetheless still become entirely dependent on them. We know they can cause wars and suffering, yet they can also drive prosperity and growth. They can destroy the environment and, at the same time, be the solution to a better world. They have shaped our history; they determine how nations interact and they will define our future. For all of us, they are and will be an inevitable part of our life.

To understand their behaviour, we need to think about commodities differently. They are not like equities or bonds and do not often form part of the occasionally fragile fabric that binds so many financial assets together. They are not restricted by our rules, our regulations, or our expectations and are instead free to track the ebb and flow of global trade. Prices are mostly always driven by supply and demand fundamentals; they behave intuitively, and these relationships are intuitive and repeatable.

Occasionally, these relationships breakdown and being able to disentangle fundamental price drivers from non-fundamental price drivers can be difficult. Commodities can also become swayed by shifts and trends in sentiment that may be driven by a variety of factors, either exogenous or endogenous. These have the power to decouple prices from their fundamentals for considerable periods of time and sometimes by significant degrees.

For over 20 years, I have tried to better understand commodity price behaviour, and it is indeed extremely challenging. I believe that irrespective of the extent to which non-fundamentals may be driving prices, or the degree to which shifts in sentiment may have caused them to decouple from prices, fundamentals ultimately win. The realignment occurs not only because commodities are tangible goods, but because they exhibit specific behavioural patterns and relationships that are driven by factors linked to physical attributes and structural dynamics within the asset class. Their positive serial correlation, or the strong persistence in changes in these factors, not only drive sustained moves in price, but also provide time for them to be identified and for these relationships to be traded and monetised. This rarely occurs in other asset classes because of the high degree of contemporaneity, meaning that price drivers typically need to be forecasted.

The serial correlation is driven by how commodities are transported and stored – in turn, a product of the extreme differences in the production and consumption locations that characterise commodities. It is also a function of how they are affected by seasonality and weather and their vulnerability to supply shocks. The nature of their demand drivers – our need to eat, our desire to be clothed, our fight to stay warm in winter and cool in summer, our obsession with fuel and power, and our dependency on commodities like metals with their unique and often non-substitutable properties.

The liquidity, depth, and complexity of commodity derivatives markets also allow for different facets of price behaviour to be effectively traded. In addition to directional price changes, the shape of the forward curve, the volatility profile, and the numerous relative relationships between commodities, all increase the optionality of how these relationships can be captured.

I have written this book to provide some hopefully new and alternative insights in an area of analysis largely agnostic to whether fundamentals or non-fundamentals are driving prices. Embracing many of the factors mentioned above that are specific to commodity markets, the approach focuses entirely on how changes in positioning and flow affect price behaviour, and on new and innovative ways to track and evaluate sentiment and behavioural dynamics in the market.

The signals, indicators, models, and analyses presented throughout the book have proved influential in helping clients better understand commodity price behaviour to improve trading, investment, hedging, and risk management strategies. In most cases, these improvements have been significant, but without exception, the analyses and the approach have proven to be fresh, original, unconventional, and intuitive.

Mark Keenan

A companion website accompanies this book. The objective of the site is to provide the reader with an online platform consisting of a wide range of analytical tools that can be customised in a variety of ways. The underlying data will be updated regularly and will cover 24 different commodities and a variety of other data. The analyses may also be downloaded for the site. Each of the analytics is explained in the book. The book and website have been designed to work together.

The website has been designed to run on a desktop computer (PC or MAC), rather than a mobile device. The address of the site is:

www.shadwellanalytics.com.

The online platform

The analytics in the book include trading signals, indicators, models, and analyses. One of the main objectives of the book is to provide all the necessary formulae and explanations of how they can be built and implemented. The purpose of the website is to provide the reader with an online platform where many of the analytics can be run in an online format, customisable for different commodities, different time periods, and in some cases with different variables.

This is made possible by having all the analytics for the website in Tableau, a powerful application primarily for data visualisation, but also for generating 'dashboards', or pages that allow data to be organised and accessed by users in a customisable and interactive framework.[1] For this to work, the analytics also need to be hosted on a Tableau server, which enables all the necessary functionality to be accessed by multiple users simultaneously.

Each of the analytics in the book that have been included on the website have been clearly labelled in the book. To make comparisons between the book and the website identical, Tableau has also been used to generate all the relevant charts and diagrams for the analytics in the book. This also means that everything in the book done in Tableau and included on the website can be replicated online.

---

[1]www.tableau.com.

There are, however, several Tableau charts in the book that have not been included on the website as they are mostly for illustrative purposes rather than analytical tools. These have been clearly labelled in the footnote of each chart as not being included on the website. There are also charts and tables that have been done in Excel that have also not been included on the site. These are also either for illustrative purposes or include specific types of data, such as newsflow data. **These have been clearly labelled in the footnote of each chart as not being included on the website.**

This website also includes some analytics that have not been shown in the book that provide additional background insight and information. They are generally intuitive, and do not require a full explanation as they are similar to other analytics in the book; and in the interest of space, they have been omitted in the book. It is also possible that new or modified analytics will be added to this website going forward. If an explanation is required, this will be given on the site.

A complete list of all the current analytics included on the website can be found under the 'metadata' list at the bottom of the homepage or 'Launchpad'.

The website

A screenshot of the homepage or 'Launchpad' of the companion website is shown below. Each of the analytics can be accessed as a separate page or dashboard by clicking the black buttons next to the respective headings on the right-hand side. Each of the headings corresponds to the name or names of the analytics, as defined in the book. The chapter number where the analytics are explained in the book is also clearly shown alongside in bold.

Launchpad

Advanced Positioning, Flow and Sentiment Analysis in Commodity Markets

by Mark J. S. Keenan

Please select the black buttons on the right to access the relevant Tableau charts from the book. The charts have been organised according to their approximate order of appearance in the book. Additionally, the chapter number in which the chart occurs, has also been highlighted.

Each chart has features that can be customised. These include changing the commodity and selecting different dates or time periods for the analysis. In some cases, changing other parameters such as the trader group is possible.

All charts in the book, that are on this site, have been clearly highlighted in the book beneath each chart. All data is updated regularly.

This site also includes charts and analytics that have not been shown in the book to provide additional insight and information. A complete list of all the analytics included can be found under the "metadata" list below. It is also possible that new charts will be added to this site going forward.

ALL CHARTS AND ANALYTICS ARE EXPLAINED IN THE BOOK

ALL SYMBOLS AND COMMODITY CODES USED ON THIS SITE ARE GIVEN IN THE BOOK IN SECTION 2.4.

Any updates, changes and erratum will be published under the link on the bottom right of the launchpad.

Please contact Mark Keenan if you have any questions (contact details are in the book)

1) PP Net Open Interest Indicator, PP Net Traders Indicator, PP Concentration Indicator -

2) PP Clustering Indicator, Position Size Indicator - **Chapter 4**

3) PP Spreading Indicator - **Chapter 4**

4) DP Indicator, DP Notional Indicator, DP Seasonal Indicator, DP Time Indicator - **Chapter..**

5) DP Relative Indicator - **Chapter 5**

6) DP Indicator (Advanced) - **Chapter 6**

7) DP Net Indicator - **Chapter 5**

8) DP Concentration Indicator, DP Notional Indicator - **Chapter 6**

9) DP Concentration/Clustering Indicator, DP Position Size Indicator - **Chapter 6**

10) DP Price Indicator - **Chapter 6**

11) DP Curve Indicator - **Chapter 6**

12) DP Hedging Indicator - **Chapter 6**

13) DP Factor Indicator - **Chapter 6**

14) DP Currency Indicator - **Chapter 6**

15) DP Fundamental Indicator - **Chapter 6**

16) OBOS Concentration Indicator - **Chapter 7**

17) OBOS Charts - **Chapter 7**

18) OBOS Time Indicator - **Chapter 7**

19) OBOS Net Indicator - **Chapter 7**

20) OBOS Seasonal Indicator - **Chapter 7**

21) DP/OBOS Hybrid Indicator - **Chapter 7**

22) OBOS Clustering Indicator - **Chapter 8**

23) OBOS Position Size Indicator - **Chapter 8**

24) OBOS Hybrid Concentration/Clustering Indicator - **Chapter 8**

25) OBOS Hybrid Concentration/Clustering/Position Size Indicat..

26) OBOS VIX Factor Indicator, OBOS FCI Factor Indicator - **Chapter 8**

27) NDS & DS Sentiment Indices - **Chapter 8**

28) Mismatch Indicator - **Chapter 8**

29) General Commodity Price Chart

Updates, changes and erratum:

By way of an example, the fourth button from the top in the first column on the launchpad is titled:

4) DP Indicator, DP Notional Indicator, DP Seasonal Indicator, DP Time Indicator – **Chapter 5**
Clicking the black button to the right of this heading will access the page or dashboard containing the analytics as shown. Each of these is then explained in Chapter 5.

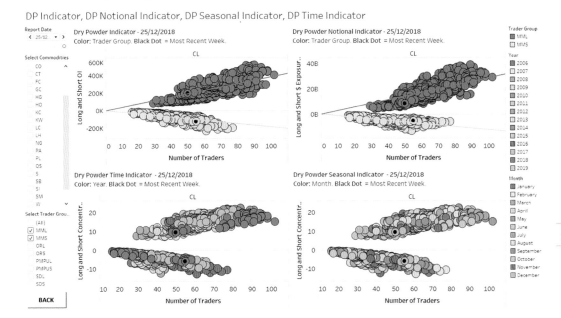

The four analytics are clearly labelled above each of the charts, which are also the same charts used in the book.

On the left-hand side of the page or dashboard, there are three customisable menus. On other pages, there will be different options depending on the type of analytic shown.

1. The top left-hand menu, titled 'Report Date', is both a sliding menu to rapidly move to an approximate date, and also a drop down menu to select an exact date for the analysis. Weekly data back to 20 June 2006 are available. This will be updated regularly as new data is released. Changing the date in this menu will change the date of analysis for all the analytics on this page. On other pages, there may be separate menus for different analytics.
2. The middle left-hand menu, titled 'Select Commodities', allows up to 24 different commodities to be selected either individually or in combination. Looking at different groups of commodities together can be useful for these analytics in particular, but for most of the analytics on the other page, only one commodity can be typically be selected at a time. A key for all the commodity symbols used in the book and on the website is given in Table 2.1. As with the date menu, selecting different commodities will change all the analytics on this page. On other pages, there may be separate menus for different analytics.
3. The bottom left-hand menu, titled 'Select Trader Groups', allows up to eight different trader groups to be selected either individually or in combination. Again, looking at combinations of trader groups together is often useful for these indicators, but for most of the analytics on the

other pages, the trader groups have been pre-selected. A key for all the COT symbols used in the book and on the website is given in Table 2.2. Again, selecting different trader groups will change all the analytics on the page.

The right-hand side of the page shows the keys for the different analytics. The top key, titled 'Trader Group', shows the colours of the trader groups selected. Note that this is only relevant for the top two indicators, the Dry Powder indicator and the Dry Powder Notional indicator, as the colour on the other two indicators, the Dry Powder Time indicator and the Dry Powder Seasonal indicator, are superseded by colours for the year and month, as made clear in Chapter 5.

The middle right key, titled 'Year', shows the colours of the years for the Dry Powder Time indicator and the bottom right key, titled 'Month', the colours of the months for the Dry Powder Seasonal indicator.

Using the small buttons/icons at the bottom of each page, the charts can also be downloaded directly from the website in a variety of different formats.

The Software and Applications Used in the Book

Although Tableau has been used extensively throughout this book for many of the reasons above, all the analytics in this book can also easily be built and run in Microsoft Excel or in a similar spreadsheet package. The book contains all the necessary explanations and calculations of how to build the analytics, but a good knowledge of Excel is required. The machine learning in Chapter 14 was done with the Excel add-in XLSTAT.[2]

All the data used in the book has been downloaded from Bloomberg directly either into Excel to generate the Excel-based analytics or uploaded into Tableau to drive the Tableau-based analytics.

Apart from the newsflow data in Chapter 11, which has been coded directly within and extracted from the Bloomberg platform, all the data used in the book is available through a variety of vendors and also straight from the relevant websites.

Please note that some of the chart axis labels and legend labels in the figures in the book have been cut short due to space constraints. The full labels are visible on the website.

Updates, Changes, and Erratum

Any updates, changes, and erratum in the book will be published under the link on the bottom right of the Launchpad. Please contact Mark Keenan at: mjsk@shadwellresearch.com with any questions or comments.

---

[2]https://www.xlstat.com/en/

INTRODUCTION

This book focuses on Positioning Analysis. It is based on new material, but also updates and builds significantly on some of the work in the previous book, *Positioning Analysis in Commodity Markets – Bridging Fundamental and Technical Analysis*, by Mark Keenan. New material includes analytics based on the analysis of flow, the decomposition of trading flows, trading activity in the Chinese commodity markets, the inclusion of newsflow into Positioning Analysis, and how machine learning can provide insight into trading relationships.[1]

The ideas, insights, and concepts behind the signals, indicators, models – collectively the analyses – in this book have been developed over the last 20 years throughout a variety of different market conditions and regime changes. In many cases, their construction is unique, but in all cases, the approach is robust, intuitive, and accessible to commodity market participants and risk managers on a variety of levels and in different areas of the market.

The book is restricted to the commodity derivatives markets only, and specifically to exchange-traded futures and options. The application of the analyses can, however, be applied to all commodity-related assets, including commodity derivatives, commodity over-the-counter (OTC) markets, associated equities, and instruments on commodity-related companies.

Behavioural patterns driven by positioning and flow dynamics can change and evolve as different types of market participants enter and leave the market and as new price drivers emerge which can lead to the formation new patterns and relationships. This book provides a wide range of different analytics to help understand them better and how to track how these relationships evolve. It is important to note that the analytics, how results and data are interpreted, and what conclusions are drawn throughout this book, are by no means exhaustive or final.

A sizeable proportion of the analysis in this book is open to interpretation, and there are often a variety of different conclusions that can be drawn from the data with various ways to respond. As will become evident throughout the book, there are numerous approaches to the analytics in

---

[1] Keenan, Mark JS (2018) *Positioning Analysis in Commodity Markets – Bridging Fundamental and Technical Analysis*. Publisher: Shadwell Publications & National Library Board – Singapore (27 January 2018).

how they can be used. This ranges from using them directly, either in isolation or in combination or incorporating them into existing trading, hedging, investment, and/or risk management processes.

The objective of the book is to show the reader new and alternative ways of thinking about commodity markets and to provide new tools and analytics to help improve trading performance and risk management. A website has also been developed that allows the reader to use many of the analytics directly, and to customise them to different commodities of interest. The book is equally relevant for a hedge fund manager trading oil or natural gas, a farmer growing coffee rearing cattle, a miner producing copper or gold, or a commodity speculator trading anything from iron ore to glass on the Chinese futures markets.

All the signals, indicators, models, and analyses throughout the book have been developed by the author and all the views and interpretations expressed are the author's own.

The following provides a summary of each of the chapters in the book.

Chapter 1

There are 14 chapters in this book, with the first chapter beginning with an introduction to Positioning Analysis and positioning data and also addressing some of the more common misunderstandings and issues in this area.

Chapter 2

The next chapter provides an overview of how positioning data is broken down and attributed between trader categories, integrating both the Legacy and Disaggregated COT reports to show how the different trader categories are related to each other.

The relationships, patterns, and dynamics between changes in open interest and changes in the number of traders both within and between trader categories are considerable and an understanding of the structure of the data and how it is reported is a prerequisite in Positioning Analysis. Robust analysis of changes in this data makes it possible to reliably isolate specific types of flow patterns, quantify shifts in sentiment, define behavioural responses, and develop tools for better trading and risk management.

The chapter also shows how COT data can be used to understand and evaluate positioning patterns and profiles between the major commodities. Data on which commodities are the most liquid – in terms of the commodities with the highest (lowest) open interest and the highest (lowest) number of traders in each category – is useful in helping to understand which commodities might be the most or least vulnerable to shifts in investor sentiment, and whether more technically driven strategies or a more fundamentally driven approach might perform better. In addition, identifying the most (least) speculatively driven commodities, and similarly, the commodities with the highest (lowest) implied consumer and producer hedging activity, can also provide a solid foundation for many of the models and analytics presented in later chapters.

Chapter 3

Speculative activity has two main channels of influence on prices: a market impact that can affect the price and a sentiment effect that can change behaviour. The interplay of these dynamics can be challenging to disentangle, but collectively they are essential in understanding how prices may evolve and where risks may lie. Consequently, speculative activity tends to attract a disproportionate amount of interest in Positioning Analysis.

Chapter 3 addresses the questions of whether speculators generate positive performance, and if so, how so and in which commodities. This is useful in providing further insight into many of the analytics throughout the book. It is also helpful in developing more profound insights into trading performance, such as whether returns are driven by a small number of large traders or whether it is more widespread, with performance driven by the majority of traders.

Chapter 4

Concentration – the size of a position as a percentage of total open interest – a measure of positioning risk; clustering – the number of traders holding a specific position as a percentage of the total number of traders in the market – a measure of sentiment; and position size – the average size of individual traders' position – a measure of conviction, are introduced in Chapter 4 as ways to help measure risk, sentiment, and conviction dynamics in commodity markets. Collectively, these metrics and the insights they generate provide a solid foundation to many of the indicators, models, and analysis covered in later chapters.

Chapters 5 and 6

Chapter 5 introduces Dry Powder (DP) analysis as a way of visualising positioning in commodity markets using a variety of different DP indicators. The indicators reconcile the historical long and short open interest in a specific trader category with the number of traders holding the position.

They are plotted as charts, which can be directly used as trading indicators to help assess the likelihood of an existing position becoming bigger or whether it is vulnerable to liquidation. DP indicators can be modified in a variety of ways to isolate specific positioning dynamics. They also work well with other indicators and models to refine trading signals and enhance risk management.

In Chapter 6, DP analysis is extended to include a variety of new types of information to better visualise positioning profiles in the context of other factors. These can include positioning data on the different trader categories, the price of the underlying commodity, the shape of the forward curve, certain types of fundamental data, and macroeconomic variables.

Chapter 7

To understand the explanatory power that changes in the positioning of individual long and short trader categories have on price, a Shapley–Owen decomposition of the regression of changes in price against changes in positioning can be used. This provides some indication of which trader groups have been determining prices on a commodity-specific basis over time. By extension, Shapley–Owen decomposition can also be used to understand the explanatory power that changes in the positioning of individual trader categories have on other trader categories. This provides an indication of the trading flows between groups.

In combination with other analytics, the overall approach described in this chapter provides meaningful insight into potential price changes, by factoring into account the trading flows and the price sensitivity. It is also possible to then back-out the possible length of time that specific changes in trader positioning could need to complete. This can dramatically enhance risk management, trading performance, and market analysis.

Chapters 8 and 9

In Chapter 8, the Overbought/Oversold (OBOS) framework is introduced as a way of generating trading signals in commodities that lie at the intersection of extremes in their long and short speculative positioning, and extremes in their price. Extremes in speculative positioning can provide useful trading insights in isolation, but it is mostly also in the context of price extremes that they become particularly powerful.

The OBOS framework uses a combination of speculative positioning data and pricing data over specific timeframes. Specific thresholds are used to define whether a commodity becomes 'Overbought' or 'Oversold', within the framework, and it is at these points that trading signals are generated.

The framework is also useful in the analysis of behavioural patterns to help manage risk more effectively and, in combination with numerous other positioning models and analytics, to produce more sophisticated and refined trading signals.

In Chapter 9, the OBOS framework is extended to include different positioning metrics such as Clustering and Position Size and also to make use of a broader set of variables within the framework, like the VIX, Financial Conditions Indices (FCIs), and the dollar index (DXY), to better underhand positioning dynamics.

The use of Positioning Analysis in the risk management of commodity risk premia strategies is also covered.

Chapter 10

Changes in the number of COT long, short, and spreading traders can be a powerful measure of sentiment and an effective way of identifying behavioural patterns in commodities.

In Chapter 10, Sentiment indices based on changes in trader number positioning – a good proxy for sentiment, plus different indicators and indices are developed to track the evolution of market sentiment. Two different indices are developed: Directional Sentiment (DS) indices, based on the number of long and short traders only; and Non-Directional Sentiment (NDS) indices, based on the number of traders holding a spreading position.

These indices can be applied to the whole commodity asset class, to specific commodity sectors, or to individual commodities.

The chapter also introduces Mismatch indicators to provide a way of visualising and identifying positioning mismatches. These occur when the direction in the net number of traders (number of long traders – number of short traders) is different to the direction of their net position (long open interest – short open interest). Mismatches frequently intersect with price inflexion points and can be useful trading signals.

Chapter 11

Chapter 11 focuses on incorporating commodity newsflow into certain areas of commodity Positioning Analysis.

Commodity positioning-related newsflow is important in helping to assess and track the current level of interest in positioning data. Like technical analysis, Positioning Analysis carries a degree of self-reinforcement, which can affect prices, shape sentiment, and influence behaviour. As positioning-related newsflow increases or decreases the more or the less pronounced these positioning-related effects often become.

When positioning is extreme in a commodity, the absolute level of commodity trading-related newsflow in that commodity, and also the direction of newsflow in terms of whether it is bullish or bearish for prices, can significantly affect behaviour. A large long or short position and bullish or bearish price-related newsflow respectively suggests the position could become bigger, or, if positioning is already extreme, less vulnerable to liquidation. Similarly, if newsflow starts to wane, prices could start to become vulnerable as positions are no longer justified and positions begin to unwind.

This chapter covers the construction of different types of newsflow indices and ways of including them into Positioning Analysis to refine signals and provide more information.

Chapter 12

Chapter 12 introduces the Flow Cube and Build ratio to organise and quantify changes in price, open interest, and volume into a framework to define the type and efficiency of trading activity. This can be done over any timeframe (daily, weekly, monthly) and for any commodity on an aggregate or individual futures contract basis.

The approach means that the recent trading activity in a commodity, or the trading activity at specific points down its forward curve, can be defined and then, in combination with the Build ratio, quantified in terms of its efficiency.

This means that in combination with some knowledge of the type of trading activity down the curve, in terms of speculative or hedging, the efficiency of trading activity can be assessed and, by extension, the extent of more fuzzy types of trading such as the level of 'High-Frequency Trading (HFT)' observed.

Chapter 13

This chapter focuses exclusively on the Chinese commodity futures markets, with the primary objective of defining, assessing, and tracking the level of trading activity, and specifically speculative activity, that frequently dominates the newsflow on these exchanges.

As there is no equivalent CFTC Commitment of Traders (COT) report for Chinese exchanges, insight on trading activity for these exchanges can be approximated using the Speculation Ratio (SR) indicator and the Build Ratio (BR) indicator.

A new Overbought/Oversold OBOS model for Chinese commodities, based on extremes in price and the SR, is also developed.

Chapter 14

The final chapter, on machine learning, introduces decision trees and random forests as ways of uncovering relationships between changes in positioning and changes in commodity prices.

The objective is to identify which aspects of positioning are the most useful in helping to understand commodity markets from a machine's perspective.

Machine learning applied to positioning data to predict prices is particularly useful in the analysis of positioning data, with 'feature importance' being a powerful way of identifying new patterns and new relationships in positioning.

These are insights that can help improve how other positioning signals, indicators, and models are interpreted and used.

Symbols used in the book

Symbols for commodities used throughout the book are given in Table 2.1. Symbols for other variables, including all Commitment of Traders (COT), data are given in Table 2.2.

CHAPTER 1

Advanced Positioning, Flow, and Sentiment Analysis in Commodity Markets

Chapter objectives

This book focuses on Positioning Analysis. It is based on new material, but also updates and builds significantly on some of the work in the previous book, *Positioning Analysis in Commodity Markets – Bridging Fundamental and Technical Analysis*, by Mark Keenan.

New material includes analytics based on the analysis of flow, the decomposition of trading flows, trading activity in the Chinese commodity markets, the inclusion of newsflow into Positioning Analysis, and how machine learning can provide insight into trading relationships.

This chapter introduces Positioning Analysis and positioning data and addresses some of the more common misunderstandings and issues in this area.

1.1 Positioning Analysis – What Is It?

Positioning Analysis is one area of research that provides a powerful framework to better understand price dynamics, risk, sentiment, and behaviour in commodity markets.

Based on standard positioning data and bridging aspects of fundamental and technical analysis, the approach builds on how certain types of positioning patterns – both within the data and in the context of changes in variables like price, curve structure, fundamentals such as inventory, seasonal factors, exchange rates, changes in the broader macroeconomic environment, and the levels of risk and uncertainty in the market – can be used to develop models, indicators, and analyses. These lead to the generation of robust trading signals that can be either used directly or integrated into a variety of different trading, investment, and risk management programmes to enhance performance.

Positioning data shows us who is trading what, and how much they are trading. Positioning Analysis helps us identify behavioural patterns in the data and to understand how changes in specific variables can affect positioning, impact sentiment, and drive price.

1.1.1 Positioning Data

Positioning data in commodity markets is generated by attributing exchange-traded futures and options positions between specific groups or categories of traders. It gives an idea of what each category of trader has been doing and the extent to which they have done it.[1]

Positioning data is the breakdown of open interest on a weekly basis, between traders in each category according to their long, short, and, where reported, spreading positions. Futures open interest and combined futures and options open interest are typically reported separately, with the options positions reported on a delta-adjusted basis. Only reportable positions, defined as those positions that exceed specific reporting thresholds, are broken down, meaning that between 70% and 90% of open interest, on average, is categorised. The remaining positions are reported as a single group called non-reportables. Importantly, positioning data also includes the number of traders in each long, short, and spreading category.

1.1.2 Positioning Analysis – Bridging Fundamental and Technical Analysis

The analysis of changes in positioning data – Positioning Analysis – makes it possible to define behavioural responses, quantify shifts in sentiment, isolate specific types of flow patterns, and develop tools and signals for better trading, investment and risk management.

In this respect, it is like technical analysis but with more emphasis on behavioural patterns. In many cases, behavioural patterns take a long time to change, so understanding how traders have behaved in the past with the help of Positioning Analysis allows useful decisions to be made in the future.

[1]The terms 'trader groups' and 'trader categories' are used interchangeably through this book.

Positioning Analysis bridges fundamental and technical analysis in two ways; firstly, it is agnostic to whether a position was established because of a fundamental or technical reason; and, secondly, insights from Positioning Analysis can be used to enhance both fundamentally and technically driven trading strategies.

1.1.3 Positioning Signals, Indicators, Models, and Analyses

Positioning Analysis makes up a substantial proportion of this book and COT data is therefore used extensively.

Most of the trading signals, indicators, and models in this book use speculative positioning data. This has been done both in the interest of space and also because the motivation behind the data is intuitive, meaning that we understand speculators are seeking to profit from their trading, as opposed to it being a function of hedging activity. Unless otherwise specified, all the signals, indicators, models, and analyses in this book can be applied to the positioning data in other trader groups to help formulate a complete picture of the overall positioning landscape in a commodity. In doing so, however, an understanding of the trade motivation behind all the different trader categories is essential in helping to gauge how price, curve structure, and sentiment may evolve.

The ideas, insights, and concepts behind the signals, indicators, models, and analyses, collectively the 'analytics', in this book have been developed over the last 20 years by the author. In many cases, their construction is unique, but in all cases, the approach is robust, intuitive, and accessible to commodity market participants and risk managers on a variety of levels.

A sizeable proportion of the analysis in this book is open to interpretation, and there are often a variety of different conclusions that can be drawn from the data with different ways to respond. Commodity price action driven by positioning dynamics is often linked to sentiment and behavioural patterns, which can change and evolve over time. This can lead to the formation and establishment of new patterns and relationships as different types of market participants enter and leave the market, and as new price drivers emerge.

This book provides a wide range of different analytics to help understand positioning dynamics and to track how relationships evolve. It is important to note that the analytics, how results and data are interpreted, and what conclusions are drawn throughout this book are by no means exhaustive or final.

Significant literature and several excellent books already exist that cover many of the areas of how positioning data is defined and generated.[2] The aim of this book is not to re-do this work in any capacity, but is instead to establish and develop Positioning Analysis as a trading, investment, and risk management tool.

In Chapter 2, however, a complete overview of how positioning is broken down on every level for a commodity is given. Section 2.1 is vital as it shows how different positioning categories are related to each other. Appendix 2, taken directly from many of the official sources including the CFTC, the ICE, and the LME, also provides valuable information.

---

[2]Including: *The Commitments of Traders Bible: How to Profit from Insider Market Intelligence* by Stephen Briese; *Commitments of Traders: Strategies for Tracking the Market and Trading* by Floyd Upperman; and *Trade Stocks & Commodities with the Insiders – Secrets of the COT Report* by Larry Williams.

1.2 The History of Positioning Data, the COT Report, and the Agencies that Provide the Data

The Commodity Futures Trading Commission (CFTC) website explains that positioning data in commodities has been around since 1924 when the Grain Futures Administration of the US Department of Agriculture (USDA) published its first comprehensive annual report of hedging and speculation in regulated futures markets.[3,4]

In 1962, positioning or commitment of traders (COT) data, as it became referred to, was published each month. In 1990, the CFTC started publishing data mid-month and month-end, in 1992 every two weeks, and then in 2000 on a weekly basis. Current and historical COT data is now available on the CFTC website, going back to 1986 for futures-only reports, to 1995 for futures and options combined reports, and to 2006 for the supplemental and disaggregated reports. A more detailed history of the CFTC COT data is also given in Appendix 1.

In addition to the COT data published by the CFTC, almost identical COT data is published by the Intercontinental Exchange (ICE) for the commodity markets traded on the ICE. The ICE includes markets like Brent and gasoil.

The London Metal Exchange (LME) also publishes a COT report for industrial metals which, as shown in Section 2.2, has some significant differences to the CFTC and ICE COT reports. The Shanghai Futures Exchange (SHFE) publishes a form of positioning data called Daily Ranking data, where the volume and open interest (long and short) rankings, including changes from the previous day, are reported for the top 20 members in each commodity.[5] This data is, however, entirely different from the CFTC, ICE, and LME COT reports and is covered briefly in Section 2.3.2.

1.3 Misunderstandings and Issues in Positioning Analysis

Positioning data can provoke strong opinions about its validity and usefulness – and is therefore not unlike technical analysis in this respect. This occurs even though it is widely accepted that information relating to the trading activity of competitors and other market participants can be useful and can provide an edge in most areas of business and finance.

Many of the more idiosyncratic issues and misunderstandings in positioning will be covered in detail throughout the book, but in this section, it is useful to address some of the more significant and more widespread issues at the outset.

There are four primary areas of concern:

- The issue of lag. This specifically refers to the time between when the open interest is broken down, and when it is reported.

---

[3]The USDA's Grain Futures Administration was the predecessor to the USDA Commodity Exchange Authority, which in turn was the predecessor to the Commodity Futures Trading Commission (CFTC).

[4]The Commodity Futures Trading Commission (CFTC) was created by Congress in 1974 as an independent agency of the federal government to administer the Commodity Exchange Act (CEA). www.cftc.gov

[5]Each member is reported as a numeric code: www.shfe.com.cn/en/MarketData/dataview.html?paramid=week.

- The issue of trader classification. This relates to how traders are classified – a critical component in Positioning Analysis.

- The motivation behind the positions. Being able to disentangle positions to try and understand the underlying objective and motivation behind a trader category's position can be challenging.

- Concerns about the 'age' of positions, although this becomes less of an issue when looking at changes in positioning, rather than absolute levels.

1.3.1 The Issue of Lag

In finance, and specifically in trading and investment-related areas, lag generally refers to the delay between when data was measured and when it is reported. This type of lag is structural and is typically present in all kinds of data to some degree. Unfortunately, the word 'lag' does, however, imply that the data has in some way been compromised or is less valuable in some way, thereby inferring that un-lagged data would be more useful. Whilst this may be the case, if un-lagged data does not exist, the issue of lag becomes less of an issue as all positioning data is released to all market participants at the same time. Any sense that that data has therefore been compromised in some way, perhaps by some market participants being aware of the data beforehand, is not valid. In this respect, positioning data is like corporate earnings data or macroeconomic data.

This stands in contrast to most types of fundamental data, like inventory data, imports, exports, crop status reports, and certain types of transport data, where typically those entities that either report it or that make up the data have a good idea of the data beforehand. Firms that own storage or warehouse facilities, for example, will know their inventory or stock levels (and invariably also be aware of that of their competitors) before the agencies that collect it and release it to the public.

In this sense, fundamental data, whilst also structurally lagged, has also been compromised.[6] Positioning data is in fact one of the only data sources in commodity markets where all market participants are equal in how and when they receive the data. The main lag-related issue arises from whether the data has changed between its measurement and its release – a problem common to most types of data. With positioning and sentiment often intertwined, as discussed in many of the following chapters, one of the most powerful linkages between positioning and price comes from changes in sentiment, which tend to be driven by trends in positioning rather than precise positioning levels. Positioning data also generally exhibits positive serial correlation as positions can take time to unwind and change. Overall, this makes the structural lag in positioning data less critical than in other types of data where sentiment is less important.

---

[6]This is often given as a reason to explain why physical commodity traders and merchants (commodity trade houses) are considered more successful than hedge funds and speculators, which typically only have a lagged window into the physical world. This is not to say that the analysis of fundamental data is therefore not valuable in commodity market analysis, but rather that it is hypocritical to dismiss positioning data simply because it is structurally lagged.

1.3.2 The Issue of Trader Classification

Positioning data is based on the categorisation of traders, rather than the aim or motivation behind their trades. This means that a producer using futures to hedge production, but that may also have a speculative trading book, will be classified as a Producer/Merchant/Processor/User (PMPU) trader, irrespective of whether a specific trade is initiated for hedging or speculative purposes. This can sometimes lead to confusion when trying to interpret positioning activity. It is especially important to be aware that positions may not always be consistent with the trader's category definition.

Appendix 2 details the official trader categories used in the COT reports. For ease of reference, an extract from the CFTC website for the categories used in the CFTC Disaggregated COT report (and those most frequently used throughout this book) is given in Box 1.1.

Box 1.1 Disaggregated COT categories

Producer/Merchant/Processor/User (PMPU)

A 'producer/merchant/processor/user' is an entity that predominantly engages in the production, processing, packing, or handling of a physical commodity and uses the futures markets to manage or hedge risks associated with those activities.

Swap Dealer (SD)

A 'swap dealer' is an entity that deals primarily in swaps for a commodity and uses the futures markets to manage or hedge the risk associated with those swap transactions. The swap dealer's counterparties may be speculative traders, like hedge funds, or traditional commercial clients that are managing risk arising from their dealings in the physical commodity.

Money Manager (MM)

A 'money manager', for the purpose of this report, is a registered commodity trading advisor (CTA); a registered commodity pool operator (CPO); or an unregistered fund identified by CFTC. These traders are engaged in managing and conducting organised futures trading on behalf of clients.

Other Reportables

Every other reportable trader that is not placed into one of the other three categories is placed into the 'other reportable' category.

Source: Based on data from www.cftc.gov/MarketReports/CommitmentsofTraders/index.htm.

1.3.3 The Motivation Behind the Positions

While the disaggregated COT category definitions are mostly well defined, it can sometimes also be difficult to know how a trader is categorised, and changes in positioning within a specific category can sometimes also be confusing and difficult to interpret. A Swap Dealer (SD), for example, could be hedging its exposure to a crude oil swap that may be for a consumer or producer; or it could be for a hedge fund, particularly with many hedge funds trading swaps to avoid futures position limits.

A few of the most common sources of confusion, as well as some important characteristics of each of the categories, are highlighted in more detail below. The more idiosyncratic aspects of positioning are discussed throughout the book as they arise.

1.3.3.1 The PMPU Category – Not Always Hedging

A sizeable proportion of the PMPU category are consumers and producers, but it is possible (and often quite common) for them to engage in a degree of speculative activity, as speculative trades at the outset often become part of legitimate hedging trades later. Speculation may occur in timing the market, to try and capture the lowest (highest) prices to strike a hedge, or in changing the hedge quantity based on a price outlook to maximise or optimise the profitability or efficiency of the hedge. The flexibility in timing will invariably still be subject to a specific overall timeframe (usually linked to some logistical constraint such as loading time of a vessel or the transport time), and flexibility on the hedge quantity will often be driven by accounting or risk management policies in terms of how much ultimately should be hedged. Maximising the profitability of the hedge is a type of speculation which has the effect of making changes in PMPU positioning more sensitive to price than they would otherwise be expected to be. In contrast, a PMPU trader hedging with zero speculation would, for instance, initiate or lift a fixed or predetermined hedge when the physical deal is done, without acknowledgement of the market outlook and at the current price level.

It is important to be aware that, aside from trying to optimise the efficiency of the hedge, PMPU traders are mostly seeking to make money out of the physical commodity, or a product related to the physical commodity. Overall, the hedge is expected to lose money; therefore, positioning often runs counter to price trends in the market. A hedging loss should, therefore, typically suggest that the overall trading activity was profitable.[7]

An understanding of hedging dynamics and their rationale can make the analysis of positioning data in the PMPU category a powerful indicator of price direction. Despite seeking to make money out of the physical commodity, changes in positioning can be highly informative. An increase, for example, in the long (short) positioning in the PMPU category could suggest that consumers (producers) believe that prices have bottomed (topped), indicating a good level to hedge or to undertake a physical trade.

It is often assumed that physical trading activity is not very opportunistic in nature, as supply and demand dynamics are always under way, and positioning patterns in the PMPU category are therefore always relatively rigid. This assumption is driven by a variety of commercial relationships. Airlines, for example, do not just fly when fuel prices are low, deep-water oil production

---

[7]This is also the case because it is rare for a consumer or producer to hedge their entire commodity price liability.

rigs do not just produce oil when it is profitable, and Easter egg demand does not halt if cocoa prices are too high.

In reality, however, physical trading is more opportunistic than expected, a trend that is arguably increasing. A mine, for example, increases (decreases) supply when prices are high (low) as they become increasingly more efficient and more automated. With the recent growth of shale oil production, oil producers are also taking price increasingly more into account as they seek to optimise drilling and fracking activity – shale oil production is more closely related to manufacturing than to conventional oil production. Changes in price can therefore drive changes in physical trading activity, which in turn can drive more price-sensitive PMPU activity.

This is also particularly evident in the context of inventory management. As prices change and as the forward curve shifts, traders will optimise storage to take advantage of prices and the price outlook. As crude oil (WTI) inventories rise (fall), the size of the short PMPU position usually rises (falls). Any optimisation around these hedges, for example a decline in the PMPU short position, can often point towards a potential decrease in stocks.

The PMPU category is a complex category, but the visibility and access of PMPU traders into the physical world, in contrast to most of the speculative community, can, however, make changes in PMPU activity disproportionately informative.[8]

1.3.3.2 The MM category – Not Always Speculating   In the same way that a PMPU trader may engage in speculative activity, a MM trader may engage in hedging activity.

A macro fund trading equities, for example, might sell crude oil (WTI) oil futures to hedge against downside oil price risk in a portfolio of US energy stocks.

In a similar way, a commodity fund will end up selling crude oil (WTI) futures to express a bullish view on a crack (a trade seeking to profit from the spread between related products, such as gasoline and heating oil to crude oil) or because they expect it to fall more (rise less) than Brent in an arbitrage trade. These trades are a departure from pure directional speculation, and may not be bearish on an absolute basis, but are bearish on a relative basis with the short position in crude oil (WTI) behaving like a hedge. This type of trading activity can make MM analysis more complicated.

The MM category can also be clouded by index activity and ETF trading. A trader replicating a commodity index with futures, in either a long or a short capacity, will typically fall under the MM category.[9] A commodity pool operator (CPO) managing an ETF, such as the US Oil Fund, designed to track the price of crude oil (WTI), will need to hedge its exposure in the futures market according to the demand for the ETF.

---

[8]In many cases, a physical trader, for example a commodity merchant, may also speculate on the price of a commodity with no underlying physical exposure to the commodity. This type of speculative activity clearly clouds this category, but due to their visibility into the physical market, their speculative trading activity can be considered different from the speculative activity in the MM category, with limited visibility into the physical market. Whilst this activity may question the accuracy of the PMPU classification, the PMPU positioning is nonetheless equally valuable. It could be argued, for example, that a speculative trade taken by a physical trader could be disproportionally informative. Depending on how the trade house is structured, this type of trading activity can also be reported in the OR category.

[9]If they were, however, to buy the same index from a bank via swap, then the bank would be classified as a SD.

Index investment activity, and to a certain extent ETFs, are often longer-term investments as part of long-term asset allocation strategies. These positions can be vulnerable to change as portfolios rebalance, meaning that changes in positioning may not be directly driven by market views usually associated with MMs. Despite this, index and ETF positioning is mostly in alignment with the underlying directional view for that commodity.

Despite the edging and relative value trading activity, positioning in the MM category can be interpreted as one of the 'purest' categories in terms of it being representative of the underlying price view in the commodity. MM traders are also mostly all aligned in their objective of generating positive returns in the commodity.

This generates the important question of whether MMs have any skill in their approach, and by extension, whether changes in their positioning are useful in predicting commodity price direction. Anecdotally, it is widely assumed that they do, and this is analysed in detail on a commodity-specific basis in Chapter 3.

1.3.3.3 The SD Category – Difficult to Define

The SD category is difficult to disentangle because any swap position that is hedged using futures will fall into this category. This means that a hedge fund speculating on an increase in the price of Brent using a lookalike, an airline locking in its fuel prices using a Brent swap, or a sovereign wealth fund with long-term exposure to Brent prices via a commodity index will all fall in the long SD category for Brent.[10] It is also the swap dealer (typically a bank) that reports the position to the CFTC as the underlying futures position is taken by the swap dealer. This means that positions are typically netted off, making it even harder to interpret.

The majority of SD activity is commercially driven, but with the recent proliferation of position limits, many speculators have been forced to turn to the swap market to avoid these restrictions.[11] This trend is, however, being partially offset by many of the largest index investors, including pension funds and endowments that previously invested in commodity indices exclusively via swaps, turning to the futures market to replicate the indices themselves. Their objective is to reduce counterparty risk and/or to increase the flexibility they have over their exposure.

The varied activity in the SD category means that it is the least reliable category in helping to understand commodity price and sentiment dynamics. Moreover, commodity swap index exposure can be a large component of the SD category, particularly in the smaller markets, which can change significantly as portfolios rebalance and asset allocation models change. This means that changes in SD positioning may not always be directly driven by, or reflective of, market views. In the Supplemental Report, index positions drawn from the non-commercial and commercial categories, are provided for selected agricultural markets, which can help identify the index activity. This is explained further in Chapter 2.

Changes in the SD and PMPU positions are often related when swap positions are linked to hedging. Due to differences between futures and swaps, however, different PMPU and SD

---

[10]Jet fuel, for example, is often hedged using Brent.
[11]Many commodity exchanges impose specific position limits, to curb excessive speculation by restricting the exposure in specific contracts. It is typically the contracts at the front of the curve that are most impacted.

positioning profiles can be useful in understanding different hedging dynamics in a market. It is also true to say that the choice of hedging instrument, a swap or a future contract, can be a function of the size of the company looking to do the hedge. Some examples are as follows:

- A small or developing oil producer looking to secure financing will typically use a swap to lock in prices for future oil sales and to provide some stability. It is also common to have the swap position tied into the financing deal to reduce risk in the financing.

- Smaller companies often prefer swaps as the cash management of the hedge position can be less demanding than an equivalent futures position. A small producer (consumer) will have to finance a short (long) position if the forward curve is backwardated (in contango) as the short (long) futures rolls up (down) the curve. This can be demanding on cash flow.

- Larger companies often prefer to use futures in order to reduce counterparty risk and increase flexibility. Cash management here is less of an issue as many of these companies typically use credit lines to finance their futures position.[12]

The type of hedging activity can also be important in choosing between swaps and futures:

- A company with oil storage facilities is often more likely to use futures to hedge and manage its inventory, as futures can often be more flexible and cost-effective.[13]

These examples are by no means always the case, as companies can flip between using swaps and futures at different times for many reasons. Considering the diversity of swap users, however, and how easily speculative and index activity can cloud this category, it is mostly true to say that changes in the PMPU category give more reliable insights into consumer and producer activity. Consequently, throughout this book, the PMPU long (short) positions are almost always used to proxy consumer (producer) activity.

1.3.3.4 The OR Category – Becoming Increasingly More Significant   The OR category is a broad category and includes 'every other reportable trader that is not placed into one of the other three categories'. It is likely that most of the activity in this category is speculative in nature – specifically speculation that is done with proprietary capital. OR speculation is different from MM speculation within the Disaggregated COT report as the MM category relates explicitly to the management of third-party assets. The OR category therefore mostly includes corporates and trade houses speculating with their own capital (using their balance sheet, for example) and large private investors.

If a trader classified in the OR category undertakes hedging activity to any meaningful degree, it is likely that they will ultimately be re-classified into the PMPU or indirectly into the SD category, or they may establish a separate entity for hedging. The motivation to do this is that

---

[12]Swap trading is an OTC (over-the-counter) transaction and therefore entails counterparty risk. By trading futures directly, this risk is transferred to the clearing house and is therefore negligible.

[13]Changes in the PMPU short position are often closely related to changes in inventory – the larger the inventory, the larger the hedge needs to be, as explained in Section 1.3.3.1.

legitimated hedging activity typically means that lower initial margins can be paid, making it more cost-effective.[14]

The level of speculative activity in the OR category and the size of the category means that it is often sensible to consider or to include OR data in the analysis of speculative positioning data. The OR category is becoming increasingly more significant as a positioning category, and more closely watched. As such, it is also starting to influence market sentiment – especially in the oil market.

1.3.4 Concerns About the 'Age' of Positions

Long-term investment positions – for example, positions that underpin commodity indices and commodity ETFs and long-term hedging positions – can make certain positioning profiles and patterns very difficult to interpret, especially as notional values change over time.

Many of the analytics in this book, however, only focus however on changes in positioning or make use of dynamic short-term ranges. In many cases, the data is also normalised in a variety of ways. Collectively, this mitigates some of these concerns and this is discussed in detail where relevant throughout the book.

1.4 Futures and Options Data

Combined futures and options open interest is also reported in the CFTC and ICE COT reports, where options positions are included on a delta-adjusted basis. On the LME, only combined futures and options data is reported.

Combined futures and options data is generally unsatisfactory because positioning can change without any trading activity if the underlying market changes. An out-of-the-money long-call (put) position, for example, will 'increase' as the delta increases if the market rises (falls). This implies that traders have increased their long (short) futures positioning, when they may not have, and indeed could even have reduced it. The opposite applies to short option positions.

As options positions are included in a delta-adjusted capacity, it makes it difficult to reliably use the combined futures and options data in Positioning Analysis. One solution is to use the number of options traders, calculated by subtracting the number of futures-only traders from the number of futures and options combined traders. Whilst this does not give any indication of the option position size, it provides some insight into the number of options traders which can be useful in sentiment analysis.

There are also several other option-related factors that make it difficult to understand the underlying view in the market, and which make the use of option-related positioning data unsatisfactory:

■ Options traders may be trading volatility or using options in combination with futures to delta trade the market. This type of trading activity is typically agnostic of market direction, which makes it challenging to use in Positioning Analysis.

---

[14]Initial margin refers to capital or deposit per futures contract that needs to be paid to the broker and clearing house to be able to hold the position. For hedgers, this amount is typically less than for speculators due to hedge margining, as hedging activity is considered less risky than speculative activity.

- Traders can use options to hedge other positions that they may not want to liquidate. Whilst this is useful information, potentially indicating a shift in sentiment, and perhaps a change in future market direction, the positions can be challenging to disentangle.

- Speculators often use options to bet on price spikes and other low-probability but high-reward scenarios. This type of activity can obscure current trends and patterns.

- Options are often used by firms for corporate risk management reasons. This type of trading activity can sometimes be significant and may have nothing to do with their daily trading or hedging activity. It can nonetheless cloud other positioning data.

- As option trades tend to be 'stickier' than futures trades, a degree of asymmetry is introduced when looking at changes in options positioning. This means that a trader might buy a call option because they are bullish, but they may not sell it when the market falls or if they change their view. Instead, the position will typically be left to expire worthless.

- By extension, the risk management of an options position is also different from the risk management of futures. Options positions, for example, rarely have stop losses, whilst losing futures trades are often swiftly liquidated.

- Options are used in structured products that can have complicated payoff structures. Understanding the view behind a series of structured products based on options position would be extremely challenging.

For these reasons, options tend to complicate Positioning Analysis. The combined futures and options data is therefore rarely used in this book.

CHAPTER 2

The Structure of the Positioning Data

Chapter objectives

This chapter provides an overview of how positioning data is broken down and attributed between trader categories, integrating both the Legacy and Disaggregated COT reports together to show how the different categories are related to each other. The relationships, patterns, and dynamics between changes in open interest and changes in the number of traders both within and between trader categories are considerable and an understanding of the structure of the data and how it is reported is a prerequisite in Positioning Analysis. Robust analysis of changes in this data makes it possible to reliably isolate specific types of flow patterns, quantify shifts in sentiment, define behavioural responses, and develop tools for better trading and risk management.

The chapter also shows how COT data can be used to understand and evaluate positioning patterns and profiles between the major commodities. Data on which commodities are the most liquid – in terms of the commodities with the highest (lowest) open interest and the highest (lowest) number of traders in each category – is useful in helping to understand which commodities might be the most or least vulnerable to shifts in investor sentiment, and whether more technically driven strategies or a more fundamentally driven approach might perform better. In addition, identifying the most (least) speculatively driven commodities, and, similarly, the commodities with the highest (lowest) implied consumer and producer hedging activity, can also provide a solid foundation for many of the models and analytics presented in later chapters.

2.1 The Structure of Positioning Data

The positioning data used in this book is mostly taken from the Commodity Futures Trading Commission (CFTC) and the Intercontinental Exchange (ICE). For the reasons explained in Section 1.4, only futures data is used, as opposed to combined futures and options data. Details on the new COT data from the London Metal Exchange (LME), reported under the new MiFID requirements, are covered in Section 2.2, but are not used in this book for the reasons explained in Section 2.2.1.

Positioning data is generated by attributing the open interest in a commodity, at a specific point in time, between defined trader categories by long and short positions. This attribution is also done on a trader level, where the number of entities or 'traders' is given in each category.[1] The many relationships, patterns and dynamics between changes in open interest and changes in the number of traders both within and between trader categories are extensive and can often be surprising. As explained in Section 1.1, in Positioning Analysis, the relationship between these changes and changes in exogenous variables, including price and the levels of risk and uncertainty in the market, are considerable. A clear understanding of positioning data, specifically the classifications, and how the data is structured and reported, is a prerequisite in Positioning Analysis.

2.1.1 The Commitments of Traders (COT) Reports

Full descriptions of each COT report (CFTC and ICE) are given in Appendix 2. Not everything mentioned in the Appendix is covered in the book, but all relevant definitions, classifications, and terminology used in the book are explained in the Appendix. Appendix 2 was produced in January 2019, with links included to the related websites to ensure that the most up-to-date information is accessible.

2.1.1.1 The COT Release Schedule Understanding the release schedule is essential in Positioning Analysis and is particularly important when translating the data into trading signals.

All the positioning data used in this book is released on a weekly basis and is available on the source websites, Bloomberg, and other similar service providers. All the data in this book has been sourced from Bloomberg.

- The CFTC COT report is released every Friday at 3.30 p.m. Eastern Time (ET). The data is based on the open interest and trader numbers for the previous Tuesday. The data is, therefore, lagged by three trading days, as explained in Section 1.3.1. Note that 3.30 p.m. ET is after the markets close for all the markets covered in the report. This means that the earliest that any potential trading signals or strategies based on the data could be implemented would be on the following Monday.

- The ICE COT report is released every Friday at 6.30 p.m. London time – before the close of the markets.[2] The data is based on the open interest and trader numbers for the previous Tuesday and is therefore also lagged by just less than three trading days. It is, however, possible to trade ICE COT-related signals on Friday as the markets are still open.

---

[1]The CFTC and the ICE break the number of traders down between long and short traders within a specific category, whereas the LME reports only the total number of traders in the category (long and short combined).
[2]Previously, ICE COT data was released on the following Monday.

2.1.2 The COT Report Overview – Breaking It Down

Despite the existence of significant literature on COT data, it is worthwhile giving an example of the complete breakdown in positioning for one single commodity to show how all the data is derived and how all the trader groups are related.

A top-down approach, starting with total open interest in the market and the total number of registered traders and then moving into the various sub-categories, is taken. The corn market is used in the example as it is an agricultural market, and therefore includes several additional reports, including the old crop/other crop data, which are not included for non-seasonal commodities, and also commodity index data, which are included for selected agricultural markets.

For a comprehensive and accurate insight into the data, to ensure that all the numbers add up, combined futures and options data is used. The points raised in Section 1.4 do not apply, as the objective here is to only show how all open interest is broken down between all categories. As index data, which is part of the CIT supplement, is only reported as futures and options combined data, combined data is used for all categories.

The breakdown is shown in the form of a series of 'waterfall' charts that show how long and short open interest and trader numbers are attributed between the various categories. Categories from both the Legacy COT report and the Disaggregated COT report are also blended together to provide a complete picture and also to show how the data is related.[3]

As explained on the CFTC website, 'The Disaggregated COT report increases transparency from the Legacy COT reports by separating traders into the following four categories of traders: Producer/Merchant/Processor/User (PMPU); Swap Dealers (SD); Managed Money (MM); and Other Reportables (OR). The Legacy COT report separates reportable traders only into Commercial (C) and Non-Commercial (NC) categories.'

A detailed explanation of both reports, including the necessary reporting thresholds and category descriptions, is given in Appendix 2.

2.1.2.1 Breakdown into Long and Short Registered Positions On 25 December 2018, the last reported date of 2018, the total open interest (futures and options) in CME (Chicago Mercantile Exchange) corn was 1,856,868 contracts.[4] Figure 2.1 (Figure 2.2) shows the breakdown of total open interest into long (short) reportable positions and non-reportable (NR) positions. By definition, the total open interest of the long position will always be the same as that of the short position.

FIGURE 2.1 Breakdown of total open interest into long positions.
This chart is not shown on the website.
Source: Based on data from Bloomberg.

---

[3]The CFTC began publishing the Disaggregated COT report on 4 September 2009 alongside the legacy COT report, with disaggregated data dating back to 13 June 2006.
[4]25 December is a holiday, so the open interest data is for the day prior, 24 December.

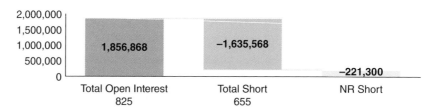

FIGURE 2.2 Breakdown of total open interest into short positions.
This chart is not shown on the website.
Source: Based on data from Bloomberg.

The total number of unique traders (of futures and options) in CME corn was 825, as shown under the *x*-axis labels. As only reportable traders are disclosed in the COT report, Figure 2.1 and Figure 2.2 show that there are no non-reportable traders. The number of long (short) traders is 660 (655), which adds up to 1315, which is higher than the total reported number of 825. This is because some long (short) traders also hold short (long) positions and are consequently included in both the long and short categories in the COT report.

This does not happen with open interest data as it is netted out. This can be seen in the example in Box 2.1, where there are four unique traders, but three traders with a long position and two traders with a short position.

Box 2.1 Example showing how trader numbers are reported

Assume a commodity futures market with four traders (A, B, C, and D).
    Assume:

- trader A is long 50 contracts of the January contract,
- trader B is short 100 contracts of the January contract,
- trader C is long 50 contracts of the January contract and short 100 contracts of the February contract, and
- trader D is long 100 contracts of the February contract.

The total number of unique traders is four, but there are three long traders (A, C, and D) and two short traders (B and C).

The total open interest is 200 contracts. The long open interest is 200 (50 January (A) + 50 January (C) + 100 February (D)) contracts. The short open interest is 200 (100 January (B) + 100 February (C)) contracts.

2.1.2.2 Breakdown into Non-Commercial (NC) and Commercial (C) Positions
Figure 2.3 (Figure 2.4) shows the breakdown of long (short) reportable positions open interest, into NC long (short), NC spreading, and C long (short) positions.

Figure 2.3 (Figure 2.4) also shows the breakdown of the long (short) traders into NC long (short), NC spreading, and C long (short) traders under the labels on the *x*-axis. The sum of the long (short) traders in the NC and C categories will not necessarily be equal to the total number

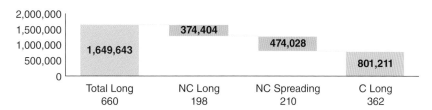

FIGURE 2.3 Breakdown of long position into NC and C positions.
This chart is not shown on the website.
Source: Based on data from Bloomberg.

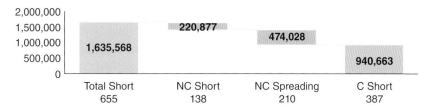

FIGURE 2.4 Breakdown of short position into NC and C positions.
This chart is not shown on the website.
Source: Based on data from Bloomberg.

of long (short) traders because of the duplication between the NC long (short) and NC spreading categories (some traders are both NC longs (shorts) and NC spread traders).[5]

2.1.2.3 Breakdown of the Commercial (C) Positions into Producer/Merchant/Processor/User (PMPU) and Swap Dealer (SD) Positions   Figure 2.5
(Figure 2.6) shows the breakdown of the C long (short) positions into the Producer/Merchant/Processor/User (PMPU) and Swap Dealer (SD) categories. These categories are provided in the

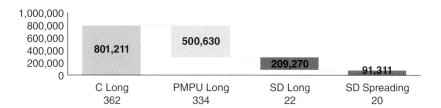

FIGURE 2.5 Breakdown of long C position into PMPU and SD positions.
This chart is not shown on the website.
Source: Based on data from Bloomberg.

---

[5]For the futures-only report, spreading measures the extent to which a trader holds equal long and short futures positions. For the options-and-futures-combined report, spreading measures the extent to which a trader holds equal combined-long and combined-short positions. For example, if a corn futures trader holds 2,000 long contracts and 1,500 short contracts, 500 contracts will appear in the 'Long' category and 1,500 contracts will appear in the 'Spreading' category.

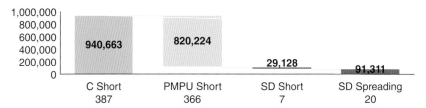

FIGURE 2.6 Breakdown of short C position into PMPU and SD positions. This chart is not shown on the website.
Source: Based on data from Bloomberg.

Disaggregated COT report, which includes more detailed trader classification categories than the commercial and non-commercial categories in the Legacy report.

Figure 2.5 (Figure 2.6) also shows the breakdown of the C long (short) traders into the PMPU and SD categories. Again, the sum of the long (short) traders in the PMPU and SD categories will not necessarily be equal to the total number of long (short) C traders because of the duplication between the SD long (short) and SD spreading categories (some traders are both SD longs (shorts) and SD spread traders).

2.1.2.4 Breakdown of the Non-Commercial (NC) Positions into Money Manager (MM) and Other Reportables (OR) Positions Figure 2.7 (Figure 2.8) shows the breakdown of the C long (short) positions into the MM and OR categories. As described in Section 2.1.2.3, these categories are in the Disaggregated COT report.

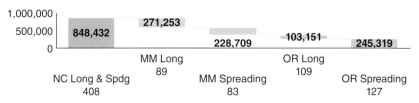

FIGURE 2.7 Breakdown of long NC position into MM and OR positions. This chart is not shown on the website.
Source: Based on data from Bloomberg.

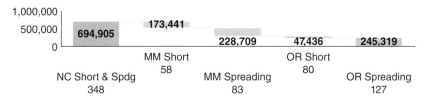

FIGURE 2.8 Breakdown of short NC position into MM and OR positions. This chart is not shown on the website.
Source: Based on data from Bloomberg.

Figure 2.7 (Figure 2.8) also shows the breakdown of the NC long (short) traders into the MM and OR categories. Again, the sum of the long (short) traders in the MM and OR categories will not necessarily be equal to the total number of long (short) NC traders because of the duplication between the MM long (short) and MM spreading categories and the OR long (short) and OR spreading categories (some traders are both MM longs (shorts) and MM spread traders, and some traders are both OR longs (shorts) and OR spread traders).

2.1.2.5 Breakdown into Commodity Index Traders (CIT) Positions
The CIT supplement to the COT was first published in January 2007 for 12 agricultural commodities.[6] Commodity indices include products like the S&P GSCI and the BCOM (Bloomberg Commodity) Index.[7] These are investment products that offer exposure to a basket of just over 20 different commodity futures. The commodities are weighted according to specific rules (typically based on variables such as production and liquidity) and the underlying futures contracts are rolled and rebalanced according to a strict methodology. Société Générale estimated the total investment in commodity indices at the end of 2018 at approximately $150 billion.

There are a wide variety of different commodity indices in the market, including sophisticated products based on complex roll methodologies and specific trading strategies. The latest generation of indices is referred to as 'risk premia' products that are often market-neutral and seek to generate returns from certain structural aspects of the market. Collectively, all these products are referred to as commodity indices. Most investments into commodity indices are long-only, but there is a small proportion that is short, as shown in Figure 2.9 and Figure 2.10. The short exposure can be investors that are short commodity indices or, more commonly, investors that are short as part of a risk premia strategy. These are explained in more detail in Section 9.3.

Figure 2.9 (Figure 2.10) shows the proportion of CIT long (short) open interest, including the number of long (short) CIT traders in the CME corn market.

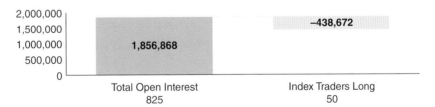

FIGURE 2.9 Breakdown of total open interest into long commodity index positions. This chart is not shown on the website.
Source: Based on data from Bloomberg.

---

[6]There is some relationship between 'index traders' positions in that supplement and 'swap dealer' positions in the Disaggregated COT, but there are notable differences. The 'swap dealer' category of the Disaggregated COT includes swap dealers that do not undertake any commodity index trading activity and are, therefore, not in the Index Traders category of the CIT Supplemental. Also, the 'index trader' category of the CIT supplement includes pension and other investment funds that place their index investment directly into the futures markets rather than going through a swap dealer. Those traders are classified as 'managed money' or 'other reportables' in the Disaggregated COT, depending on their business activity.

[7]https://us.spindices.com/index-family/commodities/sp-gsci and www.bloombergindices.com/bloomberg-commodity-index-family/.

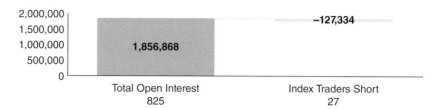

FIGURE 2.10 Breakdown of total open interest into short commodity index positions. This chart is not shown on the website.
Source: Based on data from Bloomberg.

2.1.2.6 Breakdown of Commodity Index Traders (CIT) Positions into Non-Commercial (NC) and Commercial (C) Positions Figure 2.11 (Figure 2.12) shows the breakdown of the long (short) index (CIT) positions into NC long (short) CIT, NC spreading CIT and C long (short) CIT positions.

Figure 2.11 (Figure 2.12) shows the breakdown of the long (short) index (CIT) traders into NC long (short) CIT, NC spreading CIT and C long (short) CIT traders. The sum of the long (short) traders in the NC long (short) CIT, NC spreading CIT and C long (short) CIT categories will not necessarily be equal to the total number of long (short) index traders because of the duplication between the NC long (short) CIT and NC spreading CIT categories.

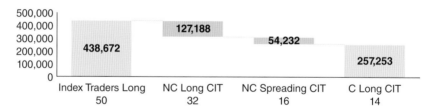

FIGURE 2.11 Breakdown of long index position into NC and C positions. This chart is not shown on the website.
Source: Based on data from Bloomberg.

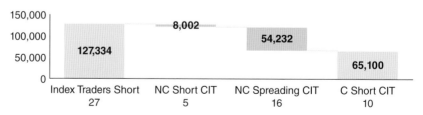

FIGURE 2.12 Breakdown of short index position into NC and C positions. This chart is not shown on the website.
Source: Based on data from Bloomberg.

2.1.2.7 Breakdown of Old and Other Data Positions

For selected commodities, where there is a well-defined marketing season or crop year, the COT data is broken down by 'old' (old data) and 'other' (other data) crop years.[8] This is described in Appendix 2.

Figure 2.13 shows the breakdown of total open interest and traders into 'old' crop years and 'other' crop years. The Old Data and Other Data traders will not necessarily add up to the total number of traders because some traders may be holding a spreading position between the old and other crop years.

Figure 2.14 shows the position (trader) distribution between the legacy COT report categories and Figure 2.15 shows the position (trader) distribution between the Disaggregated COT report categories.

FIGURE 2.13 Breakdown total open interest/traders into old and other crop year positions.
This chart is not shown on the website.
Source: Based on data from Bloomberg.

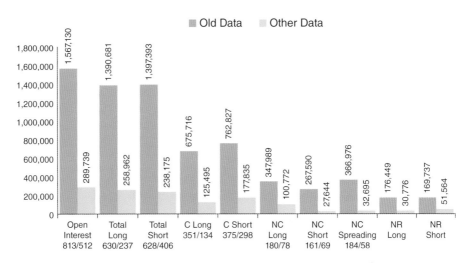

FIGURE 2.14 Position distribution between Old Data and Other Data – legacy COT report categories.
This chart is not shown on the website.
Source: Based on data from Bloomberg.

---

[8]These classifications are also referred to as 'old' crop and 'new' crop.

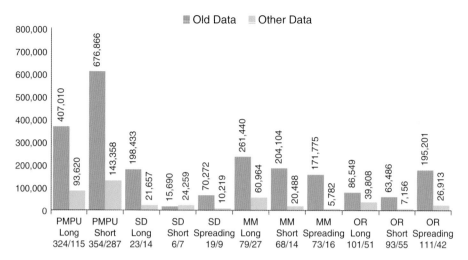

FIGURE 2.15 Position distribution between Old Data and Other Data – Disaggregated COT report categories.
This chart is not shown on the website.
Source: Based on data from Bloomberg.

2.1.2.8 The Top Four and Eight Largest Gross and Net Positions The CFTC and the ICE also report a concentration ratio, which shows the percentages of gross and net open interest held by the largest four and largest eight reportable traders respectively, but, importantly, without regard as to whether they are classified as commercial or non-commercial. The 'concentration ratio' is different from 'Concentration', introduced in Chapter 4.

These ratios are reported with trader positions computed on a 'gross long' and 'gross short' basis, and also on a 'net long' or 'net short' basis. The 'net position' ratios are computed after off-setting each trader's equal long and short positions. A reportable trader with large, balanced long and short positions in a single market, therefore, may be among the four and eight largest traders in both the gross long and gross short categories, but will probably not be included among the four and eight largest traders on a net basis.

This data can be interesting to see which markets are holding the largest positions, and how substantial positions have historically been. It can also be useful in providing information to either support or dispel rumours that certain traders might be holding or amassing disproportionally large positions.

2.2 Positioning Data for the London Metal Exchange (LME) – The MiFID Classifications

The Markets in Financial Instruments Directive II (MiFID II) regulation came into effect on 3 January 2018 with one objective being to improve the transparency of financial markets. Accordingly, Article 58 of MiFID II requires trading venues such as the London Metal

Exchange (LME) to publish weekly reports with aggregate positions held by different categories of persons.

In accordance with the new MiFID II regulation, the LME introduced a new Commitments of Traders report that replaced the pre-MiFID II COT (legacy COT) report. The new COT report was published in parallel with the legacy COT report for a four-week period (26 January 2018 to 23 February 2018) before the legacy COT report was discontinued entirely. The new report is now referred to as the LME COT report.[9]

The key features of this report are:[10]

- It is published every Tuesday at about 1.00 p.m. (UTC) with the data based on the open interest as of the close of business of the previous Friday. The report is therefore weekly and released with a lag of two business days.[11] A separate COT report is produced for each metal.

- For each trader classification, the report provides the number of long (short) positions, the percentage of total open interest represented by long (short) positions, and changes in the long (short) positions since the previous report. The total number of traders in each category (long and short combined) is also reported. Individual long and short trader numbers are not, however, reported.

- The COT report classifies traders into the following categories, defined in Box 2.2.
  1. investment firms or credit institutions (IF/CI)
  2. investment funds (IF)
  3. other financial institutions (OFI)
  4. commercial undertakings (CU)
  5. Directive 2003/87/EC (DCO).

- The LME COT report provides data on the futures positions on LME traded contracts combined with the delta-equivalent traded option positions, but warrants or Traded Average Price Option (TAPO) figures are not included.[12] Members are required to calculate the delta equivalent for all option positions. Futures data is not provided in isolation.

- Positions within each of the categories are reported according to whether they are risk-reducing or not. This is explained in Box 2.3.

---

[9]The ICE Futures Europe also launched a COT report in the new format on 2 February 2018. However, here the Exchange plans to continue publishing the existing CFTC format COT reports.

[10]Information extracted and sourced from the LME: www.lme.com/Market-Data/Reports-and-data/Commitments-of-traders#tabIndex=0.

[11]The legacy COT report was published weekly at the close of business each Tuesday, with daily reports for each business day of the previous week (Monday through Friday). The data was therefore daily but released only on a weekly basis with a lag of two business days.

[12]Option data was also included in the legacy COT report.

Box 2.2 The LME COT categories

Investment firms or credit institutions (IF/CI)

Investment funds (IF)

Investment funds, either an undertaking for collective investments in transferable securities (UCITS) as defined in Directive 2009/65/EC, or an alternative investment fund manager as defined in Directive 2011/61/EC.

Other financial institutions (OFI)

Other financial institutions, including insurance undertakings and reinsurance undertakings as defined in Directive 2009/138/EC and institutions for occupational retirement provision as defined in Directive 2003/41/EC.

Commercial undertakings (CU)

In the case of emission allowances and derivatives thereof, operators with compliance obligations under Directive 2003/87/EC. (Not applicable for the LME.)

Source: Based on data from www.lme.com/-/media/Files/Regulation/Mifid-ii/17.344-Appendix-6-LME-Position-Reporting-Guide.pdf.

Box 2.3 Risk-reducing positions

Under MiFID II, there is an obligation for reporting entities to categorise positions as risk-reducing or not. Risk-reducing positions are defined as 'Positions objectively measurable as reducing risks directly related to the commercial activity'. The standard developed for the purpose of MiFID II states that a derivative contract is objectively measurable as reducing risks directly relating to the commercial activity when, by itself or in combination with other derivative contracts, it meets one of the following criteria:

1. it reduces the risks arising from the potential change in the value of assets, services, inputs, products, commodities, or liabilities that the non-financial entity or its group owns, produces, manufactures, processes, provides, purchases, merchandises, leases, sells, or incurs or reasonably anticipates owning, producing, manufacturing, processing, providing, purchasing, merchandising, leasing, selling, or incurring in the normal course of its business;

2. it qualifies as a hedging contract pursuant to International Financial Reporting Standards (IFRS) adopted in accordance with Article 3 of Regulation (EC) No 1606/2002 of the European Parliament and of the Council.

Source: Based on data from www.lme.com/-/media/Files/Regulation/Mifid-ii/17.344-Appendix-6-LME-Position-Reporting-Guide.pdf.

2.2.1 The LME COT Report

The LME COT report is a new report which, as at the end of 2018, has only about one year of historical data available. This makes the data difficult to use in many of the analytics described throughout this book, as more extended periods of data are often required for defining the ranges and for calibration.

The sub-division of open interest into risk-reducing (RR) and non-risk-reducing positions (NRR) within each category in this new MiFID report is particularly interesting. For the first time in positioning data, an indication of the speculative activity of commercials and the hedging activity of investors becomes visible. This new report could, therefore, potentially provide new insights into the behaviour of metal prices.

The general expectation for a commercial trader, classified in this report as CU, would be only to use the LME to hedge their underlying metal price exposure – consequently, all trading activity would, therefore, be RR. Interestingly, their NRR trading activity is also reported, which, by definition, gives an indication of their speculative activity (on the basis that this would not reduce their risk). Theoretically, this gives a view of what CU traders might be thinking about future price direction.

CU traders, the equivalent of PMPU traders in the CFTC and ICE COT reports, are widely considered to be better informed than other trader categories on where prices are going, due to their proximity, exposure, and visibility to the underlying supply and demand dynamics of the market. This suggests that if a zinc CU trader – for example a zinc producer – were to take a large long NRR position in zinc, they are bullish prices and they might know something about future supply – potentially a supply cutback or a strike.

Conversely, with the trading activity of IF/CI traders mostly considered to be speculative, a long RR position in copper might have been taken as a hedge, against a client's option position or against an investment product such as a commodity index, or, if a short position, perhaps to protect a portfolio of mining equities. When assessing the speculative activity of traders in this group, it makes sense to remove these positions and consider only positions that are purely speculative, just the NRR open interest.

2.2.1.1 Refining the Speculative Activity of LME Participants In the legacy COT format, either MM positions or MM+OR (equivalent to the NC category) positions were used to measure speculative activity with the OR category in isolation becoming increasingly more interesting. This category included speculators trading on their own account; for example, propriety trading houses, family offices, and large individual speculators.

In the LME COT report, there are several alternative approaches to measure speculative activity:

1. **The most similar to the legacy report:** aggregate the long (short) positions across the IF/CI+IF+OFI categories to generate an equivalent measure of NC long (short) open interest.
2. **Refining point (i):** aggregate only the NRR long (short) positions across the IF/CI+IF+OFI categories to generate a more refined measure of only the speculative (NRR) open interest amongst the equivalent NC traders.
3. **Taking the NRR positions across all categories:** aggregate the long (short) NRR positions across the IF/CI+IF+OFI+CU categories to generate a measure of total speculative open interest – removing all hedge-related activity.
4. **Taking only the NRR in the CU category:** long (short) NRR positions for the CU category to isolate speculative open interest amongst the group considered to have increased visibility into the underlying market.

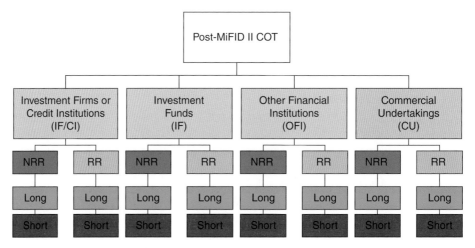

FIGURE 2.16 Overview of the LME COT report.
Source: Based on data from www.lme.com/-/media/Files/Regulation/Mifid-ii/17-344-Appendix-6-LME-Position-Reporting-Guide.pdf.

Figure 2.16 gives an overview of the LME COT reporting framework. The NC trader groups are shown in grey.

Collectively, the interplay between these groups combined with an ability to isolate speculative and hedging activity more precisely could potentially provide a more accurate set of signals, indicators, models, and analyses for the LME market. As the data history develops, time will tell whether this is the case.

One impediment, however, to LME Positioning Analysis lies in the report's inclusion of options data, without also separating out the futures-only data. As explained in Section 1.4, this can lead to problems in Positioning Analysis. There is also a risk, with position holders being able to calculate their own delta values when reporting positions, that the delta exposure might not be accurate.[13]

A further impediment lies in reconciling the COT data with the open interest in the market. Attempts to do this have so far revealed differences that are difficult to disentangle from potential option-related issues and/or from potential misclassification problems, and/or from reporting issues. Some of the patterns and profiles in the LME COT data are unusual and not intuitive.

For these reasons, LME positioning data has not been included in the analytics in this book. As the report becomes more established and these issues become clearer, the LME COT report is well placed to become a valuable addition to the positioning landscape.

---

[13]Source: LME Position Reporting Guide – Version 1.1.
www.lme.com/en-GB/About/Regulation/MiFID-II/Documents#tabIndex=0.

2.3 Other Types of Positioning and Flow Data

2.3.1 The London Bullion Market Association (LBMA) LBMA-i Trade Reporting Data

The London Bullion Market Association (LBMA) started publishing a weekly report on market activity on the London gold and silver over-the-counter (OTC) market on 20 November 2018. The report gives insight on the trading patterns and size of one of the world's oldest and largest markets. It provides data on the trading volumes and outstanding interest on the gold and silver OTC market.[14]

LBMA-i market data makes it possible for market participants to gauge the size and shape of the precious metals market for the first time in history.[15] The data represent all LBMA Market Makers' and some Full Members' share of the Loco London and Loco Zurich OTC markets. Data is displayed as a total over a business calendar week and is released each Tuesday at 9 a.m. (London time) aggregating trading data over the previous calendar week (Friday to Friday).

Trading volumes and outstanding interest on an array of different products including spot, forward and swaps, options, and leased gold, and on different maturity buckets, spot, 1-week, 2w, 1-month, 3m, 6m, 9m, 12m, and beyond 12m are provided in the report.

All LBMA trading members are required to report to the LBMA transactions on the LBMA spot, forwards, and options OTC markets, with the exception of small or exotic trades. As such, the report is compiled from the reported trades of the 13 market makers and some 44 other reporting entities (full members). It is, therefore, only partial in the sense that it does not include OTC trading flows outside of the LBMA precious metals markets and thus represents only the LBMA's members' share of the market rather than the global OTC gold market.

Whilst LBMA-i trade reporting data does not classify trading activity by trader group like the CFTC/ICE COT reports, and is therefore entirely flow driven, many of the signals, indicators, models, and analyses discussed in the book will not be applicable. The flow models and indicators like the speculation ratio, however, are applicable and this is discussed further in Section 12.3.

2.3.2 Shanghai Futures Exchange (SHFE) Member Volume, Open Interest Rankings

As stated on a report on the SHFE website, in June 2013 the exchange adopted an improved information publication approach pertaining to the ranking by trading volume and open interest, by revising the relevant provisions of the Trading Rules of the Shanghai Futures Exchange.

---

[14] Outstanding interest includes open interest in the swap, forward, options, and leasing market as well as spot transactions that have yet to be settled.

[15] LBMA-i is the transparency service for the precious metals market, delivered by Simplitium. The service collates trades from LBMA members and publishes anonymous and aggregated trading data to the market. Simplitium was appointed as LBMA's trade reporting service provider following an exhaustive selection process.

Simplitium's market-leading OTC trade reporting technology was the ideal foundation for this transparency service, which is shining a light on a sector that has until now been opaque. LBMA member reporting launched in Q1 2017. Weekly market data was disseminated from 20 November 2018 and daily from April 2019 onwards.

Source: www.simplitium.com/lbma-i-market-data.

The revised trading rules of the Shanghai Futures Exchange provide that the member-related trading information to be disseminated shall include: 'the total trading volume and open interest in the active futures contract months of futures firm members, the total trading volume and open interest in the active months of non-futures firm members, the trading volume and open interest in the active months of top 20 futures firm members'.[16]

This data is provided on a daily basis, with each member firm assigned a 4-digit code which can be identified on the SHFE website.[17] For example, the code 0049 is for the broker Jinrui Futures Co., Ltd, which is a holding subsidiary company for Jiangxi Copper. This does not, however, mean that all the trading activity by Jinrui Futures is from Jiangxi Copper only. Jiangxi Copper can execute their future orders with any brokerage firm, and similarly, Jinrui Futures can execute orders for many different clients.

This data lends itself well to clustering studies, with one aim being to reverse engineer any information in the holdings of the most significant positions in each commodity, to identify whether any trading patterns exist – particularly around expiry. Otherwise this data is difficult to use in Positioning Analysis as no classifications are given. An analysis of the trading activity on the SHFE and the other Chinese futures exchanges is covered in Chapter 13.

2.4 The Structure of Commodity Markets

Data on which commodities are the most liquid – in terms of the commodities with the highest (lowest) open interest and the highest (lowest) number of traders in each category – is useful in helping to understand which commodities might be the most or least vulnerable to shifts in investor sentiment, and whether more technically driven strategies or a more fundamentally driven approach might perform better. In addition, identifying the most (least) speculatively driven commodities, and similarly, the commodities with the highest (lowest) implied consumer and producer hedging activity, can also provide a solid foundation for many of the models and analytics presented in later chapters.

2.4.1 The Total Value of Each Commodity Market

Open interest gives useful information on one aspect of the liquidity of the market, but to evaluate the total value of the market – approximately equivalent to the market capitalisation in equity markets – the notional value of the open interest also needs to be determined. Using value instead of open interest is also an effective way of normalising the commodities for comparison purposes.

---

[16]Source: www.shfe.com.cn/en/content/cxxc/7wsxx.pdf.
[17]www.shfe.com.cn/en/aboutus/membership/memberlist/#.

The average value can be calculated by multiplying the average open interest over a period, for example 2018, by the average price of the commodity during the same period and then by the point value of the futures contract.[18] Using a one-year period is often sensible, as seasonal effects, which can cause significant variations in intra-year pricing for some commodities, are mitigated.

Using Brent as an example, and based on weekly data from the COT report, the average open interest in 2018 was 2,378,890 contracts. Using the settlement price of the second-month futures contract to reduce expiry-related volatility, and a point value of $1000, the average price in 2018 was $71.44. The average notional value of Brent for 2018 is therefore $169bn (2,378,890 × 71.44× 1000).[19]

Figure 2.17 shows the average notional value for 2018 across the major commodity markets in USD billions in a bubble diagram. This type of chart is good to highlight the vast differences in value between the most liquid commodities in the COT universe. Brent and crude oil (WTI) are the most liquid, with a combined average notional value over 2018 of $323bn.

The LME markets (copper, aluminium, nickel, zinc, lead, and tin) have been included only at the bottom of Figure 2.17 as the LME markets have not been included in many of the positioning analytics in the book for the reasons discussed in Section 2.2.1.

TABLE 2.1   **List of the commodity symbols used throughout the book.**

CO	Brent	KW	Kansas wheat
CC	Cocoa	LH	Lean hogs
KC	Coffee	LC	Live cattle
HG	Copper	NG	Natural gas
C	Corn	PA	Palladium
CT	Cotton	PL	Platinum
CL	Crude oil (WTI)	SI	Silver
FC	Feeder cattle	BO	Soybean oil
QS	Gasoil	S	Soybeans
XB	Gasoline (RBOB)	SM	Soymeal
GC	Gold	SB	Sugar
HO	Heating Oil	W	Wheat

---

[18]The point value of each commodity can be found on the exchange or on Bloomberg. It simply refers to the value of one point and is a function of the contract size. For Brent, the point value is $1000 as the futures price in $/barrel is based on a contract for 1000 barrels. This is different from the tick value (value of the smallest move in price) – which is $10 for Brent.

[19]To increase the accuracy of this figure, daily data would need to be used, and the price of each contract down the curve would need to be used in the proportion of the open interest distribution down the curve. This data is available on Bloomberg.

Total Value ($bn) – All Commodities

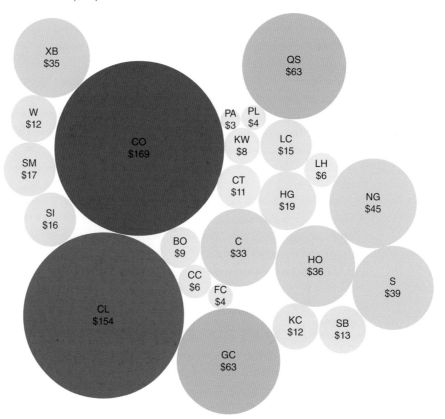

FIGURE 2.17 Average market value (2018) for major commodities (USD bn).
Commodity symbols: As listed in Table 2.1.
This chart is not shown on the website.
Source: Based on data from Bloomberg.

2.4.1.1 The Value of Each Commodity Market by Long Trader Group

Figure 2.18 shows a tree diagram of the same data in Figure 2.17 but broken down across the long trader groups. Total long and short open interest must equal each other, but the long and short trader distribution between groups does not. Figure 2.19 shows the breakdown by short open interest. Only the largest segments are labelled in these charts for clarity.

TABLE 2.2 List of the COT symbols used through this book.

SYMBOL	
C	Commercials
NC	Non-Commercials
NR	Non-Reportables
PMPU	Producer/Merchant/Processor/User
MM	Money Managers
OR	Other Reportables
SD	Swap Dealers

| **TABLE 2.2** | *(Continued)* |

SUFFIX

L (LT)	Long Open Interest (Long Number of Traders)
S (ST)	Short Open Interest (Short Number of Traders)
D (DT)	Spreading Open Interest (Spreading Number of Traders)
TOI	Total Open Interest
LPS	Long Position Size
SPS	Short Position Size

MML, therefore, refers to Money Manager long (open interest), and MMLT refers to the number of long Money Manager traders.

Total Value ($bn) by Trader Group (Long + Spreading) – All Commodities

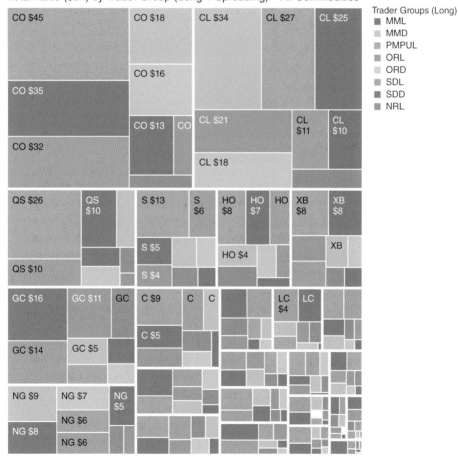

FIGURE 2.18 Average market value (2018) for major commodities by long trader group (USD bn).
Commodity symbols: As listed in Table 2.1.
COT symbols: As listed in Table 2.2.
This chart is not shown on the website.
Source: Based on data from Bloomberg.

Focusing on the Brent block in the top left of Figure 2.18, the long open interest is broken down into the seven major groups (MML, MMD, PMPUL, ORL, ORD, SDL, SDD, and NRL). The open interest is converted into dollar value and will equal the $169bn value for Brent shown in Figure 2.17. The PMPUL group is the largest, with a $45bn value, followed by the MML group at $35bn and the SDL category at $32bn. Compared to crude oil (WTI) in the right-hand block of Figure 2.18, the positioning structure is quite different. For crude oil (WTI), the largest proportion of long open interest is in the MMD category at $34bn. The relative differences in the ORL category are also significant; in Brent, the ORL category is $6bn and in crude oil (WTI) it is $21bn.

Differences in the positioning structure between these two very related markets can often be a driver of both differences in price behaviour and also in the structure of the forward curve.

2.4.1.2 The Value of Each Commodity Market by Short Trader Group
Figure 2.19 shows the same tree diagram but now broken down by short trader groups. The open interest is again converted into dollar value and will equal the $169bn value for Brent shown in Figure 2.17.

Total Value ($bn) by Trader Group (Short + Spreading) – All Commodities

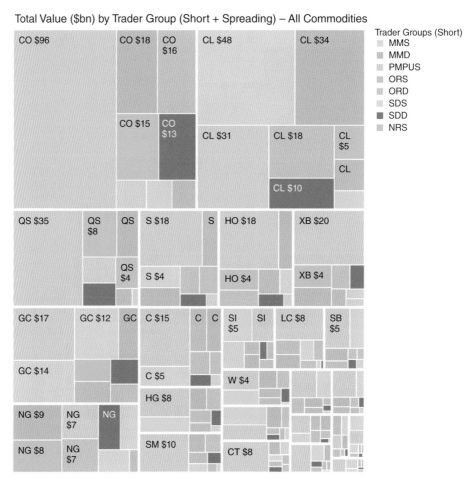

FIGURE 2.19 Average market value (2018) for major commodities by short trader group (USD bn).
Commodity symbols: As listed in Table 2.1.
COT symbols: As listed in Table 2.2.
This chart is not shown on the website.
Source: Based on data from Bloomberg.

Figure 2.19 shows a different structure to Figure 2.18. In general, there are larger boxes within each of the blocks – suggesting the short positioning is less diversified and arguably has a more straightforward structure than the long profile. Focusing again on Brent in the top left block, the PUPUS is more than 50% of the total open interest at $96bn. Looking at crude oil (WTI), the SDS group is the largest at $40bn (compared to $4bn for Brent), with the PMPUS group the third largest at $31bn.

The PMPUS and SDS groups are related to each other in that producer hedging makes up a sizeable proportion of their activity. The difference between PMPUS and SDS hedging is that the PMPUS group will hedge via futures directly, whereas for the SDS group the hedge is via a swap with a swap dealer.

Collectively, Figure 2.18 and Figure 2.19 provide an essential foundation in understanding the structure of the positioning between different commodities and also between the long and short positioning within the same commodity. These differences can be helpful in explaining behavioural differences between the markets.

2.4.1.3 Different Ways of Cutting the Data

To increase the visibility of the data in Figure 2.18 and Figure 2.19, and to build a better understanding of the underlying positioning structure for all commodities, Figure 2.20, Figure 2.21, Figure 2.22, and Figure 2.23 organise the data by long, short and, where applicable, spreading, for the MM, PMPU, OR, and SD groups respectively, as a percentage of total open interest (Concentration), and then by commodity.[20] Only the largest segments in each chart are labelled for clarity.

This provides excellent insight into which commodities are likely to be more speculatively driven and which are likely to be more fundamentally driven.[21] Figure 2.20 also shows that the MML and MMS proportions of total open interest are also very different, with the MML group being on aggregate larger than the MMS group. This is intuitive as long-only inventors in commodities are more widespread than short investors due to the general preference for a long exposure rather than a short exposure to the asset class.

The MML position palladium is significant at 52% of long open interest on average for 2018 – the largest for all commodities. In contracts, the MMD position for palladium is the smallest for all commodities (not labelled on the chart for clarity) but is approximately 3% of open interest. This information clearly points to a high level of directional speculative activity in palladium. In Figure 2.22, the ORL group for palladium is also significant at 27%, suggesting that most of the long length in the market is speculative in nature. This speculative composition of the ORL category is explained in Section 1.3.3.4.

Figure 2.24, Figure 2.25, Figure 2.26, and Figure 2.27 show the same data, but organised by the number of long, short, and spreading traders for the MM, PMPU, OR, and SD groups respectively, and then by commodity. This also provides excellent insight into which commodities are likely to be more sentiment driven – with a higher number of traders suggesting the propensity towards a higher proportion of sentiment activity.[22] Again, only the largest segments are labelled for clarity.

---

[20]Concentration is discussed in detail in Section 4.1.
[21]Commodities with a lower proportion of speculative open interest tend to be more fundamentally driven.
[22]This could contrast with a small number of traders holding exceptionally large positions, for example, which would not necessarily be indicative of the overall sentiment in the market. Furthermore, for sentiment to develop, many like-minded participants are needed to develop the herd-like characteristics that sentiment implies.

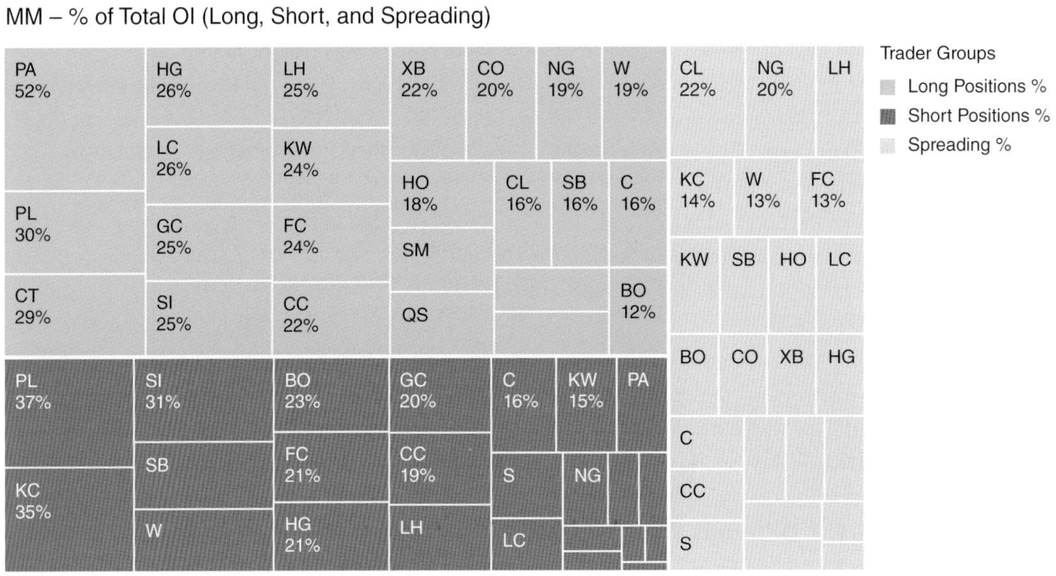

MM – % of Total OI (Long, Short, and Spreading)

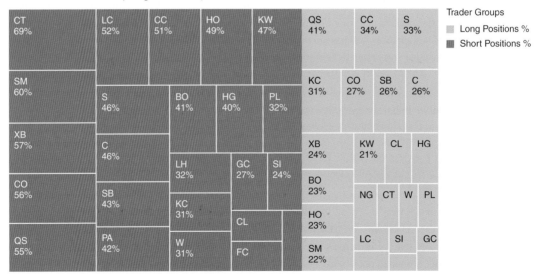

FIGURE 2.20 Average MM Concentration (2018 data) for major commodities.
Commodity symbols: As listed in Table 2.1.
This chart is not shown on the website.
Source: Based on data from Bloomberg.

PMPU – % of Total OI (Long and Short)

FIGURE 2.21 Average PMPU Concentration (2018 data) for major commodities.
Commodity symbols: As listed in Table 2.1.
This chart is not shown on the website.
Source: Based on data from Bloomberg.

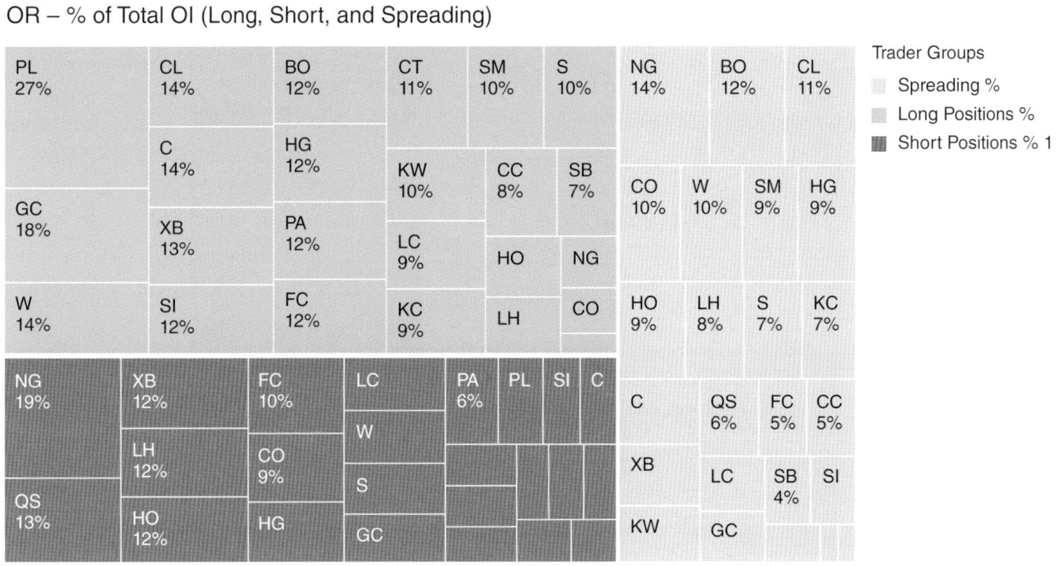

OR – % of Total OI (Long, Short, and Spreading)

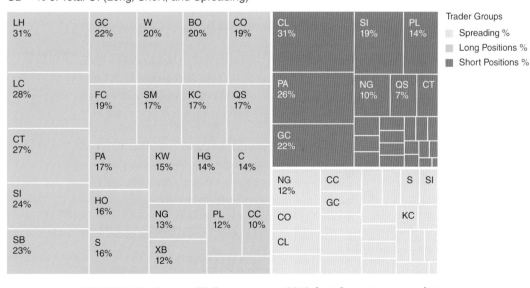

FIGURE 2.22 Average OR Concentration (2018 data) for major commodities.
Commodity symbols: As listed in Table 2.1.
This chart is not shown on the website.
Source: Based on data from Bloomberg.

SD – % of Total OI (Long, Short, and Spreading)

FIGURE 2.23 Average SD Concentration (2018 data) for major commodities.
Commodity symbols: As listed in Table 2.1.
This chart is not shown on the website.
Source: Based on data from Bloomberg.

MM – Traders (Long, Short, and Spreading)

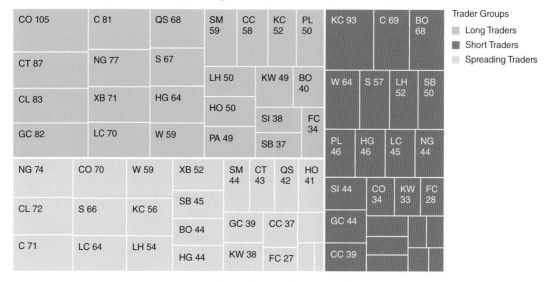

FIGURE 2.24 Average number of MM traders (2018 data) for major commodities.
Commodity symbols: As listed in Table 2.1.
This chart is not shown on the website.
Source: Based on data from Bloomberg.

PMPU – Traders (Long and Short)

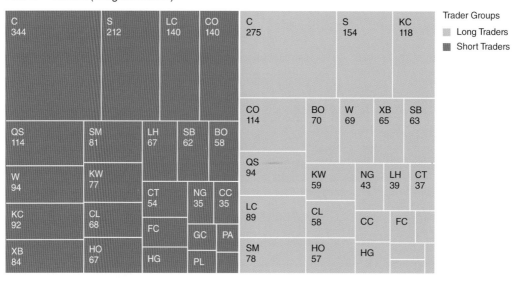

FIGURE 2.25 Average number of PMPU traders (2018 data) for major commodities.
Commodity symbols: As listed in Table 2.1.
This chart is not shown on the website.
Source: Based on data from Bloomberg.

OR – Traders (Long, Short, and Spreading)

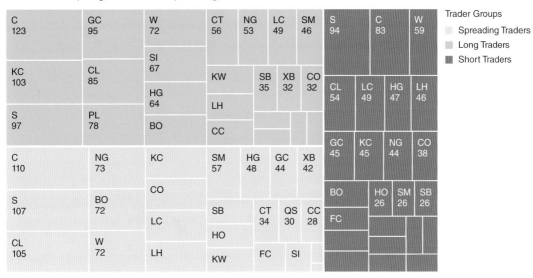

FIGURE 2.26 Average number of OR traders (2018 data) for major commodities.
Commodity symbols: As listed in Table 2.1.
This chart is not shown on the website.
Source: Based on data from Bloomberg.

SD – Traders (Long, Short, and Spreading)

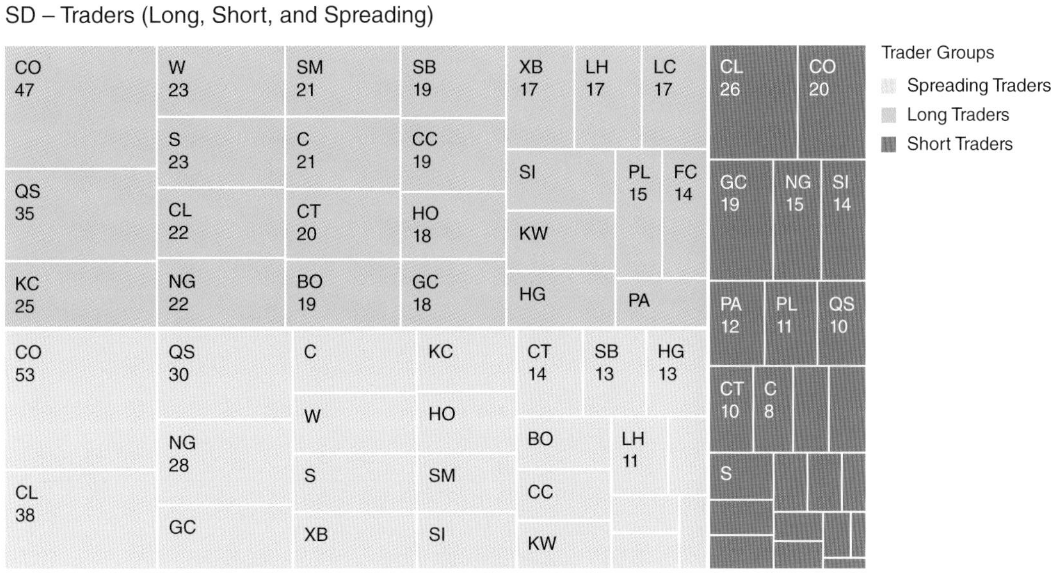

FIGURE 2.27 Average number of SD traders (2018 data) for major commodities.
Commodity symbols: As listed in Table 2.1.
This chart is not shown on the website.
Source: Based on data from Bloomberg.

By dividing the data in Figure 2.20 by the data in Figure 2.24, the average implied position sizes can be derived.[23] In the MM category, palladium has the largest implied long position size, with each trader on average holding 1.06% of the open interest (52%/49 traders). The largest implied short position size, with each trader on average holding 0.80% (37%/46 traders) of the open interest, is in platinum.

Collectively, these similarities and differences between markets provide a solid reference and foundation in being able to better understand and explain the behaviour of commodities in many of the models and analytics presented in later chapters.

---

[23]Position Size is discussed further in Section 4.1.

CHAPTER 3

Performance Attribution — An Insight into Sentiment and Behavioural Analysis?

Chapter objectives

Changes in positioning, especially speculative positioning, can impact prices through different channels. This can either be directly – due to the actual trade flow in the market, or indirectly – by shaping sentiment and affecting the behaviour of market participants. The interplay between these dynamics can be challenging to disentangle, but together they are important in understanding price evolution and risks in the market. An awareness of how effective speculators have been at generating profits in a particular market is also important in being able to provide a degree of conviction to the analysis.

Whilst the focus of this chapter is on speculative activity, how other trader groups perform can also be useful when trying to understand other aspects of price.

A robust and intuitive model to show the markets where speculators have performed best is developed. The objective in doing this lies in the assumption that the markets in which speculators have historically generated positive returns should be markets where they are likely to continue to perform. Future trends and shifts in the positioning in these markets could, therefore, provide useful trading indicators and signals.

The model captures and attributes performance between two aspects of their positioning – whether their net futures position is long or short and whether the net trader number positioning is long or short. The results from these analyses provide valuable insights into whether positive MM returns have on balance been generated by a few large traders or more widely across all MMs.

The model also shows whether MMs are better in generating absolute or relative returns, and then by extending the analysis to other trader groups, which are the best trader groups to look at.

3.1 The Proliferation of Speculative Positioning Data

Figure 3.1 shows how positioning-related newsflow has increased since 2014. The chart plots the evolution of a newsflow index that measures the number of stories or reports each week, recorded on the Bloomberg terminal that includes COT-related terminology in the context of commodity markets. The number of stories per week increased significantly from about 5–10 per week in 2015 to approximately 50 per week in 2018. The grey line, which shows the total number of Bloomberg stories per week, has stayed roughly constant, indicating that there has been no structural increase in the number of stories overall.

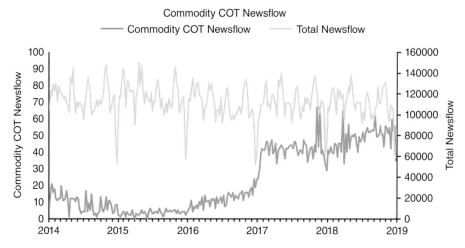

FIGURE 3.1 Commodity positioning newsflow.
This chart is not shown on the website.
Source: Based on data from Bloomberg.

3.2 Why is Positioning Data Interesting

Positioning data and, in the context of newsflow, mostly speculatively driven positioning data have several attributes that help explain why it so widely followed.

1. Speculators, and more specifically hedge funds, are widely viewed as specialists in their field. This is invariably due to the view that they often have significant research and technical resources at their disposal and are known for developing highly sophisticated trading models and algorithms. Trends and changes in their positioning are often viewed as indicators of future price direction and the size of their position as an indication of their conviction.

2. Most other market participants have an interest in speculative activity. Commercial traders that are typically quite fundamental in their trading approach are often particularly interested in speculative activity, as the methodologies used by speculators can be quite different from their own. This is particularly true when it comes to more quantitative trading strategies that might be based on complex trading algorithms or strategies implemented via a risk premia approach.[1] The recent growth in high-frequency trading (HFT), Big Data, machine learning, and artificial intelligence (AI) has been a key driver of this interest.

3. In general, the direction (whether long or short) of speculative positioning data is mostly stable, with positions not changing significantly from week to week. It would, for example, be unusual to see MM positioning flip successively between net long and net short in a market. Instead, changes in positioning often show a high degree of positive serial correlation as the trading algorithms and systems that are increasingly driving the investment, trading, and rebalancing decisions, seek to minimise market impact and trading costs by building and adjusting positions over time. Consequently, changes in positioning may sometimes not have a significant effect on price, but they can be important drivers of sentiment and behaviour over extended periods of time.

4. The opposite is mostly true when speculative positions are unwound, and particularly so when speculative positions are extreme in size. In contrast to point 3, these changes can be very sudden, often exacerbated by the same algorithms and systems that established them, but now designed to swiftly exit a position. Here the impact on both price, sentiment, and behaviour can be considerable.

Speculative activity has two main channels of influence on prices: a market impact that can affect the price and a sentiment effect that can change behaviour. The interplay of these dynamics can be challenging to disentangle, but collectively, they are essential in understanding how prices may evolve and where risks may lie. Consequently, speculative activity in particular tends to attract a disproportionate amount of interest in Positioning Analysis.

In this chapter, questions on whether speculators generate positive performance, and if so, how so and in which commodities are addressed. This is useful in providing further insight into many of the analytics throughout the book. It is also helpful in developing more profound insights into trading performance, such as whether the performance is likely driven by a small number of large traders or whether it is more widespread.

---

[1] Risk premia strategies are discussed further in Section 9.3.

3.3 Measuring the Skill or Performance of MMs

The CFTC COT report is published every Friday (the 'Release date') at 3.30 p.m. Eastern Time (ET) and gives a complete breakdown of the open interest in all major commodities by trader category as at the close on the previous Tuesday (the 'Report date'), meaning that the data is lagged by three full trading days (Wednesday, Thursday, and Friday). Importantly, it is also is released after the close of all commodity futures markets, so as shown throughout this book, trading signals based on the data can only be implemented on the following Monday. The release for ICE data, including Brent and gasoil, is, however, released on Friday (6.30 p.m. London time), and is also as at the previous Tuesday, but technically only lagged by just under three full trading days. This is explained in Section 2.1.1.1.

3.3.1 The Reporting Timeline

Section 1 in Figure 3.2 displays the weekly CFTC reporting timelines. At the end of a trading week, running from Tuesday to Tuesday, the open interest at the close of the day (red line) is broken down, attributed between the various trader categories, and reported at 3.30 p.m. ET on Friday (blue line) by the CFTC. The three-day lag period is illustrated in grey. For simplicity, the ICE COT timeline is taken to be the same as the CFTC COT report for use in the model below.

3.3.2 Developing a Performance Model

To evaluate the historical performance of the MMs, representative of much of the speculative activity in a market, a robust and intuitive model to evaluate the performance in each commodity is developed.[2] The approach is as follows:

- Every week, the net MM position for each commodity at the start and end of the trading week (running from Tuesday to Tuesday) is recorded. The lag is ignored, as the model is

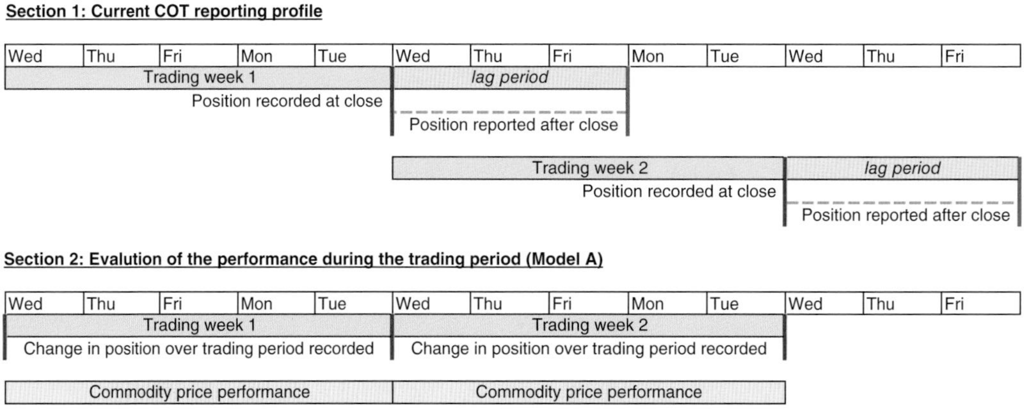

Section 1: Current COT reporting profile

Section 2: Evalution of the performance during the trading period (Model A)

FIGURE 3.2 Overview of the reporting timeline and the evaluation periods. *Source:* Author.

[2]The OR category is also largely speculative, as explained in Section 1.3.3.4.

backwards-looking and will not be used as a trading strategy. This period is shown in Section 2 of Figure 3.2 as the periods between the two red lines.

■ If the net MM position is directionally the same (long or short) at the start *and* end of the trading week, it is assumed that the position remained directionally the same throughout the week. Note that only the net direction of the position is considered, as there is no way of knowing if, or how, the size of the position changed intra-week.

■ If the net position is directionally different at the end of the trading week from the start of the week, that week is ignored from the evaluation as there is no way of knowing when the position changed. For each commodity, the total number of ignored weeks is recorded, with the balance reported as a percentage of the total number of weeks used in the evaluation. This gives an idea of how representative the final results are of the entire period.

■ The change in the price of the underlying commodity is then recorded for the Trading week. This is shown as the yellow box in Section 2 of Figure 3.2. Bloomberg Commodity (BCOM) Excess Return (ER) mono-indices are used to calculate the price changes to remove any issues relating to futures contract expiry.[3]

■ The objective of the model is to evaluate MM performance, specifically whether MMs were successful in the directionality of their positioning. This performance is gauged by cumulating the price changes during the weeks when their positioning was 'correct' and subtracting the price changes during the weeks when it was 'incorrect'. If, for example, MMs were net long during a week, and the change in price was up (down) 1% over that week (Tuesday to Tuesday), a +1% (-1%) price change would be recorded. If the MMs were net short during that week, and the change in price was up (down) 1% over that week, a -1% (+1%) price change would be recorded.

■ The MM positioning is then evaluated in two ways: in terms of the net long and short futures open interest; and, in terms of the net number of long and short traders. This data is required to be able to evaluate differences in performance between the net futures positioning and the net trader positioning.

■ To evaluate the performance over more prolonged periods: – for example, a year – the weekly price changes are cumulated. This means that if MMs were net long over the first three weeks of 2007, and the performance of the BCOM crude oil ER Index over these three weeks was 0.24%, -9.04%, and -8.42%, the total performance of MMs in crude oil for the three-week period would be recorded as -17.22% (0.24% + -9.04% + -8.42%). No compounding is performed to mitigate against any path dependency in the analysis. It is also assumed that there is no leverage.

■ The cumulative returns of the MMs are finally compared to the cumulative long-only returns in the market (calculated in the same way) to evaluate the relative performance of the MMs. Box 3.1 provides an example of the approach.

---

[3] https://data.bloomberglp.com/indices/sites/2/2017/10/BCOM_methodology_20171013.pdf.

Box 3.1 A hypothetical example showing the model's approach

Assume that at the beginning and end of Trading week 1, MMs were net long cotton (the size of the position is not considered). The model assumes that MMs were net long throughout the week and that the size of their position did not change. If during that week the BCOM cotton ER index rose by 1%, a +1% price change would be recorded.

If at the end of Trading week 2, the MMs were net short cotton, the position must have changed intra-week from net long to net short. As there is no way of knowing when this change occurred, this week is removed from the study.

If at the end of a 52-week year there were:

- 30 weeks where the MM positions were net long throughout the week, and the market was up 1% in each of those weeks, a cumulative price change of 30% will be recorded for those weeks;
- 10 weeks where the MMs were net long throughout the week, but the market was down by 1% in each of those weeks, a cumulative price change of -10% will be recorded;
- 5 weeks where the MMs were net short throughout the week, and the market was down by 1% in each of those weeks, a cumulative price change of +5% will be recorded.

This gives a total cumulative return for the year of +25% (+30% -10% + 5%). For the remaining seven weeks of the year, the position changed intra-week, and so these weeks are ignored. This means that only 45 of the 52 weeks (86.5% coverage) were evaluated by the model.

The model is simple, and any conclusions based on the results need to be mindful of the assumptions, constraints, and limitations in the data and approach. The approach does, however, give broad insight into the speculative performance of MMs across a wide range of commodities.

3.3.3 Absolute Performance Based on Net Futures Positioning

Figure 3.3 shows the results of the analysis over the last 10 years across 24 different commodity markets using net MM futures positioning data.

The 'Average' column to the right of the table shows the average price change over the entire 10-year period for each commodity, and the 'Average' row at the bottom of the table, the annual averages across all commodities. The 'Success' column shows the percentage of years where a positive price performance was generated. The 'Cover' column indicates the number of weeks evaluated for each commodity over the period. As explained in Section 3.3.2, weeks where the net futures position at the beginning of the week was different from that at the end of the week were ignored.

Figure 3.3 shows that on average, 94% of weeks over the 10-year period were evaluated. There were only five full years of data for Brent and gasoil (shaded orange) and seven full years of data for palladium and platinum (shaded light orange).

	2009	2010	2011	2012	2013	2014	2015	2016	2017	2018	Average	Success	Cover
Crude oil	28%	8%	5%	−16%	12%	−49%	−48%	14%	6%	−26%	−7%	60%	99%
Brent						−61%	−51%	30%	15%	−20%	−17%	40%	100%
Gasoline	77%	9%	21%	22%	5%	−55%	−6%	−5%	−5%	−36%	3%	50%	98%
Heating oil	35%	8%	14%	−10%	−14%	38%	47%	−1%	−3%	−17%	10%	50%	95%
Gasoil						−22%	40%	33%	19%	−10%	12%	60%	96%
Natural gas	55%	54%	50%	24%	−14%	8%	50%	21%	−27%	15%	24%	80%	95%
Corn	6%	28%	6%	24%	5%	−17%	−14%	−11%	−11%	3%	2%	60%	97%
Wheat	−19%	38%	−14%	7%	32%	−7%	−22%	26%	−7%	−13%	2%	40%	94%
Kansas wheat	−21%	28%	−24%	3%	−22%	0%	−17%	10%	−3%	−10%	−6%	30%	96%
Soybeans	29%	24%	−6%	26%	10%	−2%	−19%	13%	−19%	−9%	5%	50%	97%
Beanoil	−6%	37%	−17%	−11%	23%	−24%	16%	12%	−2%	21%	5%	50%	93%
Soymeal	38%	36%	−14%	40%	19%	16%	7%	1%	−6%	−5%	13%	70%	98%
Cotton	30%	78%	−22%	9%	9%	−28%	−1%	12%	12%	−5%	9%	60%	94%
Coffee	3%	51%	−8%	25%	36%	15%	−15%	−8%	18%	26%	14%	70%	96%
Sugar	74%	42%	−10%	−15%	−4%	7%	36%	14%	−9%	11%	15%	60%	95%
Cocoa	26%	−23%	17%	−3%	17%	10%	9%	−25%	2%	−10%	2%	60%	99%
Gold	24%	25%	14%	4%	−30%	0%	−2%	4%	11%	2%	5%	80%	99%
Silver	49%	62%	4%	7%	−13%	15%	2%	16%	−12%	−1%	13%	70%	97%
Palladium			5%	7%	12%	−34%	24%	47%	10%	10%	86%	67%	
Platinum			8%	−10%	−11%	−30%	4%	−9%	2%	−7%	43%	67%	
Copper	−47%	28%	−5%	−11%	15%	3%	27%	3%	25%	−1%	4%	60%	91%
Live cattle	−11%	15%	2%	−4%	−5%	22%	−15%	−5%	10%	1%	1%	50%	99%
Feeder cattle	−10%	20%	12%	−15%	6%	30%	−20%	15%	17%	−9%	5%	60%	94%
Lean hogs	41%	1%	1%	2%	−5%	−2%	−28%	−1%	8%	−24%	−1%	50%	96%
Average	20%	28%	1%	5%	4%	−4%	−4%	8%	3%	−4%	5%	58%	94%

FIGURE 3.3 Absolute performance attribution based on net futures positioning.
Source: Based on data from Bloomberg.

The 'Cover' column also gives insight into the commodities where MMs have switched positions (between net long and net short) most frequently. Historically, platinum and palladium have had the highest number of changes, and Brent, crude oil (WTI), cocoa, gold, and live cattle have had the least.

The 'Average' column shows that the average cumulative absolute price performance was positive for all the commodities except crude oil (WTI), Brent, Kansas wheat, platinum, live cattle, and lean hogs.

The best performance for MMs has been in natural gas, sugar, and coffee, with palladium, gold, and natural gas having the highest percentage of successful years. The worst performance for MMs has been in Brent, platinum, and crude oil (WTI), with Kansas wheat, Brent, and platinum having the lowest percentage of successful years.

As most MMs have the flexibility to be net long or short (and hence could be positioned oppositely to the market's direction), positive performance on an absolute basis is an important and informative metric. Assuming this profile continues, it could make sense to track the positioning profile of MMs in the commodities with both strong positive and negative performance statistics. The logic being that given the strong historical performance of natural gas, a net long position on natural gas could suggest that the MMs have made a correct decision and prices would move higher. Conversely, given the poor performance in Brent, a net long position could suggest that the MMs have got it wrong and prices could fall.

It is also noteworthy that the commodities that generally attract the highest degree of attention with respect to changes in their positioning, such as crude oil (Brent and WTI), are among the poorest performing commodities in the model. It is also interesting that natural gas, one of the commodities most feared by speculators due to its volatility, is the best-performing commodity.

3.3.4 Relative Performance Based on Net Futures Positioning

In Figure 3.4, the relative price performance is shown. This is calculated by taking the absolute performance of the MMs in Figure 3.3 and subtracting the price performance of the underlying market.[4]

To give an example: if MMs were net short, and the price of the commodity fell by 1%, an absolute price change of +1% would be recorded in Figure 3.3 as described in Section 3.3.2, but a relative price change of +2% would be recorded in Figure 3.4. A positive relative performance shows that MMs have 'outperformed' the market. As this model assumes no leverage, 'outperformance' can only be generated in falling markets.

	2009	2010	2011	2012	2013	2014	2015	2016	2017	2018	Average
Crude oil											0%
Brent											0%
Gasoline		−7%					−2%	−17%	−11%		−4%
Heating oil	−4%	−3%		−15%	−17%	85%	94%	−34%	−18%		9%
Gasoil						36%	84%	3%			25%
Natural gas	111%	108%	102%	55%	−23%	32%	99%	6%	26%	−13%	50%
Corn	5%	−3%			39%	−7%	5%	−3%	2%	7%	5%
Wheat	4%	11%	22%	−10%	64%	−2%	−1%	51%	5%	−23%	12%
Kansas wheat	−2%	−13%		−11%	8%		19%	38%	11%	−15%	4%
Soybeans		−7%	8%				−4%	−4%	−10%	4%	−1%
Beanoil	−25%	4%	−5%	−2%	46%	−6%	24%	1%	7%	43%	9%
Soymeal			3%	−7%			24%	−17%	−2%	−1%	0%
Cotton	−3%			12%		−9%	−4%	2%			0%
Coffee	−16%	−5%		71%	73%	−26%	19%	−13%	35%	52%	19%
Sugar					15%	41%	39%	−9%	15%	33%	13%
Cocoa		−16%	48%	−10%				7%	20%	−28%	2%
Gold							9%	−3%		5%	1%
Silver					26%	31%	16%		−15%	12%	7%
Palladium										−5%	−1%
Platinum									−12%	19%	1%
Copper	−142%		18%	−16%	20%	19%	54%	−14%		21%	−4%
Live cattle	0%				1%						0%
Feeder cattle	−5%	−2%		−7%	9%		2%	27%		−11%	1%
Lean hogs	60%			3%	−2%					−14%	5%
Average	−1%	3%	10%	3%	12%	8%	20%	1%	2%	4%	6%

FIGURE 3.4 Relative performance attribution based on net futures positioning.
Source: Based on data from Bloomberg.

[4]The underlying market performance is the cumulative weekly performance of all weeks in the year – approximately equivalent to a long-only exposure, using the same calculation methodology as the model, i.e. without compounding.

In Figure 3.4, the cumulative relative average price performance was positive for all commodities except gasoline, copper, soybeans, and palladium, which shows that, on average, MMs generated positive relative returns across most commodities.

The best outperformance for MMs occurred in natural gas, gasoil, and coffee. Negative outperformance occurred in gasoline, copper, and soybeans.

3.3.5 Absolute Performance Based on Net Trader Number Positioning

Figure 3.5 and Figure 3.6 show the cumulative absolute and relative price performances using positioning data based on the net trader number positioning – specifically, the difference between the number of traders that are reported long and those that are reported short.

The difference between these results and the results generated in Section 3.3.3 and Section 3.3.4 is significant. Performance based on the net number of traders improves significantly for nearly all markets except natural gas, heating oil, cocoa, and feeder cattle. The 'Success' metric is also either the same or higher for all nearly all markets.

Figure 3.5 shows that, on average, 89% of weeks were evaluated for each commodity – less than the 94% in Figure 3.3. This means that net trader positioning data is, on average, more dynamic than net futures positioning data. Palladium and platinum switched trader positions

	2009	2010	2011	2012	2013	2014	2015	2016	2017	2018	Average	Success	Cover
Crude oil	10%	7%	19%	−40%	12%	−34%	−4%	25%	−7%	1%	−1%	60%	85%
Brent						16%	−9%	30%	8%	−20%	5%	60%	90%
Gasoline	77%	16%	21%	22%	5%	−55%	−4%	13%	8%	−36%	7%	70%	99%
Heating oil	−8%	5%	14%	−3%	−11%	13%	22%	12%	−11%	−7%	3%	50%	88%
Gasoil						49%	47%	−13%	19%	9%	22%	80%	92%
Natural gas	14%	20%	23%	27%	18%	−25%	42%	29%	−15%	16%	15%	80%	81%
Corn	24%	39%	6%	−2%	19%	15%	−13%	−8%	−8%	−8%	6%	50%	93%
Wheat	14%	24%	−4%	5%	31%	1%	−39%	32%	−10%	−15%	4%	60%	88%
Kansas wheat	−17%	52%	−24%	24%	−34%	0%	5%	14%	11%	0%	3%	60%	95%
Soybeans	25%	21%	−13%	24%	10%	14%	−3%	12%	−19%	−12%	6%	60%	93%
Beanoil	−14%	37%	−14%	−13%	21%	10%	9%	14%	1%	20%	7%	70%	89%
Soymeal	38%	34%	−14%	40%	19%	16%	2%	14%	−9%	−4%	14%	70%	96%
Cotton	30%	78%	−16%	2%	13%	11%	−3%	12%	12%	2%	14%	80%	92%
Coffee	−3%	33%	−3%	40%	29%	22%	−18%	0%	16%	26%	14%	70%	90%
Sugar	74%	42%	−10%	−5%	9%	14%	31%	16%	−6%	−1%	16%	60%	91%
Cocoa	13%	−35%	10%	−18%	1%	10%	9%	−5%	−2%	−4%	−2%	50%	94%
Gold	24%	25%	14%	4%	−12%	−1%	−8%	6%	11%	−3%	6%	60%	96%
Silver	49%	62%	4%	19%	11%	6%	−7%	16%	4%	8%	17%	90%	93%
Palladium				10%	7%	12%	−17%	17%	47%	8%	12%	86%	63%
Platinum				8%	−10%	−11%	−16%	−4%	12%	8%	−2%	43%	64%
Copper	48%	28%	11%	−19%	11%	14%	33%	9%	25%	−8%	15%	80%	88%
Live cattle	−8%	15%	−6%	−14%	2%	22%	−13%	20%	10%	−5%	2%	50%	90%
Feeder cattle	−5%	18%	−1%	−3%	7%	30%	−1%	−11%	15%	−10%	4%	40%	89%
Lean hogs	71%	−1%	9%	4%	4%	−2%	−7%	17%	4%	11%	11%	70%	88%
Average	23%	26%	1%	5%	7%	6%	2%	11%	5%	−1%	8%	65%	89%

FIGURE 3.5 Absolute performance based on net trader number positioning (trader alignment). *Source:* Based on data from Bloomberg.

(between net long and net short) the most often, and gasoline, soymeal, and gold the least. The cumulative absolute average price performance was positive for all commodities except cocoa, platinum, and crude oil (WTI).

Based on net trader positioning, the best performance for MMs occurred in gasoil, silver, and sugar, with silver, palladium, gasoil, natural gas, cotton, and copper having the highest percentage of positive years. The worst performance occurred in platinum, cocoa, and crude oil (WTI).

3.3.6 Relative Performance Based on Net Trader Number Positioning (Trader Alignment)

In Figure 3.6 the relative price performance is shown. This is calculated in the same way as Figure 3.4. The cumulative relative average price performance was positive for all commodities except cocoa, showing that based on net trader positioning, MMs generated positive relative returns across most commodities.

The best outperformance for MMs occurred in natural gas, gasoil, and Brent. Negative outperformance occurred in cocoa.

Consistent with the net trader performance on an absolute basis, the net trader performance on a relative basis is also generally better than the net futures performance on a relative basis.

	2009	2010	2011	2012	2013	2014	2015	2016	2017	2018	Average
Crude oil	−18%	−1%	13%	−25%		16%	44%	11%	−13%	27%	5%
Brent						78%	42%		−7%		23%
Gasoline								1%	3%		0%
Heating oil	−47%	−7%		−8%	−14%	60%	69%	−21%	−26%	11%	2%
Gasoil						107%	91%	−43%	0%	20%	35%
Natural gas	69%	74%	75%	58%	9%	−1%	92%	13%	38%	−12%	41%
Corn	23%	9%		−26%	53%	25%	7%	0%	5%	−3%	9%
Wheat	37%	−2%	32%	−11%	63%	6%	−18%	58%	1%	−24%	14%
Kansas wheat	2%	11%		11%	−4%		41%	42%	25%	−5%	12%
Soybeans	−4%	−11%	0%	−2%		16%	13%	−6%	−10%	1%	0%
Beanoil	−33%	4%	−2%	−4%	45%	28%	17%	3%	10%	42%	11%
Soymeal		−2%	3%	−7%			19%	−4%	−5%	0%	0%
Cotton	−3%		6%	5%	4%	30%	−6%	2%		7%	4%
Coffee	−22%	−23%	6%	86%	66%	−19%	16%	−4%	32%	52%	19%
Sugar		0%		9%	27%	48%	34%	−6%	18%	21%	15%
Cocoa	−14%	−29%	41%	−26%	−16%			28%	16%	−23%	−2%
Gold					19%	−2%	4%	−1%		0%	2%
Silver				12%	50%	22%	7%		0%	21%	11%
Palladium				5%			17%	−6%		−8%	1%
Platinum				0%			14%	−8%	10%	24%	6%
Copper	−48%	0%	34%	−24%	15%	30%	60%	−7%		14%	8%
Live cattle	2%		−8%	−10%	7%		3%	25%		−6%	1%
Feeder cattle	0%	−4%	−13%	5%	9%		21%	1%	−2%	−13%	0%
Lean hogs	90%	−2%	7%	5%	8%		20%	18%	−4%	21%	16%
Average	2%	1%	10%	2%	16%	18%	25%	4%	4%	7%	10%

FIGURE 3.6 Relative performance based on net trader number positioning (trader alignment). *Source:* Based on data from Bloomberg.

3.4 Net Futures Positioning vs Net Trader Number Positioning or Alignment

The difference in performance attribution between net futures data and net trader number data highlights important behavioural and sentiment dynamics in commodity markets.

The difference lies in what each set of data represents. Net trader positioning reflects the overall positioning in the markets and to a degree is representative of the sentiment in the market. This information can be easily obscured when looking at net futures positioning, especially when there are large futures positions in the market. This is illustrated in the following example.

Consider a hypothetical group of ten traders, where nine traders are long 100 contracts each, and one trader is short 3000 contracts. The net futures position would be reported as short 2100, and the net trader position as long 8. In this example, based on the model described in Section 3.3.2, a move higher in the market would be recorded as negative performance based on the net futures position, but a positive performance when the positioning is based on the net trader number position. In this example, the large short trader was wrong, whereas the wider group of all traders were correct despite them all having smaller positions.

Figure 3.7 shows the difference between Figure 3.5 and Figure 3.3 (net traders positioning – net futures positioning) and the generally superior performance based on net trader number positioning.

Differences between these two performance numbers could also suggest that the following dynamics are at play: if the net futures performance is better (worse) than the net traders performance, it might be the case that a small number of MM traders, or even a single MM trader, with a large position as illustrated in the example above are generating positive (negative) performance. This is particularly evident in natural gas, heating oil, and cocoa, where the net futures performance is greater than the net trader performance, suggesting some MMs are taking large positions, opposite to the net trader position, and they are generating positive returns. This is discussed further in Section 10.3.

Collectively the results also show a diverse level of MM skill across the different commodities. This suggests that a trading approach or strategy that might incorporate aspects of MM positioning data could be enhanced by recognising these profiles and focusing on the commodity markets where performance is better. A trading model, for example, that factors into account the directional MM position in Brent would likely benefit from the knowledge that MMs are poor at trading Brent relative to many other commodities. Conversely, a trading model trading natural gas that does not consider MM positioning might be better placed doing so.

In general, the results show that positioning based on net trader numbers have historically generated better absolute and relative performance than positioning based on net future data. This suggests that for many markets, tracking changes in the net trader number data leads to more useful results in terms of understanding market direction, positioning, and sentiment dynamics than tracking changes in the net futures position. Changes in trader numbers are the basis of many of the sentiment indices presented in Chapter 10.

	2009	2010	2011	2012	2013	2014	2015	2016	2017	2018	Average
Crude oil	−18%	−1%	13%	−25%		16%	44%	11%	−13%	27%	5%
Brent						78%	42%		−7%		23%
Gasoline		7%				2%	18%	13%			4%
Heating oil	−43%	−4%		7%	3%	−25%	−25%	13%	−8%	11%	−7%
Gasoil						71%	7%	−47%	0%	20%	10%
Natural gas	−41%	−34%	−27%	3%	32%	−33%	−8%	8%	12%	1%	−9%
Corn	19%	12%		−26%	14%	32%	2%	4%	3%	−11%	5%
Wheat	33%	−13%	10%	−1%	−1%	7%	−17%	7%	−3%	−1%	2%
Kansas wheat	4%	24%		22%	−12%		22%	4%	13%	10%	9%
Soybeans	−4%	−4%	−7%	−2%		16%	16%	−1%	0%	−3%	1%
Beanoil	−8%		3%	−2%	−2%	34%	−7%	1%	3%	−1%	2%
Soymeal		−2%					−5%	13%	−3%	1%	0%
Cotton			6%	−7%	4%	39%	−2%			7%	5%
Coffee	−6%	−18%	6%	15%	−7%	8%	−2%	8%	−3%		0%
Sugar		0%		9%	12%	7%	−5%	2%	3%	−12%	2%
Cocoa	−14%	−12%	−7%	−15%	−16%			20%	−4%	6%	−4%
Gold					19%	−2%	−6%	2%		−5%	1%
Silver				12%	24%	−9%	−9%		16%	9%	4%
Palladium				5%			17%	−6%		−2%	2%
Platinum				0%			14%	−8%	21%	6%	5%
Copper	94%	0%	16%	−8%	−4%	11%	6%	6%		−7%	11%
Live cattle	3%		−8%	−10%	7%		3%	25%		−6%	1%
Feeder cattle	5%	−2%	−13%	12%	0%		19%	−26%	−2%	−1%	−1%
Lean hogs	30%	−2%	7%	1%	10%		20%	18%	−4%	35%	12%
Average	3%	−2%	0%	0%	4%	10%	5%	3%	2%	3%	3%

FIGURE 3.7 Performance difference between net trader number positioning and net futures positioning.
Source: Based on data from Bloomberg.

3.4.1 Dynamic Performance Tables – Who's the Best

Extending the analysis to other trader groups such as the OR and the PMPU categories can add more insight into the best-performing groups. Figure 3.8 shows the best-performing trader group after looking at three different trader categories using both net futures and net trader positioning. The best-performing groups are defined here as those generating the highest 'Average' performance across the same 10-year periods shown in Figure 3.3 and Figure 3.5.

On average, the MMT shows the best results, reflecting the conclusion in Section 3.4, but other trader categories also frequently feature. For crude oil (WTI), for example, tracking the net trader position in the PMPU category and for Brent tracking the net futures position in the PMPU category generate the best results. In gasoline, for example, tracking the net futures position in the OR category produces the best results.

Note that all the data in this chapter has been based on annual figures – these could be changed to weekly or monthly to provide a more granular and dynamic set of results.

	MM	MMT	OR	ORT	PMPU	PMPUT		Best
	Average	Average	Average	Average	Average	Average		
Crude oil	−7%	−1%	−8%	−15%	2%	7%		PMPUT
Brent	−17%	5%	8%	2%	17%	17%		PMPU
Gasoline	3%	7%	10%	8%	−6%	−6%		OR
Heating oil	10%	3%	0%	−1%	−1%	−1%		MM
Gasoil	12%	22%	11%	−9%	13%	13%		MMT
Natural gas	24%	15%	25%	4%	14%	−27%		OR
Corn	2%	6%	3%	8%	3%	3%		ORT
Wheat	2%	4%	1%	10%	11%	7%		PMPU
Kansas wheat	−6%	3%	−2%	5%	10%	8%		PMPU
Soybeans	5%	6%	8%	4%	−6%	−6%		OR
Beanoil	5%	7%	−1%	−4%	4%	−5%		MMT
Soymeal	13%	14%	9%	0%	−13%	−3%		MMT
Cotton	9%	14%	−15%	0%	−9%	−10%		MMT
Coffee	14%	14%	4%	6%	7%	−15%		MM
Sugar	15%	16%	2%	−7%	−1%	−18%		MMT
Cocoa	2%	−2%	4%	−4%	3%	1%		OR
Gold	5%	6%	2%	4%	−4%	−14%		MMT
Silver	13%	17%	8%	4%	−6%	−17%		MMT
Palladium	10%	12%	1%	12%	−11%	−11%		MMT
Platinum	−7%	−2%	−7%	−7%	8%	4%		PMPU
Copper	4%	15%	−17%	−15%	−8%	−8%		MMT
Live cattle	1%	2%	−3%	5%	−1%	−1%		ORT
Feeder cattle	5%	4%	−4%	−3%	0%	−4%		MM
Lean hogs	−1%	11%	2%	−4%	5%	5%		MMT
Average	5%	8%	2%	0%	1%	−3%		

FIGURE 3.8 Best-performing groups (net futures and net traders) for each commodity. *Source:* Based on data from Bloomberg.

Concentration, Clustering, and Position Size — Price Risks and Behavioural Patterns

Chapter objectives

Concentration, Clustering, and Position Size are positioning metrics that can be used to help measure risk, sentiment, and conviction dynamics in commodity markets. They can be thought of as broadly representative of the following:

- **Concentration:** a measure of positioning risk.

- **Clustering:** a measure of sentiment.

- **Position Size:** a measure of conviction.

In this chapter, these metrics are explained and Positioning Price charts are introduced as a useful way to visualise the evolution of these metrics over time, how they are related to each other, and their relationship to changes in price and curve structure.

Collectively Concentration, Clustering, and Position Size dynamics provide a solid foundation to many of the indicators, models, and analyses covered in later chapters.

4.1 Concentration, Clustering, and Position Size

Concentration, Clustering, and Position Size are ways of measuring and tracking the evolution of certain aspects of risk, sentiment, and conviction in commodities for each trader group (MM, PMPU, SD, OR) on a long and short basis, for example, MML or MMS. They can be defined and summarised as follows:

- **Concentration:** the size of a futures position as a percentage of total futures open interest – a measure of positioning risk.

- **Clustering:** the number of futures traders holding a specific position as a percentage of the total number of futures traders in the market – a measure of sentiment.

- **Position Size:** the average size of individual traders' positions calculated by dividing the size of the futures position by the number of traders holding it – a measure of conviction. A variant of Position Size can also be calculated by dividing Concentration by the number of traders, to show the average percentage of open interest each trader in a group is on average holding.

4.1.1 Formulae and Calculations

4.1.1.1 Concentration

This is a useful indicator of positioning risk in a market, showing the proportion of open interest held by specific groups of traders in the overall market. If it becomes too concentrated, significant moves can occur if these positions unwind too quickly.

Concentration is also a way of normalising positions. This is important when comparing positioning profiles between markets and also in the historical analysis of various positioning profiles.

In general, open interest has risen for most commodities over time, which can lead to unintentional biases in calculations unless Concentration is used. It is also true that many traders, especially speculative traders, adjust their notional exposure as prices change, which affects the open interest they hold. By looking at Concentration, this effect is reduced.

Concentration is calculated for each group, on a long or short basis, as follows:

$$Concentration_{trader\ category}\ (\%) = \frac{Open\ Interest_{trader\ category}}{Total\ Open\ Interest}$$

where

$$trader\ category = MM(L, S), PMPU(L, S), OR(L, S), SD(L, S)$$

See Table 2.2 for abbreviations.

4.1.1.2 Clustering Clustering is related to Concentration in that it provides another way of normalising the data. It gives a good measure of the 'crowding' or 'herding' activity in a market, which can also be a powerful measure of sentiment in the market.

Clustering is also one metric that has successfully adapted to and embraces the increasing regulation on Position Size, diversification requirements, and leverage constraints. Traders that previously might have been able to hold a sizeable single position in a commodity, now run into certain restrictions in terms of exchange-driven position limits, or if running an investment fund such as a UCITS structure, certain diversification and leverage constraints often apply. As such, the impact that a large position might have previously had on the market becomes less of an issue. Instead, small positions that might have been previously overlooked now need be considered, as they might hold the same conviction as a once larger position. Clustering adapts to this, being agnostic to Position Size, but able to capture trader positioning.

Clustering is calculated for each group, on a long or short basis, as follows:

$$Clustering_{trader\ category}(\%) = \frac{Number\ of\ traders_{trader\ category}}{Total\ number\ of\ traders}$$

where

$$trader\ category = MM(L,\ S), PMPU(L,\ S), OR(L,\ S), SD(L,\ S)$$

See Table 2.2 for abbreviations.

One interesting attribute of Clustering compared to Concentration is that the number of long and short traders does not have to be equal, whereas the long and short open interest across all trader groups in the market, must be equal.[1] This property increases the level of directionality in trader number data and net trader number data, which can add additional insight above analytics based on open interest. If, for example, the long (and short) open interest in a market was 100,000 lots, the total number of long traders could be 90, whereas the total number of short traders could be 10.

This information can become particularly useful when inferring the average long and short position sizes when assessing potential risk in the market. In this example, 10 traders exiting a position of 100,000 contracts would be expected to have a more significant price impact than 90 traders exiting the same size position.[2]

4.1.1.3 Position Size By blending open interest data with trader number data, the average Position Size can be calculated. Position Size gives a more specific insight into the average level of trader conviction by blending the size of the position with the number of traders holding it. Naturally, the calculation assumes that each trader holds the same size position, which in practice will not be the case, but with the proliferation of speculative position limits over time, Position Sizes have become more uniform, particularly towards the upper end of Position Sizes.

---

[1]This assumes the NR group is also included. Trader numbers are not included in the NR category. This is shown in Section 2.1.2.1.

[2]Many of the reasons and arguments behind differences in open interest and trader numbers are covered in detail in Section 10.1. These include conviction differences, timing differences, regulatory differences, style differences, size differences, and information differences.

Position Size is calculated for each group, on a long or short basis, as follows:

$$Position\ Size_{trader\ category} = \frac{Open\ Interest_{trader\ category}}{Number\ of\ Traders_{trader\ category}}$$

where

$$trader\ category = MM(L, S), PMPU(L, S), OR(L, S), SD(L, S)$$

See Table 2.2 for abbreviations.

When combined with data on position limits, the location of trading activity down the curve can be inferred. The position spot month limit for crude oil (WTI) for example, as detailed by the CME, is 3000 lots.[3] On 25 December 2018, the long MM open interest was 268,886 contracts, held by 66 long MM traders. The implied position size is 4074 lots (268,886/66), but with the largest position a trader may hold in the spot month being 3000 lots, at least 1074 contracts per trader must be held further down the curve. Put differently, on 25 December 2018, the maximum size of the MM speculative long position in the front month cannot be more than 198,000 contracts for the 66 long traders (66 × 3000), which means that there must be a minimum of 70,886 contracts of speculative length, distributed down the curve. This information could be useful in better assessing the impact on price and curve structure if this position were to unwind.

Different types of position limits also apply in various ways down the curve (such as limits on total exposure). In general, they all have the effect of capping position sizes and making positions more uniform in size.

4.2 Concentration, Clustering, Position Size, and Their Relationship to Price Over Time

Positioning Price indicator charts are a useful way to visualise the evolution over Concentration, Clustering, and Position Size over time. These charts help in understanding how there are related to each other and also their relationship to changes in price and curve structure.

4.2.1 Positioning Price (PP) Concentration Indicator

Figure 4.1 shows a PP Concentration indicator chart for gold based on MML data. Each bubble represents a week (plotted as of COT Report date) with its size a function of the total open interest the market, and the colour a function of the long Concentration. The darker the green (blue) shading, the higher (lower) the Concentration, with the scale showing that the long Concentration ranges from 14.74% (dark blue) of open interest to 49.66% of open interest (dark green).[4]

The purpose of including the total open interest is to ensure that the market is sufficiently liquid, and to show that that the open interest has not shifted too much over time so that meaningful historical comparisons can be made and to make sure the Concentration data is relevant.

---

[3]www.cmegroup.com/market-regulation/position-limits.html.

[4]For PP charts that have range data, the entire dataset is used in the range calculation – it does not recalculate based on the data shown the chart. Simply – if a chart that is shaded based on a price range and the highest price occurred 10 years ago, a chart showing only the last 5 years will still factor into account the highest price. This is the same for all charts that include similar range data plotted using Tableau.

Positioning Price Concentration Indicator (MML) – 25/12/2018
Colour: Darker Green (Blue) Shading = Higher (Lower) Long Concentration.
Size: Larger Bubbles = Higher Total OI.

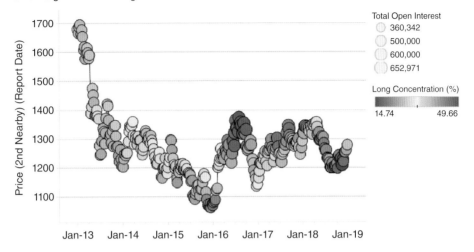

FIGURE 4.1   Positioning Price Concentration indicator – MML in gold.
This chart has been plotted using the application Tableau. The chart is on the companion website, where it can be plotted for any commodity over any timeframe. It is updated regularly.
Source: Based on data from Bloomberg.

Figure 4.2 shows the same PP Concentration indicator chart for gold for MMS data. The darker the red (blue) shading, the higher (lower) the short concentration, with the scale showing that the short Concentration ranges from 1.98% (dark blue) of open interest to 41.20% of open interest (dark red).

Positioning Price Concentration Indicator (MMS) – 25/12/2018
Colour: Darker Red (Blue) Shading = Higher (Lower) Short Concentration.
Size: Larger Bubbles = Higher Total OI.

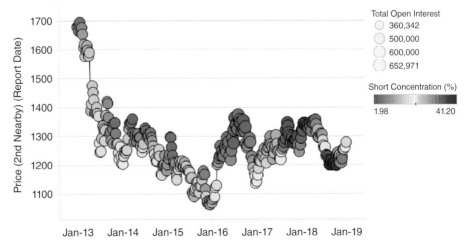

FIGURE 4.2   Positioning Price Concentration indicator for gold – MMS in gold.
This chart has been plotted using the application Tableau. The chart is on the companion website, where it can be plotted for any commodity over any timeframe. It is updated regularly.
Source: Based on data from Bloomberg.

The colour patterns at the peaks and troughs suggest an elevated level of momentum trading in the gold market, with high levels of MML Concentration coinciding with many of the peaks, suggesting MML are buying price strength. There is also a high level of MMS Concentration at many of the troughs, suggesting MMS are selling weakness. To be clear, the profile suggests they are buying strength and selling weakness, and they likely did not build these positions beforehand; otherwise the dark green (red) would have been evident before prices rose (fell). In both charts, there is little follow through in prices from these points, with prices instead mostly reversing.[5]

High MM trader Concentration, specifically when it becomes extreme and the green and red shading is darkest, indicates a high level of risk to prices. When highly concentrated positions start to unwind, they often lead to large moves in price. This behaviour is the core philosophy behind the Overbought/Oversold (OBOS) framework covered in Chapter 8.

The OBOS framework provides a highly structured way of trading these extremes, whereas PP Concentration indicator charts give an overview of positioning behaviour in the context of prices and provide information into how traders have generally behaved over time.

PP Concentration indicator charts can also be used in conjunction with technical analysis, where extreme Concentration in the context of certain price levels, trends, and the value of key moving averages and the level of oscillators like an RSI can add further insight into price behaviour. PP Concentration charts based on PMPU data can also be useful in identifying price levels where hedging activity has historically been high.

4.2.2 Positioning Price Clustering Indicator

Figure 4.3 (Figure 4.4) is a PP Clustering indicator chart for copper based on MML (MMS) data. Each bubble represents a week (plotted as of COT Report date) with its size a function of the total number of traders in the market and the colour a function of the degree of Clustering. The darker the green (blue) shading, the higher (lower) the long Clustering in Figure 4.3, and the darker the red (blue) shading, the higher (lower) the short Clustering in Figure 4.4.

The purpose of including the total number of traders is to ensure that there are sufficient traders in the market, and that the number has not changed too much over time, so that meaningful historical comparisons can be made and to make sure the Clustering data is relevant.

The long Clustering ranges from 8.97% (dark blue) of the total number of traders to 31.75% % of the total number of traders (dark green). The short Clustering ranges from 5.35% (dark blue) of the total number of traders to 30.04% of the total number of traders (dark red).

The colouring patterns show good alignment with price, with high levels of long and short clustering associated with rising and falling prices, respectively. This suggests that traders on aggregate have some ability to predict price activity and on balance position themselves according.

Clustering is a good measure of the 'crowding' or 'herding' activity in a market and is by extension a reliable indicator of bullish and bearish sentiment in the market, a key driver of prices. This is discussed further in Chapter 10 in the development of various sentiment indices.

---

[5]Concentration is calculated by dividing the MM position by the total open interest in the market – if the latter changes to activity in other trader groups, this will naturally impact the MM Concentration.

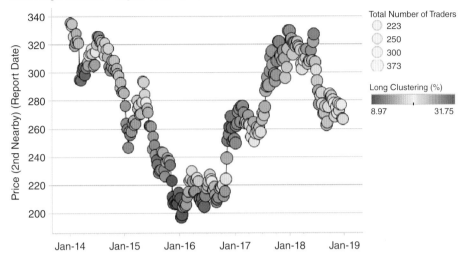

Positioning Price Clustering Indicator (MML) – 25/12/2018
Colour: Darker Green (Blue) Shading = Higher (Lower) Long Clustering.
Size: Larger Bubbles = Higher Total Number of Traders.

FIGURE 4.3 Positioning Price Clustering indicator chart – MML in copper.
This chart has been plotted using the application Tableau. The chart is on the companion website, where it can be plotted for any commodity over any timeframe. It is updated regularly.
Source: Based on data from Bloomberg.

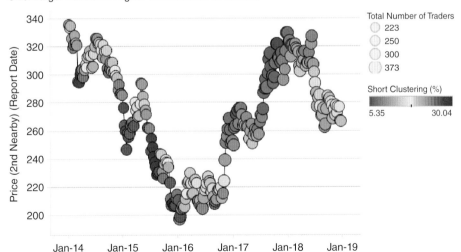

Positioning Price Clustering Indicator (MMS) – 25/12/2018
Colour: Darker Red (Blue) Shading = Higher (Lower) Short Clustering.
Size: Larger Bubbles = Higher Total Number of Traders.

FIGURE 4.4 Positioning Price Clustering indicator chart – MMS in copper.
This chart has been plotted using the application Tableau. The chart is on the companion website, where it can be plotted for any commodity over any timeframe. It is updated regularly.
Source: Based on data from Bloomberg.

4.2.3 Positioning Price Position Size Indicator

Figure 4.5 (Figure 4.6) is a PP Positioning Size indicator chart for sugar based on MML (MMS) data. Each bubble represents a week (plotted as of COT Report date), with its size a function of the total number of long (short) traders in the market and the colour a function of the average Position Size. The darker the green (blue) shading, the larger (smaller) the average long Position Size in Figure 4.5 and the darker the red (blue) shading, the larger (smaller) the average short Position Size in Figure 4.6.

The purpose of including the total number of long and short traders is to show how many traders are on average holding each position, respectively. It is also useful to ensure that the number has not changed too much over time, so that meaningful historical comparisons can be made and to make sure the data is relevant.

The long Positioning Size ranges from 2,251 lots/trader (dark blue) to 6,667 lots/trader (dark green). The short Positioning Size ranges from 756 lots/trader (dark blue) to 5,731 lots/trader (dark red).

Figure 4.5 shows the average long Position Size was particularly high between January 2013 and March 2015, even during periods of significant price weakness. Position Size provides insight into the average level trader conviction, suggesting that over this period, traders were holding above average size long positions and were presumably convinced prices would rebound.[6,7]

PP Clustering and Concentration indicator charts for sugar (charts not shown) over the same period show that the long Clustering and long Concentration were low. This means that despite the average long Position Size being high, bullish sentiment was still weak and that on average, MML traders were not holding large positions in the market. This suggests that there were only a small number of long MMs with large long positions over this period, which increased the average position size significantly. On the short side, the large short Position Size over this same period in Figure 4.6 coincided with a high level of short Clustering and Concentration (charts also not shown), suggesting that sentiment and conviction were more aligned.

This mismatch in bullish sentiment and long Position Sizing highlights the importance of using a wide variety of indicators to isolate different aspects of the positioning structure in the market to develop a more detailed understanding of the positioning in the market.

---

[6]One issue with these charts is that the size of a position will also be a function of the notional value of the futures contract, which is in turn a function of price. This can cloud the conviction argument as MMs typically hold more (less) contracts when the price is low (high) to maintain the same notional exposure. One way to control for this is to compare the Position Size PP chart with a Concentration PP chart to check the bubble size. Small (large) bubbles at high (low) prices would indicate that the open interest is low (high), which would likely be a function of notional effects.

[7]Periods where the Position Size is high can also be a function of 'insider knowledge' where a small number of traders (or even a single trader) might be holding disproportionately large positions because they may be in possession of price-sensitive information that may be difficult to obtain. This is not technically different from conviction, but it clearly has another connotation.

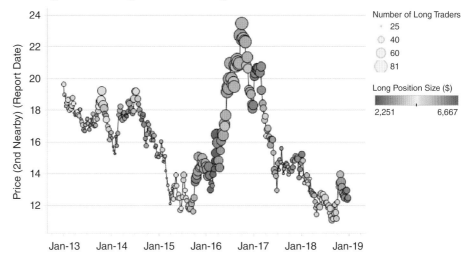

Positioning Price Position Size Indicator (MML) – 25/12/2018
Colour: Darker Green (Blue) Shading = Higher (Lower) Long Position Size.
Size: Larger Bubbles = Higher Number of Long Traders.

FIGURE 4.5 Positioning Price Position Size indicator – MML in sugar.
This chart has been plotted using the application Tableau. The chart is on the companion website,
where it can be plotted for any commodity over any timeframe. It is updated regularly.
Source: Based on data from Bloomberg.

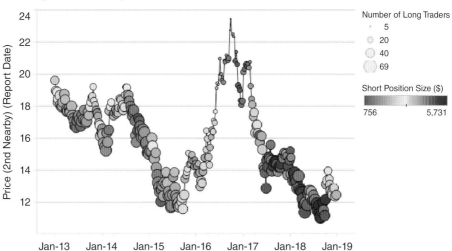

Positioning Price Position Size Indicator (MMS) – 25/12/2018
Colour: Darker Red (Blue) Shading = Higher (Lower) Short Position Size.
Size: Larger Bubbles = Higher Number of Short Traders.

FIGURE 4.6 Positioning Price Position Size indicator chart – MMS in sugar.
This chart has been plotted using the application Tableau. The chart is on the companion website,
where it can be plotted for any commodity over any timeframe. It is updated regularly.
Source: Based on data from Bloomberg.

Long and short average Positions Sizes were both low during the spike in prices in September 2016, suggesting a low degree of conviction amongst MML and MMS traders. Bullish sentiment was high; however, as the long Clustering was high (chart not shown), but low Position Size suggested weak conviction and a probable reason for the quick decline in prices.

4.2.4 Positioning Price Spreading Charts

Closely related to the analysis of Concentration, Clustering, and Position Size in the commodity market is the study of the proportion of spreading activity in a market.

As discussed in Chapter 10, the proportion of speculative spreading activity relative to directional speculative activity can provide useful information into the underlying view, often in terms of directional conviction, and also the trading activity of speculators.

Typically, a high proportion of spreading activity suggests traders are focused on changes in curve structure, rather than market direction, but it could be because market conditions may not support a directional view due to volatility being too high, conviction being low due to market uncertainty being elevated, or, in some cases, because liquidity might be too low. During these periods, the proportion of speculative spreading activity relative to directional trading activity gives an idea of the directional conviction held by speculators. The interplay between the number of long, short, and spreading traders is a powerful indicator in tracking these dynamics.

Figure 4.7 is a PP Spreading indicator chart for copper based on both Clustering and Concentration – a variation to the PP Clustering and PP Concentration indicator charts in Figure 4.1 to Figure 4.4. Each bubble represents a week (plotted as of COT Report date) with larger (smaller) bubbles a function of higher (lower) spreading Concentration in the market. The colour is a function of the degree of spreading Clustering, with darker orange (blue) shading showing higher (lower) spreading Clustering. The size and colouring patterns in Figure 4.7 show a clear increase in both the spreading Concentration and Clustering of MM traders in mid-2018, which up until that point had been low.

The Positioning Spread (PS) Spreading indicator chart in Figure 4.8, which is the same as the chart in Figure 4.7 except that the spread between the second and third month copper futures contract has been plotted instead of the copper price, shows that the increase in spreading activity was associated with a significant change in curve structure.

Changes in structure can also be driven by specific directional activity in specific contracts on the curve, which often have a more temporary effect on structure. These charts are therefore helpful in being able to disentangle the drivers of curve structure between legitimate spreading activity and more directionally driven trading activity.

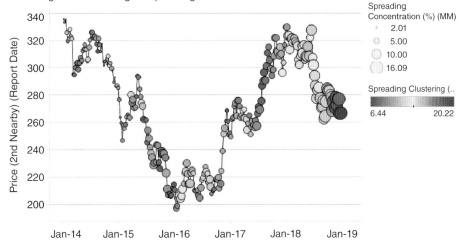

Positioning Price Spreading Indicator (MMD) – 25/12/2018
Colour: Darker Orange (Blue) Shading = Higher (Lower) Spread Clustering.
Size: Larger Bubbles = Higher Spreading Concentration.

FIGURE 4.7   Positioning Price Spreading indicator chart – MM in copper.
This chart has been plotted using the application Tableau. The chart is on the companion website,
where it can be plotted for any commodity over any timeframe. It is updated regularly.
Source: Based on data from Bloomberg.

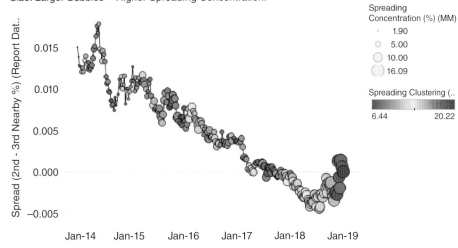

Positioning Spread Spreading Indicator (MMD) – 25/12/2018
Colour: Darker Orange (Blue) Shading = Higher (Lower) Spread Clustering.
Size: Larger Bubbles = Higher Spreading Concentration.

FIGURE 4.8   Positioning Spread Spreading indicator chart – MM in copper.
This chart has been plotted using the application Tableau. The chart is on the companion website,
where it can be plotted for any commodity over any timeframe. It is updated regularly.
Source: Based on data from Bloomberg.

CHAPTER 5

'Dry Powder (DP)' Analysis — An Alternative Way to Visualise Positioning

Chapter objectives

This chapter introduces Dry Powder (DP) analysis as a way of visualising positioning in commodity markets using a variety of different DP indicators. The indicators reconcile the historical long and short open interest in a specific trader category, with the number of traders holding the position.

DP indicators are plotted as charts which can be directly used as trading indicators to help assess the likelihood of an existing position becoming bigger or whether it is vulnerable to liquidation.

DP indicators can be modified in a variety of ways to isolate specific positioning dynamics. They also work well with other indicators and models to refine trading signals and enhance risk management.

Dry Powder

The term 'dry powder' refers to the gunpowder used in guns and artillery.

> *The allusion is to gunpowder which soldiers had to keep dry in order to be ready to fight when required. This advice reputedly originated with Oliver Cromwell during his campaign in Ireland. In Ballads of Ireland, 1856, Edward Hayes wrote:*
>
> > *'There is a well-authenticated anecdote of Cromwell. On a certain occasion, when his troops were about crossing a river to attack the enemy, he concluded an address, couched in the usual fanatic terms in use among them, with these words — "put your trust in God; but mind to keep your powder dry".*
>
> *Source:* www.phrases.org.uk.

More recently, the term in finance refers to the following:

> *Dry powder is a slang term referring to marketable securities that are highly liquid and considered cash-like. Dry powder can also refer to cash reserves kept on hand by a company, venture capital firm or person to cover future obligations, purchase assets or make acquisitions. Securities considered to be dry powder could be Treasuries, or other fixed-income investments, and can be liquidated on short notice, in order to provide emergency funding or allow an investor to purchase assets.*
>
> *Source:* www.investopedia.com.

5.1 Dry Powder (DP) Analysis

Dry Powder (DP) analysis is a simple and intuitive methodology used to visualise positioning. It reconciles the size of the long and short futures position (open interest) in a group (for example the MM group) against the number of individual long and short traders in that group. DP analysis requires that the underlying positioning data needs to report both the long and short open interest and the number of long and short traders.

DP analysis is exceptionally versatile, as shown throughout this chapter and also in Chapter 6. A few of the most useful variations include converting the open interest into notional dollar exposure and using normalised open interest (Concentration) instead of open interest, as introduced in Section 4.1.1.1.

5.1.1 DP Indicator Charts

5.1.1.1 Overview of a DP Indicator Chart

Figure 5.1 shows a chart for a classic DP indicator for crude oil (WTI). The individual long and short MM positions are plotted in the form of a scatter chart above and below the *x*-axis, respectively. Each point represents a week with the data going back to June 2006. This was the time when the CFTC first published the disaggregated form of the COT report and when MM data was first available.

The *x*-axis shows the number of MM traders, and the *y*-axis the size of the MM position in terms of the futures contracts' open interest. The open interest for the long (short) positions is a positive (negative) number on the *y*-axis, whereas the number of traders is always a positive number on the *x*-axis. This allows for the long and short clusters to be easily compared visually.

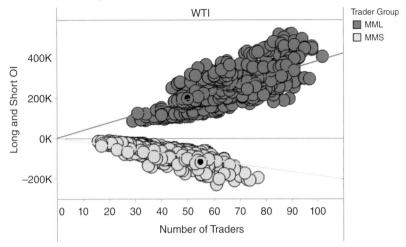

Dry Powder Indicator – 25/12/2018
Colour: Trader Group. Block Dot = Most Recent Week.

FIGURE 5.1 Dry Powder indicator – MM in crude oil (WTI).
This chart has been plotted using the application Tableau. The chart is on the companion website, where it can be plotted for any commodity on any date. It can also be customised according to trader group. Multiple groups and commodities can also be plotted together. It is updated regularly.
Source: Based on data from Bloomberg.

The position of each point in the chart is, therefore, a function of the MM position size in terms of the total open interest and the number of individual traders behind the position. The dark blue (light blue) points above (below) the *x*-axis represent all the historical long (short) positions. The point with the black in the centre above (and below) the *x*-axis indicates the long (and short) position for the most recent week. Differences between current positioning and specific aspects of the historical positioning profile – for example, the most extreme points in each cluster – give an indication of the 'dry powder' in the market.

5.1.1.2 Interpreting the Chart There are just over 650 dark blue points representing the long positions, with the cluster stretching between 29 and 102 traders on the *x*-axis and 83,540 and 519,545 contracts on the *y*-axis. This means that since June 2006, the number of individual long MM traders has always fluctuated within a 73-trader range and the total size of their long position has always been within a 436,005 range. Currently, as of 25 December 2018, the most recent data reports 50 long MM traders holding a total long position of 196,962 lots.

There are the same number of light blue dots, representing the short positions, with this cluster stretching between 16 and 77 traders on the *x*-axis and -14,132 and -232,202 contracts on the *y*-axis. This means that since June 2006, the number of individual short MM traders has fluctuated within a 61-trader range and the total size of their short position has always been within a 218,070 range. Currently, as of 25 December 2018, the most recent data reports 55 short MM traders holding a total position of -120,752 lots.

The trendline drawn through the long cluster with intercept zero has an equation $y = 3800x$ (not shown) rounded to the nearest 100. This is a way of measuring the size of the average long position that each long MM has historically held. From the equation, the average long position size per MM in crude oil (WTI) has been approximately 3,800 contracts.

On the short side, the trendline through the short cluster with intercept zero and equation $y = -1900x$ (not shown) rounded to the nearest 100 indicates that the average short position size per MM in crude oil (WTI) has been approximately 1,900 contracts. Collectively, this information provides some insight into the size of a 'normal' MM long and short position.

The location of the black dot on the trendline signifies that the current average long position is in line with the historical average. Based on the most recent data of a total long position of 196,962 contracts and 50 long MM traders, the current average is 3,939 contracts (196,962 / 50) per trader. This is 139 contracts per trader more than the historical average long position of 3,800 contracts (the equation of the trendline), which could indicate slightly more conviction than usual on average.

5.1.2 The Limits of a Position – The Essence of Dry Powder Analysis

The objective of DP analysis is to provide an indication of how much bigger a long or short position can get – simply, how much dry powder is available in that trader group to build the position further. Conversely, DP analysis also provides an idea of how small a position is likely to get – a useful metric when large positions unwind.[1]

A working assumption in Dry Powder analysis is that the size of the cluster is unlikely to change materially in the short–medium term. Specifically, that the number of traders (both those currently in the market and those out of the market) is unlikely to change significantly and that the size of their positions (existing and future) is also likely to remain reasonably constant under a typical market environment. These assumptions are required to estimate changes in how big or small positions may get.[2]

There are three ways the overall position can increase: new traders can enter the market, existing traders can increase their existing position, or a combination of both.[3] There are also three similar ways the overall position can decrease: existing traders can decrease their position, existing traders can exit the market, or a combination of both.

By way of an example of how the long position can increase, the profile of the long cluster in Figure 5.1 shows the rightmost extreme of the cluster extending to a maximum of 102 traders. The current position is long 50 traders, meaning that there is 'capacity' based on the historical positioning profile for 52 more traders, that are not currently holding a crude oil (WTI) position, to either enter or re-enter the market. Assuming the position increases by new traders entering the market only, and assuming these traders establish a long position of 3,800 contracts

---

[1]Naturally a position can fall to zero, but this is rarely the case. The MM category, for example, includes ETF exposure and certain types in index exposure that are unlikely to be liquidated completely.

[2]Technically an infinite number of new traders could enter the market. Furthermore, the implication in DP analysis that the previous traders that were in the market are always available to re-enter the market given the correct signal is also technically incorrect, as every trader could be a new trader, with no link back to any historical trading activity. It can therefore be argued that looking at the historical maximum and minimum numbers makes little sense. Whilst new (old) traders can clearly enter (exit) the market, the size of the cluster simply gives an indication of what the historical market capacity has been for that group, which can be linked to wider metrics such as the current market liquidity, a key determinant of the number of participants. The DP Time indicator in Section 5.2.2 is helpful in alleviating some of these concerns.

[3]New traders entering the market would have to have a position at least as big as the reportable threshold, otherwise they would not be counted in the COT report. This is explained further in Section 5.1.2.1.

each, equal to the historical average (from the trendline equation above), additional buying of 197,600 contracts (52 × 3,800) could occur.[4]

Looking again at the profile of the long cluster in Figure 5.1, the uppermost extreme of the cluster directly above the 50 traders point extends up to 315,519 contracts (corresponding to the largest position previously held by approximately 50 traders). Assuming the position gets bigger by existing traders increasing their position only, this means that if the existing long 50 traders increase their existing position to the historical maximum, 118,557 contracts will be bought (315,519 − 196,962), an additional 2,371 contracts per trader on average. This would mean that the average position size would be 6,171 contracts per trader.[5]

In practice, the position will increase as both the number of new traders entering the market increases and the size of the existing positions also increases with existing traders adding to their position.

In Dry Powder analysis, the top right corner of the long cluster is considered the maximum capacity of the market for that trader group. The reverse is true for the short cluster.

5.1.2.1 Position Limits in the Context of DP Analysis
The DP approach assumes that the total long (short) open interest is distributed equally across all long (short) traders. This is a reasonable assumption, as MMs typically diversify their positions to mitigate risk, and their positions are also increasingly subject to a variety of limitations and constraints that limit position sizes and drive diversification. As mentioned in Section 4.1.1.2, many of these limitations are exchange-driven, but certain fund structures also have concentration limits.

Based on the exchange position limits published by the CME, the reporting threshold 'reporting level' to the CFTC for crude oil (WTI) is 350 lots.[6] This means that each point on the chart represents at least 350 lots.

The 'initial spot month limit' for crude oil (WTI) is 3,000 contracts, which, based on the equation of the line in Figure 5.1 ($y = 3000x$), means that each trader is on average holding at least 800 contracts further down the curve.

The 'single month accountability level' is 10,000 contracts and the 'all month accountability level' is 20,000 lots. This means that each point also represents no more than 20,000 contracts, and for positions further down the curve, no trader is holding more than 10,000 in a single month.

Collectively, these limits provide further context to DP analysis by helping to visualise the positioning landscape better.

5.2 DP Indicator Variations

DP indicators based on each of the trader groups can also be plotted to provide a complete visualisation of the positioning profile for a commodity. They are perhaps most useful, however, when applied to the MM category and, to a lesser degree, also to the PMPU category. The MM category, as described in Chapter 2, represents large speculators, which include hedge funds. This group is often perceived to be the most responsive to price changes, and by extension their actions can

---

[4]In Chapter 7, the potential impact that MMs' buying of specific volumes can have on price is covered in detail.
[5]Based on a Positioning Price chart of crude oil (WTI) using Position Size (chart not shown) as described in Section 4.2.3, the largest position size of 6428 lots occurred in August 2017, so a position of this size is within the historical range.
[6]www.cmcgroup.com/nymex position-limits.

influence price and sentiment significantly. The PMPU category, whose activity is mostly driven by hedging activity, also lends itself well to the DP framework in that it provides information on the extent of hedging in the market.

Different DP indicators based on the same trader group but configured to show various aspects of the position profile are also possible. This sector shows a few of them, with Chapter 6 introducing more complex variations.

5.2.1 DP Notional Indicator

Figure 5.2 is the same as Figure 5.1, except that the long and short positions are now shown in terms of notional dollar exposure.

Charts of the DP Notional indicator are constructed by multiplying the open interest by the futures contract size and the price of the futures contract on the day the COT data is reported. For crude oil (WTI), the contract size is 1,000 barrels. As the COT report is published each Friday, but the positions are reported as of the preceding Tuesday, it is more accurate to use the futures price on the Tuesday and not the Friday.

The DP Notional indicator provides additional and occasionally conflicting insight to standard DP indicators. These situations arise when the location of the points on the two charts are significantly different, indicating that the dollar exposure is different from what would be implied by the futures position. Essentially, differences are a function of the average open P&L of a position. Significant differences are uncommon, but they can arise when a position has changed significantly in value over the lifetime of the trade and when rebalancing has not had a significant impact. When these differences occur, it is important to factor them into account when analysing a DP positioning profile. The following is an example to help better understand how these differences can occur.

At the inception of a trade, the notional value of the position and the number of contracts is linked by the price of the transaction. This is because the price often determines the number of contracts

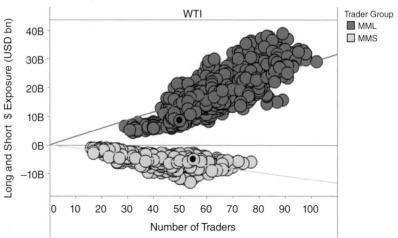

FIGURE 5.2 Dry Powder Notional indicator – MM in crude oil (WTI).
This chart has been plotted using the application Tableau. The chart is on the companion website, where it can be plotted for any commodity on any date. It can also be customised according to trader group. Multiple groups and commodities can also be plotted together. It is updated regularly.
Source: Based on data from Bloomberg.

traded for MMs, and the number of contracts and traded price together define the notional exposure. At this point, DP open interest and DP exposure charts should look very similar. Over the lifetime of the trade, as the market price rises (falls), the number of contracts stays the same (assuming the positions are not rebalanced), but the notional value increases (decreases) in alignment with the price.

Instances when a corresponding point in the long cluster on the DP Notional chart is higher (lower) than its location on the DP open interest chart, therefore, indicates on balance that positions are on average making (losing) money as the notional value of a profitable long position increases. For corresponding points in the short cluster, the same is also true. A point on the DP Notional chart that is higher (lower) than its location on the DP open interest chart indicates that positions are on average making (losing) money as the notional value of a profitable short position decreases.

The interplay between open interest and notional positioning is a critical component in assessing a position's vulnerability to both rebalancing, in order to control risk and exposure, and to either profit-taking or short covering. These dynamics are, however, mostly relevant to the MM and OR trader groups as it is unusual for PMPU or SD traders engaged in hedging activity (where trade size is typically driven by a physical volume) to rebalance the position to control risk or exposure.

5.2.2 DP Time Indicator

Colouring each point on the chart by a time variable provides insight into how the positioning profile has developed over time and by extension how much of the cluster is recent. If, for example, the extremes in the cluster occurred many years ago, this is useful to be aware of especially in the context of the arguments in Section 5.1.2.

DP Time indicators also give insight into any long-term trends and patterns in the market, such as changes in the size of specific trader groups that may have occurred over time. Figure 5.3 shows the

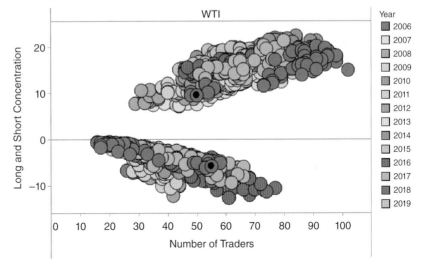

FIGURE 5.3 Dry Powder Time indicator – MM in crude oil (WTI).
This chart has been plotted using the application Tableau. The chart is on the companion website, where it can be plotted for any commodity on any date. It can also be customised according to trader group. Multiple groups and commodities can also be plotted together. It is updated regularly.
Source: Based on data from Bloomberg.

MM profile for crude oil (WTI), highlighting the extreme long and short positioning in grey evident over most of 2018. The *y*-axis has also been changed to show Concentration as explained in Section 4.1.1.1, instead of open interest. This helps to normalise the data and better isolate any changes in behaviour over time. It also eliminates any price effects, a key factor for MMs that typically hold more (less) contracts when the price is low (high) to maintain the same notional exposure.

5.2.3 DP Relative Concentration Indicator

Normalising the position by open interest and plotting Concentration is particularly useful when comparing different markets to each other, or when comparing different trader groups to each other within the same market.[7]

Figure 5.4 (Figure 5.5) shows the DP Relative Concentration indicator for all trader groups for corn (soybeans). This type of analysis is useful when comparing two related commodities and assessing how they might behave going forward under different scenarios. Crude oil (WTI) and Brent are also two excellent candidates in this respect, especially when looking at how the spread between them might evolve.

This DP indicator is also very helpful, providing a complete visualisation of the positioning profile for a commodity.

One of the most striking differences between the two markets lies in the PMPU groups (dark and light green). Corn has a significantly larger PMPUS and PMPUL profile relative

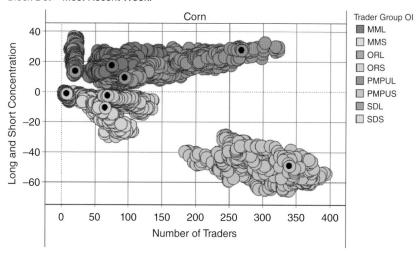

FIGURE 5.4   DP Relative Concentration indicator – all trader groups in corn.
This chart has been plotted using the application Tableau. The chart is on the companion website, where it can be plotted for any commodity on any date. It can also be customised according to trader group. Multiple groups and commodities can also be plotted together. It is updated regularly.
Source: Based on data from Bloomberg.

---

[7]Concentration in the context of DP analysis is discussed further in Chapter 6.

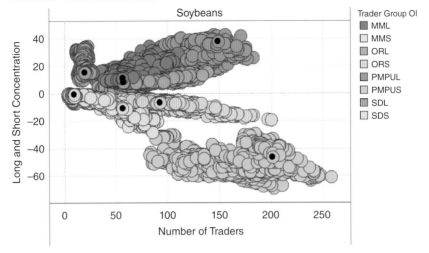

DP Relative Concentration Indicator – 25/12/2018
Block Dot = Most Recent Week.

FIGURE 5.5 DP Relative Concentration indicator – all trader groups in soybeans.
This chart has been plotted using the application Tableau. The chart is on the companion website, where it can be plotted for any commodity on any date. It can also be customised according to trader group. Multiple groups and commodities can also be plotted together. It is updated regularly.
Source: Based on data from Bloomberg.

to its other trader groups and also to soybeans, predominately in terms of the number of trading entities. In soybeans, the groups are also more balanced, except for the ORS group, which stands out as being both larger and more dynamic than its other groups, especially relative to corn.

Corn and soybeans are similar markets and compete for acreage, so their overall positioning profiles should be quite similar. The difference in the number of PMPUS entities suggests that more producers hedge corn than soybeans. This may be because some producers prefer to hedge soymeal and bean oil instead.

Looking at the positioning profile over time (chart not shown), the expansion of the ORS group occurred in the second half of 2014 – just as Latin America was starting to emerge as a significant producer the world stage. Based on this change in the market, and the definition of the OR category in Section 1.3.3.4, the expansion of the positioning profile could be a function of new OR traders, perhaps trade houses in Latin America, speculating on prices.

5.2.4 DP Seasonal Indicators

Figure 5.6 and Figure 5.7 show DP Seasonal indicator charts for Brent, where each point has also been plotted on the *y*-axis as Concentration instead of open interest. Two variations are shown; in Figure 5.6, the seasonality is in the form of the points shaded by quarter, in Figure 5.7, the points are shaded by month.

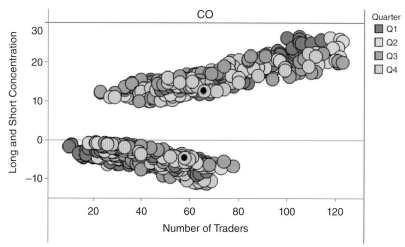

FIGURE 5.6 Dry Powder Seasonal (quarterly) indicator – MM in Brent.
This chart is not shown on the website.
Source: Based on data from Bloomberg.

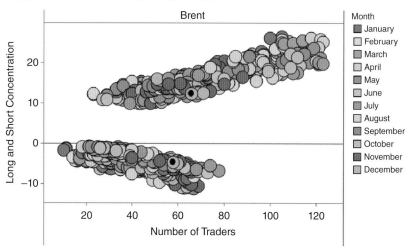

FIGURE 5.7 Dry Powder Seasonal (monthly) indicator – MM in Brent.
This chart has been plotted using the application Tableau. The chart is on the companion website, where it can be plotted for any commodity on any date. It can also be customised according to trader group. Multiple groups and commodities can also be plotted together. It is updated regularly.
Source: Based on data from Bloomberg.

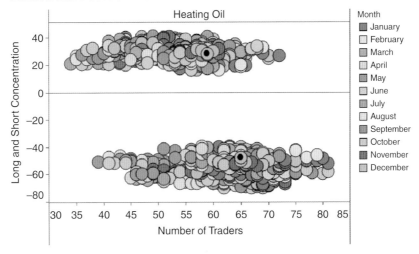

Dry Powder Seasonal Indicator – 25/12/2018
Colour: Month. Black Dot = Most Recent Week.

FIGURE 5.8 Dry Powder Seasonal (monthly) indicator – PMPU in heating oil.
This chart has been plotted using the application Tableau. The chart is on the companion website, where it can be plotted for any commodity on any date. It can also be customised according to trader group. Multiple groups and commodities can also be plotted together. It is updated regularly.
Source: Based on data from Bloomberg.

The seasonal patterns are quite vague for Brent, indicating that MMs do not generally change their exposure, either in terms of the number of traders or the size of their positions, significantly from season to season or from month to month. Frequently, established seasonal dynamics such as the refinery maintenance schedule that shapes the seasonality in the crude markets are often anecdotally perceived to be more significant than they are. Figure 5.6 shows a slight bias for larger MM long positions in Q1 and Q2 and similarly, in Figure 5.7, the smallest short positions generally occur between January and May, but the patterns are nonetheless vague.

Figure 5.8 is a DP Seasonal indicator for heating oil. This indicator shows the PMPU group instead of the MM group and can be useful in highlighting any seasonal hedging patterns and/or any developing anomalies in the market.

The light and dark blue points tend to be concentrated toward the extremes of the clusters as more PMPULs (PMPUSs), generally consumers (producers), in the top (bottom) half of the chart hedge exposure more actively during the cold winter months. It would be unusual to see blue points towards the left of the clusters, as this would suggest the market was maybe underhedged, highlighting potential price risks in the market if hedging were to suddenly start.

Seasonal position profiles are also discussed in Section 8.6.2.

5.3 DP Indicators and Trading Signals

5.3.1 The Importance of Extremes

Commodity price extremes can provoke powerful responses from market participants, often leading to increased media activity, a higher or more intense level fundamental and technical analysis, which can lead to elevated price risk and increased volatility.

Positioning extremes can provoke similar responses from market participants, with extremes in the net speculative position being the most widely followed (compared to extremes in individual long and short positioning that can sometimes go unnoticed), and by extension often responsible for shaping market sentiment, even though it is typically the changes in long and short positioning that drive the greatest price response.

Net positioning is, however, a convenient positioning metric as it gives both 'summary' and 'context' to the speculative profile within a market; for that reason, is easier to understand.

It provides 'summary' in the sense that the collective view of all speculators can be distilled into a single directional view (long or short) and it provides 'context' in the sense that individual long (short) speculative positions in isolation can be difficult to contextualise, particularly in the absence of information about the opposing short (long) position. As speculators also often hold different size positions over time depending on the price of the commodity, the market volatility, and underlying liquidity profile, despite their conviction perhaps remaining the same, net positioning provides a way of controlling for many of these factors. This occurs less in other trader categories and they are more linked to the physical market where specific volumes are usually hedged and traded.

The reason, however, why changes in extreme individual positions are often a more powerful driver of price than changes in net positioning is because the actual sizes of the underlying positions can be obscured with net positioning, whereas on an individual basis they are very clear. An offsetting long and short position where each leg is of record size will have the same net position as an offsetting long and short position where each leg is of minimal size. If one of the legs, however, starts to unwind as prices move, an awareness of the size of these individual positions become critically important in assessing the overall price response.

Focusing on individual positions also embraces the fact that long and short traders can be quite different from each other and also behave in very different ways. Commodity investors, also classified as speculators, tend not to employ leverage, have long holding periods, and are less sensitive to price swings. Long/short speculators, including hedge funds, normally use leverage and often have a more dynamic trading style. Large short speculative positions are therefore often less diversified and can often be more volatile.

In DP analysis, all aspects of long and short positioning data are embraced. By including the number of long and short traders, the long and short open interest can be evaluated in the context of another important variable. This provides 'context' and makes comparisons between their relative sizes more meaningful. Relative patterns, seasonal patterns, and differences between notional exposure and open interest patterns as mentioned in Section 5.2 collectively also add further insight into potential price direction, behaviour, and sentiment.

5.3.2 The Stability of Extremes

Trading signals in DP analysis embrace the notion of extreme positioning. An important differentiator, however, with DP analysis, is that extremes are a function of extremes in both the size of a position and also in the number of traders holding that position. These often represent points where there is simply no more dry powder available and positioning is unlikely to expand any further.

In the MM category, futures positions must be closed out before expiry, as physical delivery is in nearly all cases not an option. An awareness of when these extremes occur can be critically important in identifying price risk.[8]

Part of the philosophy behind DP analysis is that the size of the long and short positioning clusters is relatively stable over the short term, as discussed in Section 5.1.2. The most significant risk in DP analysis is that this changes and a sizeable number of new traders quickly enter the market and establish new and meaningful positions. However, the likelihood of this happening is low, especially on a weekly basis, as significant shifts in open interest and trader numbers in commodities typically take time as new positions are established. It is nonetheless possible, and this risk should not be ignored.

Looking at DP indicators of other trader groups can be useful, because traders need to trade with each other. As such, the DP profiles of other trader groups can, therefore, provide some information on which groups can potentially increase or decrease their positions. In this respect the DP relative Concentration indicator in Section 5.2.3 is useful. Combined then with the data on who trades with whom, as discussed in Section 7.4, this information can be enhanced further. Additional types of positioning analytics such as OBOS analysis, discussed in Chapter 8 and Chapter 9, can also add additional insight into the likelihood of DP clusters expanding in size.

Notwithstanding the risk mentioned above that the cluster can change in size, the working assumption remains that the size of the long and short clusters in the chart are relatively static over time, and if they start to expand, it usually happens slowly. An additional factor that can act as a stabilisation factor to the size of the cluster lies in the fact that with few liquid, exchange-traded commodities available to trade (approximately 24), there is often a requirement for commodity market speculators and funds to maintain a diversified exposure to the asset class – especially considering its inherent volatility and idiosyncrasy. This diversification often drives a continuous exposure to the major commodities, which in turn ensures that the total number of commodity traders in the market, for the major commodities at least, is kept reasonably constant (although the long and short numbers can still shift). This is particularly the case for commodity trading advisors (CTAs), a major group of commodity market speculators, where diversification is often an essential aspect of their investment process. This constancy also enhances the robustness of DP analysis, allowing for more robust analysis without the fear that the cluster will materially shift.

---

[8]Instances where futures positions can go to delivery typically occur with other trader categories such as the PMPU category.

5.3.3 The Trading Signals

Figure 5.9 illustrates the positioning profile for the most reliable trading signals in DP analysis. They occur when both the long and short positions are at opposite extremes of their respective clusters. Specifically:

■ For a **long trading signal**, the most recent long position should be at the bottom left of the cluster, with the short position at the bottom right, the logic being that the action of short covering and of new length entering the market drives prices higher.

■ For a **short trading signal**, the most recent long position should be at the top right of the cluster, with the short position at the top left, the logic being that the action of long liquidation and of new shorts entering the market drives prices lower.

Figure 5.10 shows two diagrams with similar positioning profiles to those in Figure 5.9. For these signals, it is the main price driver that needs to be at an extreme, with the other position needing only enough room to support the resultant price action. Specifically:

■ For a **long trading signal**, the most recent short position should be at the bottom right of the cluster, with the long position no higher than the centre of its cluster. In a comparable way to the long signal above, the logic is that short covering and new length entering the market drive prices higher.

■ For a **short trading signal**, the most recent long position should be at the top right of the cluster, with the short position no lower than the centre of its cluster. In a comparable way to the short signal above, the logic is that long liquidation and new shorts entering the market drive prices lower.

Typically, the initial shifts in positioning when at an extreme often come from the liquidation of an existing position rather than the establishment of a new position. The liquidation of crowded long and short positions can trigger violent price moves which make trading signals at positioning extremes highly effective.

In the context of the figures above, this means that for a short (long) signal, the existing long (short) position should be at an extreme.

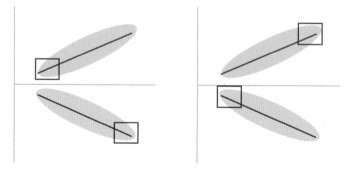

FIGURE 5.9 Long (short) trading signals on the left (right). Red boxes refer to the most reliable signal location at opposite extremes.
Source: Based on data from Bloomberg.

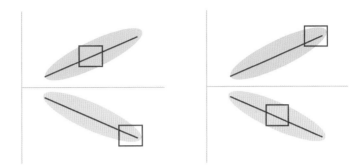

FIGURE 5.10 Long (short) trading signals on the left (right). Red boxes refer to the most reliable signal locations at a single extreme.
Source: Based on data from Bloomberg.

There is a large degree of subjectivity to these trading signals in defining exactly what constitutes an extreme. One solution to increase the signal objectivity is to use quartiles ranges, explained in Section 6.1, or a DP/OBOS Hybrid indicator, explained in Section 8.7.

CHAPTER 6

Advanced DP Analysis – Deeper Insights and More Variables

87

Chapter objectives

In Chapter 5, Dry Powder (DP) analysis was introduced as a way of visualising positioning in a commodity market.

The objective of DP analysis is to provide an indication of how much bigger long or short position can get – simply how much dry powder is available in that trader group to build the position further. Conversely, DP analysis also provides an indication of how small a position can get – a useful metric when large positions unwind.

In this chapter, DP analysis is extended to include a variety of new types of information to better visualise positioning profiles in the context of other factors. These can include positioning data on the other trader categories, the price of the underlying commodity, the shape of the forward curve, certain types of fundamental data, and macroeconomic variables.

6.1 Advanced DP Indicator Charts

In Chapter 5, Dry Powder (DP) charts were plotted as a single chart. This had the benefit of showing the sizes of the long and short clusters relative to each other, as each cluster shared the same axes. For more complex charts, the long and short clusters are plotted as individual charts. They are now bigger, more legible, and can also include different variables applied to each of the clusters.

As DP indicator charts become more complex, additional metrics can also be included. Figure 6.1 and Figure 6.2, for example, show DP indicator charts for the MML and MMS groups in Brent respectively, with grey bands that show the median with quartiles.[1] These bands are useful in being able to identify regions of the cluster and in being able to refine trading signals a little better. In Section 5.3.3, the most optimal regions within the long and short clusters for generating trading signals were highlighted, but in using more defined regions, such as quartile ranges, a more defined set of trading rules can be formulated. For example, if the most recent long point was in the top right region (the top quartiles as shown in white) and the most recent short point was in the top left region (the bottom quartiles), a sell signal could be generated.

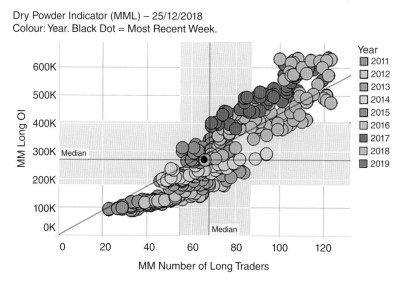

FIGURE 6.1 Dry Powder indicator – MML in Brent.
This chart has been plotted using the application Tableau. The chart is on the companion website, where it can be plotted for any commodity on any date. It is updated regularly.
Source: Based on data from Bloomberg.

---

[1]Time data has also been included in the form of years to provide more information, so these charts are therefore technically DP Time indicator charts, as originally covered in Section 5.2.2.

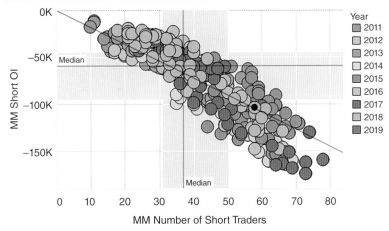

FIGURE 6.2 Dry Powder indicator – MMS in Brent.
This chart has been plotted using the application Tableau. The chart is on the companion website, where it can be plotted for any commodity on any date. It is updated regularly.
Source: Based on data from Bloomberg.

6.1.1 DP Net Indicators

Figure 6.3 shows a single DP Net indicator for Brent using net MM data – essentially a blend of Figure 6.1 and Figure 6.2, which can add a different perspective on positioning. These charts are also similar to the Mismatch indicator charts in Section 10.3 designed to highlight misalignments between net open interest and net trader positioning. In Figure 6.3, points that lie in the top left (bottom right) quadrants occur when the net positioning in terms of open interest is long (short), but the net number of traders is actually short (long). Instances when positioning falls into these quadrants can be signs of an inflexion point in the market, as covered in more detail in Section 10.3. These quadrants also have smaller variations than the long (where net open interest and net traders are both long) and short quadrants (where net open interest and net traders are both short).

DP Net indicator charts add further insight into the size of net positions, which can be helpful in interpreting DP indicators to better understand the relationship of long and short positioning to each other. Points, for example, that are at an extreme on either the long or short cluster, but not on the net cluster, could be considered overall as less extreme than if the net cluster was also at an extreme.

These single DP charts can also be used to show spreading data, where there is no long or short position. Spreading data is reported as just the number of spreading traders and the size of their position. These charts can be helpful in assessing the likelihood of a spread position becoming more extreme, especially when a curve is in steep contango or backwardation. They are by no means conclusive, and changes in structure can easily be driven by directional trading activity and not just spread-related activity. These charts are only shown on the website (the link is in the metadata list).

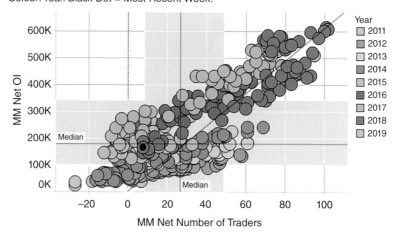

Dry Powder Net Indicator (MM) – 25/12/2018
Colour: Year. Black Dot = Most Recent Week.

FIGURE 6.3 Dry Powder Net indicator – MML in Brent.
This chart has been plotted using the application Tableau. The chart is on the companion website, where it can be plotted for any commodity on any date. It is updated regularly.
Source: Based on data from Bloomberg.

6.1.2 DP Concentration, Clustering, and Position Size Indicators

Concentration, Clustering, and Position Sizing were discussed in Section 4.1. Each of these metrics can be used in DP analysis to show various aspects of positioning and to reveal different behavioural patterns. Concentration has already been used in Chapter 5 as a way of normalising the data when using DP Time, Relative, and Seasonal indicators. Concentration is also an excellent way to isolate different patterns between the long and short trader groups

6.1.2.1 MM Concentration
Figure 6.4 (Figure 6.5) show MML (MMS) DP Concentration indicator charts for Brent, with the *y*-axes having been changed to show Concentration.

The DP indicator charts in Figure 6.1 and Figure 6.2, showing open interest, were quite similar to each other, but in switching to Concentration, the differences between the short and long clusters become quite considerable. The short cluster is now significantly more diffused – the opposite of the relatively 'neat' profile shown for the MML group. It is also important to note the Concentration scale on the *y*-axes as they are quite different. The patterns in the year distributions are also different. The year 2017 (pink) is notably different; Figure 6.2 shows that the largest short positions were held over this time, but in term of Concentration in Figure 6.5, they were significantly smaller.

By looking at Concentration, the increased volatility in the MMS relative to the MML position becomes more evident. This is likely due to the higher number of long positions that make up products like ETFs and index products, which are often less sensitive to price than short speculative positions as mentioned in Section 5.3.1. This profile also suggests that relative to the MML group, the MMS is an important driver of prices for Brent.

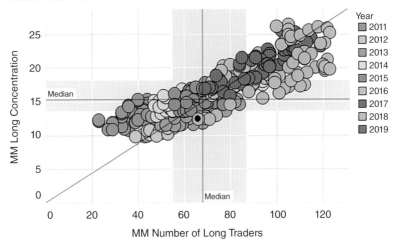

FIGURE 6.4 Dry Powder Concentration indicator – MML in Brent.
This chart has been plotted using the application Tableau. The chart is on the companion website, where it can be plotted for any commodity on any date. It is updated regularly.
Source: Based on data from Bloomberg.

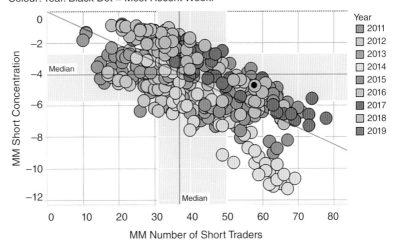

FIGURE 6.5 Dry Powder Concentration indicator – MMS in Brent.
This chart has been plotted using the application Tableau. The chart is on the companion website, where it can be plotted for any commodity on any date. It is updated regularly.
Source: Based on data from Bloomberg.

6.1.2.2 MM Concentration vs MM Clustering – Comparing Commodities

Clustering makes little sense on its own in DP analysis due to the similarity of the x-axis and the y-axis data. A DP Clustering chart would have Clustering (number of traders/total number of traders) on the y-axis plotted against the number of traders on the x-axis. This would effectively show the degree of contribution to Clustering held by each trader on average, which is not very intuitive.

DP indicator charts of Concentration vs Clustering are, however, interesting and are particularly useful when applied to different commodities together as a way of comparing different markets to each other.

One caveat is that the indicator needs to be calculated on a range basis. This is done to make the charts more dynamic and because certain commodities tend to have their own levels of Concentration (Clustering) that are relatively stable over time.[2] For example, the MML position in corn may always be about 20% of the open interest, and palladium about 50%. By using one-year rolling ranges, changes in these metrics are identified more effectively.

Ranges are covered in detail in Section 8.2.4 as part of the development of the Overbought/ Oversold (OBOS) framework, and are similarly calculated here as follows:

Concentration range:

$$long(short)\ Concentration(\%)$$
$$= \frac{current\ MML(S)\% - \min\left(MML(S)\%_{range}\right)}{\max\left(MML(S)\%_{range}\right) - \min\left(MM(S)\%_{range}\right)}$$

where

$$MML(S)\% = \frac{MML(S)\ \left(futures\ only\right)}{TOI\ \left(futures\ only\right)}$$

$$range = one\text{-}year\ rolling$$

See Table 2.2 for abbreviations.

Clustering range:

$$long(short)\ Clustering(\%)$$
$$= \frac{current\ MML(S)T\% - \min\left(MML(S)T\%_{range}\right)}{\max\left(MM(S)T\%_{range}\right) - \min\left(MM(S)T\%_{range}\right)}$$

---

[2]The Figures in in Section 2.4.1.3 show these patterns across all commodities.

where

$$MML(S)T\% = \frac{MML(S)T\ \left(futures\ only\right)}{TTF\ \left(futures\ only\right)}$$

$$range = one\text{-}year\ rolling$$

See Table 2.2 for abbreviations.

Figure 6.6 (Figure 6.7) show MML (MMS) DP Concentration/Clustering charts for all commodities using a one-year rolling range. One useful application of these charts is to identify relative value trading opportunities between commodities within the same sector, based exclusively on positioning extremes that are driven by their proximity to extremes in the proportion of open interest and the number of traders in the market.

Palladium (PA) and platinum (PL), both in the precious metals sector, show entirely different profiles to each other. Palladium is at the top right (top left) of Figure 6.6 (Figure 6.7), whereas platinum is less extreme and more toward the middle of its range. With both Concentration and Clustering at an extreme in palladium, the likelihood of it showing disproportionate weakness relative to platinum in the event of a downward price shock to the sector is high. Another example in the chart would be live cattle (LC) and feeder cattle (FC).

This analysis is very similar to the DP/OBOS Hybrid indicator in Section 8.7.2.1, where the focus is more on the generating of trading signals.

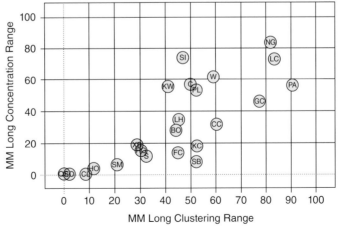

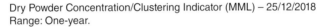

FIGURE 6.6   Dry Powder Concentration/Clustering indicator – MML all commodities.
This chart has been plotted using the application Tableau. The chart is on the companion website, where it can be plotted with any commodities on any date. It is updated regularly.
Commodity symbols: As listed in Table 2.1.
Source: Based on data from Bloomberg.

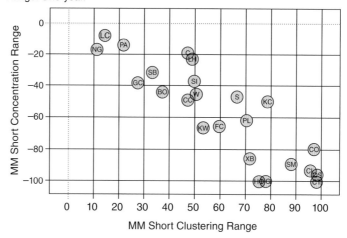

Dry Powder Concentration/Clustering Indicator (MMS) – 25/12/2018
Range: One-year.

FIGURE 6.7 Dry Powder Concentration/Clustering indicator – MMS all commodities.
This chart has been plotted using the application Tableau. The chart is on the companion website, where it can be plotted with any commodities on any date. It is updated regularly.
Commodity symbols: As listed in Table 2.1.
Source: Based on data from Bloomberg.

6.1.2.3 Position Size vs Number Traders
DP Position Size indicator charts are useful in helping to understand how position size and price are related for a commodity and how these patterns differ between long and short traders.

Figure 6.8 (Figure 6.9) shows MML (MMS) DP Position Size charts for Brent. Position Size is plotted on the *y*-axis and calculated as described in Section 4.1.1.3. The number of traders is

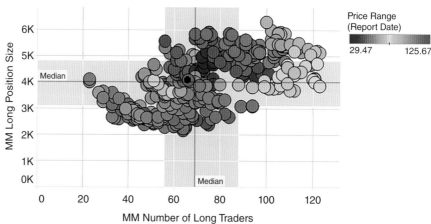

Dry Powder Position Size Indicator (MML) – 25/12/2018
Colour: Year. Black Dot = Most Recent Week.

FIGURE 6.8 Dry Powder Position Size indicator – MML in Brent.
This chart has been plotted using the application Tableau. The chart is on the companion website, where it can be plotted for any commodity on any date. It is updated regularly.
Source: Based on data from Bloomberg.

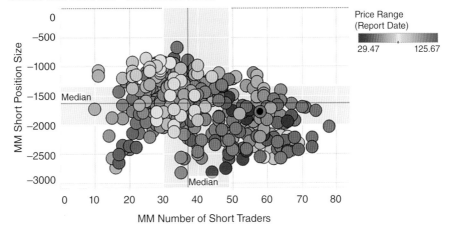

Dry Powder Position Size Indicator (MMS) – 25/12/2008
Colour: Year. Black Dot = Most Recent Week.

FIGURE 6.9 Dry Powder Position Size indicator – MMS in Brent.
This chart has been plotted using the application Tableau. The chart is on the companion website, where it can be plotted for any commodity on any date. It is updated regularly.
Source: Based on data from Bloomberg.

shown on the *x*-axis and the colour of each point reflects the price range, with red (green) points indicating prices at the bottom (top) of their one-year range.[3,4]

There is a clear difference between the two profiles; the long cluster in Figure 6.8 is well ordered, with larger (smaller) position sizes being associated with lower (higher) prices, and generally fewer traders in the market when prices are high. The short cluster in Figure 6.9 shows a more scattered profile with no clear patterns.

These differences could be due to different types of long and short market participants. The Brent MML traders look to be sizing their positions to ensure a similar notional exposure, by having larger (smaller) positions at lower (higher) prices. This is characteristic of directional trading. It could also be a function of market behaviour, with MMs having more (less) conviction at lower (higher) prices.

The mixed profile on the short side is difficult to explain, but it could be due to different types of trading activity. In commodities like Brent that are commonly traded against other commodities in the form of a spread (for example WTI/Brent) or a crack (for example Brent vs gasoil), position sizing is usually agnostic to price so the arguments above do not apply.

Overall, however, these patterns suggest more (less) directional MM exposure on the long (short) side and more (less) relative value trading exposure on the short (long) side for Brent.

---

[3]Incorporating price (and curve structure) is discussed fully in Section 6.1.2, but in the context of DP Position Size charts, it is a critical component in understanding the positioning patterns.

[4]For DP indicator charts that have range data, the entire dataset is used in the range calculation – it does not recalculate based on the data shown the chart. Simply – if a chart that is shaded based on a price range and the highest price occurred 10 years ago, a chart showing only the last 5 years will still factor into account the highest price. This is the same for all charts that include similar range data.

6.2 DP Indicators, Price, and Curve Structure

Changes in price and curve structure are often associated with changes in positioning, with the latter being a key driver of roll yield, an important factor in commodity investing.[5] Positioning patterns in the context of these variables can therefore be helpful in predicting shifts in speculative activity. Positioning at different price levels across different trader groups, such as the PMPU group, can also provide useful information on the price levels where hedging activity starts to change.

Collectively the DP analysis framework is well placed in identifying these shifts and the levels that drive changes trading activity.

6.2.1 Trader Groups vs Price

Figure 6.10 (Figure 6.11) show PMPUL (PMPUS) DP Price charts for Brent, with each point coloured according to the price of the second nearby futures contract. From the charts, approximate

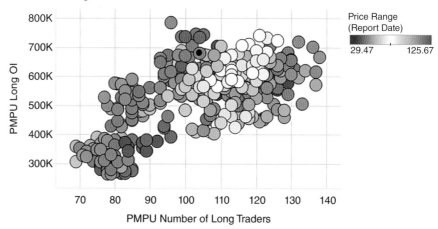

FIGURE 6.10 Dry Powder Price indicator – PMPUL in Brent.
This chart has been plotted using the application Tableau. The chart is on the companion website, where it can be plotted for any commodity on any date. It is updated regularly.
Source: Based on data from Bloomberg.

---

[5]The roll yield is the yield generated when a long or short position in a futures contract converges towards the spot price and the position is rolled forward and rebalanced. When the curve is backwardated the futures price 'rolls up' to the spot price and the roll yield is positive (negative) for long (short) positions. When the market is in contango, the futures price 'rolls down' to the spot price and the roll yield is negative (positive) for long (short) positions. Critically, roll yield is generated when a position is rebalanced – meaning that because the notional exposure is rolled forward, entirely different numbers of contacts need to be bought or sold accordingly. Assume a trader goes long 100 contracts of crude oil at $100/b (notional exposure = 10 contracts * 1,000 barrels/contract * $100/b = $10,000,000) and the price then rises to $150/b (notional exposure = $15,000,000). To scale into the position, and increase it by 10%, the trader will need to buy $1,500,000 of crude oil at $150/b. This equates to 10 new contracts.

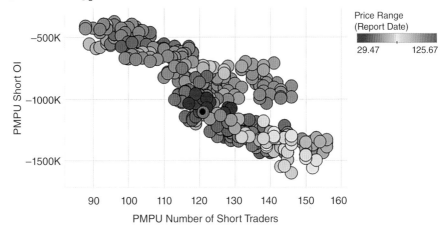

Dry Powder Price Indicator (PMPUS) – 25/12/2018
Colour. Price Range. Black Dot = Most Recent Week.

FIGURE 6.11 Dry Powder Price indicator – PMPUS in Brent.
This chart has been plotted using the application Tableau. The chart is on the companion website, where it can be plotted for any commodity on any date. It is updated regularly.
Source: Based on data from Bloomberg.

price thresholds, indicated via the shading of the points, give a general indication of the price levels where consumer and producer hedging activity are most significant. The PMPUL (PMPUS) group can be thought of as predominately consumers (producers).

It is clear, for example, that higher (lower) prices are associated with both smaller (larger) PMPUL and PMPUS positions, reflecting a more commercially-driven consumer hedging profile, but a counter-intuitive producer hedging profile, as hedging activity is expected to be higher as prices increase. This can be the case when prices are weak and where producer hedging can often take on a more of a risk management function to ensure stability in the overall business.

In wheat, for example (chart not shown), greater producer hedging occurs when prices are high as farmers seek to lock in higher prices, whereas in lean hogs, for example (chart not shown), a commodity vulnerable to price spikes, greater consumer hedging occurs when prices are high – presumably as a result of the fear that prices could spike further.

It is also interesting to see that, despite the anecdotal evidence that hedging programmes are supposed to be highly structured and mostly agnostic to price, this is not really the case for Brent. Traders appear to have quite some flexibility in adapting their hedging programmes to different price levels, or, equally possible, the hedging programmes are indeed structured, but may be driving price.

The patterns for Brent in Figure 6.10 and Figure 6.11, and also for crude oil (WTI) (not shown), are among the most pronounced for all the commodities. For most markets, there is less patterning between the red and green dots, indicating the hedging programmes are indeed agnostic to price or, alternatively, have no impact on price.

6.2.2 Trader Groups vs Curve Structure

Figure 6.12 (Figure 6.13) show MML (MMS) DP Curve charts for crude oil (WTI) with each point coloured according to the spread level, calculated as a percentage, between the second and third nearby futures contracts. Blue (white) points are the weeks in backwardation (contango).

A clear pattern is evident with large long (short) positions mostly only associated with a backwardated (contango) curve and by extension positive roll yield. Note that a binary approach has been taken to the shading, rather than shading by spread level; this simply makes identifying of backwardated period clearer.

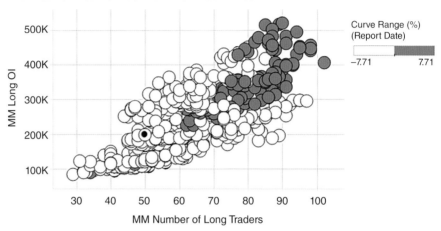

FIGURE 6.12 Dry Powder Curve indicator – MML in crude oil (WTI).
This chart has been plotted using the application Tableau. The chart is on the companion website, where it can be plotted for any commodity on any date. It is updated regularly.
Source: Based on data from Bloomberg.

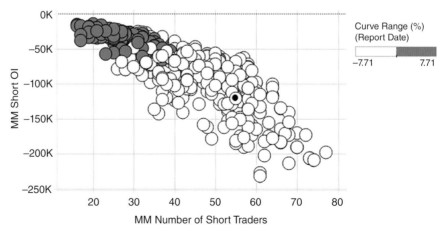

FIGURE 6.13 Dry Powder Curve indicator – MMS in crude oil (WTI).
This chart has been plotted using the application Tableau. The chart is on the companion website, where it can be plotted for any commodity on any date. It is updated regularly.
Source: Based on data from Bloomberg.

For commodities that exhibit less seasonality in their curve structure, such as oil, changes in the curve structure are typically a function of the supply/demand outlook. Backwardation (contango) is a short-term bullish (bearish) structure which is associated with long (short) MM positions. For commodities with a seasonal curve structure, such as natural gas or gasoline, the equivalent DP curve charts show a mixed profile of blue and white points throughout each cluster.

In general, the shape of the forward curve for Brent and crude oil (WTI), due to their large positions in commodity indices such as the S&P, GSCI, and BCOM (Bloomberg Commodity index), is a critically important driver of investor flows into the commodity asset class. If roll yield is negative (positive) for these commodities, flows can decrease (increase) significantly. In the case of persistent negative roll, outflows can be significant.

By looking at DP Curve indicator charts for trader categories like the SD and MM groups (the groups reflecting most of the index and ETF positions) an idea of the thresholds in curve structure where flows pivot and positioning is therefore affected can be determined. In Figure 6.12 and Figure 6.13 only two curve thresholds are shown (backwardation and contango), but these can be changed to provide more granular thresholds. In this respect a banded shading approach can be useful – this is shown in Section 6.4.3.

6.3 DP Hedging Indicators

One of the primary objectives in DP analysis is to help assess the likelihood of a position getting bigger, or if it were to unwind, how small it could get. As explained in Section 5.1.1, the philosophy behind a DP indicator charts lies in the relationship between current positioning and the historical positioning profile (the cluster) to provide an indication of the available 'dry powder' in the market.

DP analysis, however, only considers a single trader category at a time. As explained in Section 5.2.3, looking at other position groups within a DP framework shows the entire positioning landscape. By incorporating other relevant groups, for example the PMPU, directly into a MM DP chart, a clear indication of the dry powder in one group in the context of another can be seen.

Figure 6.14 shows a DP Hedging chart for natural gas in mid-November 2018 – just before a significant peak in natural gas prices, with each point coloured according the size of the PMPUL position, where dark green (blue) shows higher (lower) PMPUL open interest. The black dot (most recent week) toward the top right of the long cluster indicates an extreme MML position suggesting that prices might be nearing a top as MM dry powder is low.

PMPUL traders (mostly consumers) are another group able to buy the market and take prices higher, so their positioning is also important. The dark green shading of the point suggests that consumers already have a significant position, so the likelihood of further price upside is reduced.

Figure 6.15 shows the short positioning – the black dot (most recent week) towards the top left of the cluster shows significant MMS dry powder available to short the market, indicating that downside risk is significant, but the dark red shading, a function now of the size of the PMPUS (producer) short position, shows that producers have mostly already locked in a large short position at the higher prices. This will likely reduce the effect of any further selling pressure from producers.

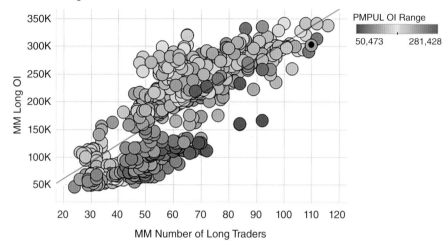

FIGURE 6.14 Dry Powder Hedging indicator – MML in natural gas.
This chart has been plotted using the application Tableau. The chart is on the companion website, where it can be plotted for any commodity on any date. It is updated regularly.
Source: Based on data from Bloomberg.

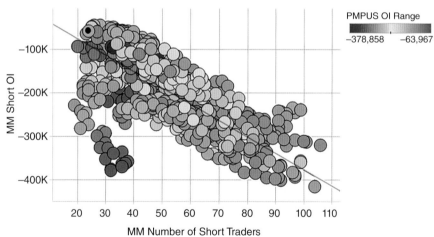

FIGURE 6.15 Dry Powder Hedging indicator – MMS in natural gas.
This chart has been plotted using the application Tableau. The chart is on the companion website, where it can be plotted for any commodity on any date. It is updated regularly.
Source: Based on data from Bloomberg.

This process can be extended to the other trader groups to develop a complete picture of the market. The PMPU group is, however, often considered to be the most useful group as they are widely viewed as having some informational edge in the market – especially the producers due to their proximity to the physical market. Their positioning profile can therefore add disproportional value in how prices could change. Interestingly, in this example, in the weeks following, natural gas prices collapsed.

6.4 DP Factor, Fundamental, and Currency Indicators

One of the most appealing attributes of DP indicator charts are their deep infographic qualities – their ability to provide a simple overview of complex relationships.

Incorporating other trader groups into the analysis framework as shown in Section 6.3 can be helpful in better assessing the likelihood of an existing position getting bigger or smaller. The inclusion of other variables able to shift positioning profiles, and by extension price and sentiment, can further refine the analysis.

Positioning data in DP indicators is plotted as of the COT Release date. When including variables into the indicator, the most recent piece of data is used.

- For variables released daily, such as the VIX, the level of the variable on the same COT Release date is used.

- For variables released weekly, either intra-week or at the end of the week, the most recent value is used.

As a rule, the value either on or immediately following the COT release data is typically used.

6.4.1 DP VIX and VVIX Factor Indicators

The VIX index is probably the most widely followed metric of financial risk in the markets today. It is also often referred to as 'the fear gauge'.

The VVIX index is less widely followed but also important. It is a measure of the implied volatility of VIX options and is therefore a good measure of the anticipation of financial risk.

The VIX index

The CBOE Volatility index® (VIX® index®) is a key measure of market expectations of near-term volatility conveyed by S&P 500 stock index option prices. Since its introduction in 1993, the VIX index has been considered by many to be the world's premier barometer of investor sentiment and market volatility. VIX futures were introduced in 2004, and VIX options were introduced in 2006. The VIX index is often referred to as the market's 'fear gauge'.

The VVIX

The VVIX index is an indicator of the expected volatility of the 30-day forward price of the VIX. This volatility drives nearby VIX option prices.

Source: www.investopedia.com.

Since their introduction, the VIX and the VVIX indices have become widely used as financial risk metrics. More recently, they have become increasingly useful in determining and defining whether financial markets, including commodity markets, are in a 'risk-on' or 'risk-off' mode.[6]

By colouring each point in the chart according to the VIX or VVIX level, the relationship between positioning and levels in the VIX or VVIX quickly becomes apparent.

Figure 6.16 (Figure 6.17) shows MML (MMS) DP Factor charts for copper, with each point shaded according to the VIX level. The darker the red shading, the higher the VIX level.[7]

The pattern clearly shows that large long MM positions very rarely occur when the VIX is elevated, a dynamic entirely consistent with the 'risk-off' effect in markets when the VIX is high. This is, however, a very one-sided relationship, meaning that, as shown in Figure 6.17, large MMS short positions are not associated with elevated VIX levels, and neither are small MMS positions associated with a low VIX level – instead a more random pattern is evident. This is because a low VIX level is not necessarily associated with risk-on.

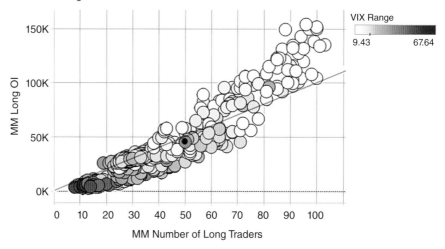

FIGURE 6.16 Dry Powder Factor (VIX) indicator – MML in copper.
This chart has been plotted using the application Tableau. The chart is on the companion website, where it can be plotted for any commodity on any date. It is updated regularly.
Source: Based on data from Bloomberg.

[6]Risk-on risk-off is an investment setting in which price behaviour responds to and is driven by changes in investor risk tolerance. Risk-on risk-off refers to changes in investment activity in response to global economic patterns. During periods when risk is perceived as low, risk-on risk-off theory states that investors tend to engage in higher-risk investments; when risk is perceived as high, investors have the tendency to gravitate toward lower-risk investments.
[7]Due the extreme range of the VIX, the red shading starts above 20 in the VIX.

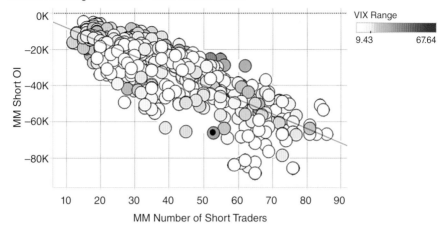

DP Factor Indicator (MMS vs VIX) – 25/12/2018
Colour: VIX Range. Black Dot = Most Recent Week.

FIGURE 6.17 Dry Powder Factor (VIX) indicator – MMS in copper.
This chart has been plotted using the application Tableau. The chart is on the companion website, where it can be plotted for any commodity on any date. It is updated regularly.
Source: Based on data from Bloomberg.

DP VVIX Factor charts are similar, except with the VVIX more driven by the anticipation of fear, or the outlook of the VIX, these charts can show a different dynamic. This can be especially interesting with commodities like gold that are often driven by safe haven dynamics, and higher VVIX levels are often associated with high gold prices.

Other Volatility indices based on the bond market, such as the MOVE index, can also be used to isolate different relationships.[8] Financial Conditions indices (FCI) can also be incorporated into the DP analysis framework in the same way, which has the benefit of portraying a more balanced view of the broader macroeconomic environment. Here it is more accurate to say that when FCIs are high (meaning Financial conditions are favourable) a 'risk-on' environment is better supported and in this respect they can complement the more one-sided nature of the VIX index. FCIs are discussed further in Section 9.2.4

Economic Policy Uncertainly indices may also be incorporated into DP analysis, although the majority of these are monthly, and subject to revision (revisions are, however, typically slight). These are discussed in more detail in Section 11.1.1.

This effect of variables like the VIX, VVIX, and EPU indices is generally most pronounced for the more industrial commodities – particularly the industrial metal and energy sectors.

---

[8]The MOVE Index (Merrill Option Volatility Estimate). This is a yield curve weighted index of the normalised implied volatility on 1-month Treasury options. It is the weighted average of volatilities on the CT2, CT5, CT10, and CT30. 'MOVE' is a trademark product of Merrill Lynch (weighted average of 1m2y, 1m5y,1m10y, and 1m30y Treasury implied vols with weights 0.2/0.2/0.4/0.2, respectively). Source: Bloomberg.

6.4.2 DP DXY Factor Indicators

Changes in the dollar can significantly affect commodity prices through a variety of different channels, including via trade linkages, export dynamics, production costs, and sentiment.

The Dollar index (DXY) indicates the overall value of the USD by taking the weighted geometric mean of six major currencies against the dollar. The composition and weights of the DXY index are as follows: Euro 57.6%, Japanese Yen 13.6%, British Pound 11.9%, Canadian Dollar 9.1%, Swedish Krona 5.2%, and the Swiss Franc 3.6%.

Weakness (strength) in the dollar index is generally bullish (bearish) for commodity prices for the following reasons:

- The trade linkage with many commodities traded in US dollars. As the dollar strengthens (weakens) against other currencies, dollar-denominated assets become more expensive (cheaper) to non-dollar-denominated buyers. Strength (weakness) in the dollar is therefore associated with lower (higher) commodity prices.

- Local (producer) currency effects – here there are two channels:[9]

  - As the dollar strengthens (weakens), commodity exporters generally receive more (less) revenue in local currency (assuming it weakens). This can increase (decrease) their incentive to export. Increasing (decreasing) exports act to elevate (reduce) global inventories, which can decrease (increase) prices.

  - As the dollar strengthens (weakens), commodity producer currencies typically weaken (strengthen), which acts to lower (raise) local production costs. Falling production costs reduce (increase) the need to cut production, which in a falling price environment can further depress prices. Falling production costs also act to keep credit channels in place, and therefore keep supply elevated.

- There are also powerful linkages between changes in the dollar and commodity prices via more sentiment-driven channels, where a rising (falling) dollar often has a powerful impact on commodity prices, especially during periods when other sources of fundamental data are scarce. These sentiment effects can be difficult to disentangle, may be bullish or bearish, and can often depend on the macroeconomic outlook.

With changes in currencies (both the dollar and producer currencies) and commodity prices heavily intertwined, many of these relationships are contemporaneous and are therefore challenging to monetise without forecasting them. By indirectly looking at the impact of changes in currencies on commodity positioning instead of on prices directly, an additional link in the chain is added, reducing some of the contemporaneity, and increasing the tradability of the relationships.

In the same way with the VIX in Section 6.4.1, colouring each point according to the DXY level reveals relationships between positioning and levels in the DXY.

Figure 6.18 (Figure 6.19) shows MML (MMS) DP Factor charts for crude oil (WTI), with each point shaded according to the DXY level. The darker the red shading, the higher the DXY level.

---

[9]Importantly, falling (rising) commodities prices also weaken (strengthen) producer currencies, which perpetuates the cycle.

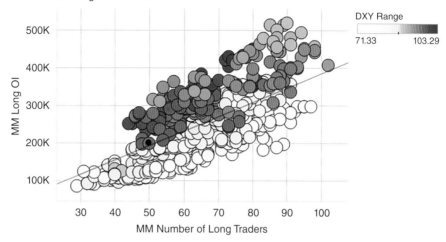

FIGURE 6.18 Dry Powder Factor (DXY) indicator – MML in crude oil (WTI).
This chart has been plotted using the application Tableau. The chart is on the companion website, where it can be plotted for any commodity on any date. It is updated regularly.
Source: Based on data from Bloomberg.

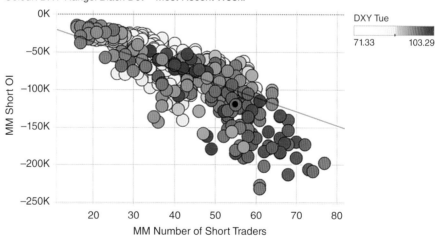

FIGURE 6.19 Dry Powder Factor (DXY) indicator – MMS in crude oil (WTI).
This chart has been plotted using the application Tableau. The chart is on the companion website, where it can be plotted for any commodity on any date. It is updated regularly.
Source: Based on data from Bloomberg.

Figure 6.18 shows a clear but counter-intuitive pattern, with none of the more conventional channels of influence explained above really applying. The chart shows that large long MM positions are mostly associated with an elevated level in the DXY, which suggest that MMs are bullish despite a higher dollar. By looking at a DP Time indicator chart of crude oil (WTI) as explained in 5.2.2 (not shown), in order to identify when this period occurred, most of these points occurred in 2015, 2016, 2017, and 2018 – a period of rising US rate expectations and of increasing US rates. This period marked a transition in the US economy as the outlook shifted to one of rising US economic growth and a stronger dollar. Positive economic growth is a key driver of higher commodity prices, and during this period was the overriding factor in determining prices.[10]

The pattern in Figure 6.19 is slightly more intuitive, although still very scattered, with larger short positions generally associated with a higher DXY index. Overall, however, these charts highlight and help to explain how some of the most established linkages in commodity markets can derail for significant periods of time and have a considerable impact on positioning profiles, price, and sentiment.

6.4.3 DP Currency Indicators

Chile is the largest copper producer in the world and the relationship between the Chilean peso and copper prices is well established and summarised under the points on producer currencies in Section 6.4.2.

Figure 6.20 (Figure 6.21) show MML (MMS) DP Currency charts for copper, with each point shaded according to the USD/CLP level. In this example, banded shading, as opposed to continuous shading, is used to divide the USD/CLP into five different levels from dark green to dark blue (very weak, weak, neutral, strong, and very strong). This is shown as an alternative and can make analysing the data easier.

Interesting patterns emerge. Figure 6.20 shows that both very strong (dark green) and very weak (dark blue) levels in the USDCLP are associated with low MML positions. This suggests that producer currency extremes, and by extension price extremes, as confirmed .with a DP Price indicator chart for copper (not shown), are associated with reduced MM activity. This could be driven by the heightened volatility in the market at these points, leading to reduced position sizing or general uncertainty surrounding the price outlook.

Figure 6.21 shows a more intuitive pattern, with the largest (smallest) MMS positions associated with weakness (strength) in the USDCLP.

6.4.4 DP Fundamental Indicators

The incorporation of fundamental data into a DP indicator can be easily included in the same way the factors and currencies have been included.

DP Fundamental indicators often reveal particularly interesting patterns and insights about the relationships between positioning and certain fundamental data.

Figure 6.22 (Figure 6.23) show a PMPUL (PMPUS) DP Fundamental chart for crude oil (WTI), with each point shaded according to the level of DOE crude oil (WTI) inventories.

---

[10]The strength in the DXY since the Federal reserve started increasing rates in late 2015 was associated with rising commodity prices due to rising economic growth prospects. Economic growth is often the most powerful driver of commodity prices.

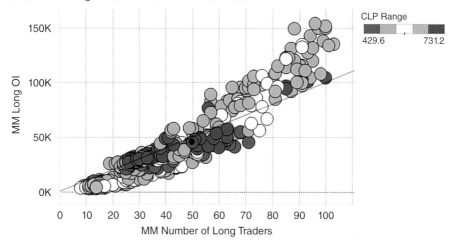

FIGURE 6.20 Dry Powder Currency (CLP) indicator – MML in copper.
This chart has been plotted using the application Tableau. The chart is on the companion website, where it can be plotted for any commodity on any date. It is updated regularly.
Source: Based on data from Bloomberg.

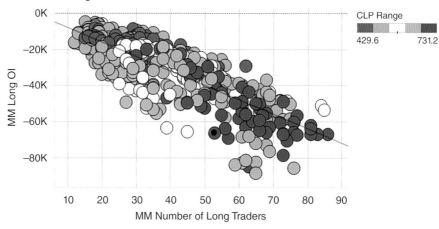

FIGURE 6.21 Dry Powder Currency (CLP) indicator – MMS in copper.
This chart has been plotted using the application Tableau. The chart is on the companion website, where it can be plotted for any commodity on any date. It is updated regularly.
Source: Based on data from Bloomberg.

Interestingly, both charts show the same relationship, but both explanations make sense. Figure 6.22 shows that larger PMPUL (including consumers) positions occur when DOE inventories are high. This is likely due to the relationship between higher inventories being associated with weaker prices, and weaker prices generally stimulating increased consumer hedging.

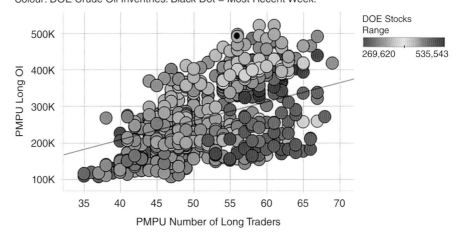

FIGURE 6.22 Dry Powder Fundamental (DOE crude oil inventories) indicator – PMPUL in crude oil (WTI).
This chart has been plotted using the application Tableau. The chart is on the companion website, where it can be plotted for any commodity on any date. It is updated regularly.
Source: Based on data from Bloomberg.

Figure 6.23 also shows that larger PMPUS positions occur when DOE inventories are high. This is due to an increase in the hedging activity needed to manage the larger inventory. The PMPU category includes both producers, merchants, and users, with the latter two groups needing to hedge and manage inventory. As inventories rise, more hedging needs to be performed.

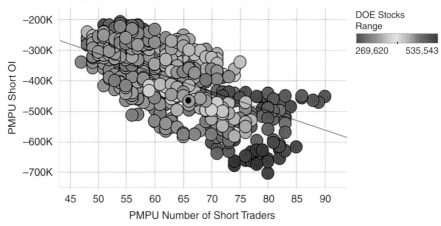

FIGURE 6.23 Dry Powder Fundamental (DOE crude oil inventories) indicator – PMPUS in crude oil (WTI).
This chart has been plotted using the application Tableau. The chart is on the companion website, where it can be plotted for any commodity on any date. It is updated regularly.
Source: Based on data from Bloomberg.

This is an interesting example, where both the PUMPUL and PMPUS groups hold larger positions when inventories are high. Interestingly, the main trading flows in crude oil (WTI) are between the PMPUL and PMPUS groups, according to the analysis in Section 7.4. This might appear counter-intuitive, as the trading activity between consumers and producers, a large proportion of the traders in the PMPUL and PMPUS categories, is usually in different areas of the curve, as discussed in Section 7.4. For oil markets, however, the PMPU groups also includes users

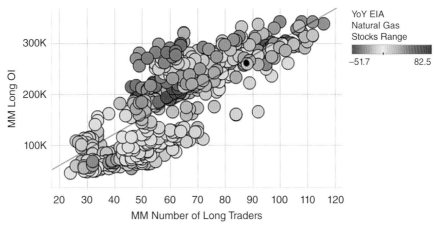

FIGURE 6.24 Dry Powder Fundamental (EIA natural gas stocks) indicator – MML in natural gas. This chart has been plotted using the application Tableau. The chart is on the companion website, where it can be plotted for any commodity on any date. It is updated regularly.
Source: Based on data from Bloomberg.

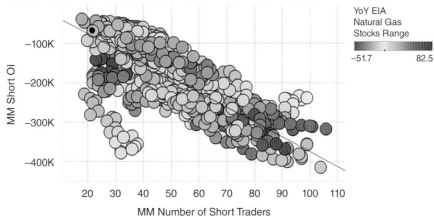

FIGURE 6.25 Dry Powder Fundamental (EIA natural gas stocks) indicator – MMS in natural gas. This chart has been plotted using the application Tableau. The chart is on the companion website, where it can be plotted for any commodity on any date. It is updated regularly.
Source: Based on data from Bloomberg.

that are active in inventory management. In the context of this example, if they did not trade with each other to hedge inventory dynamics, this would infer that other trader groups, like the MM group, would have to buy when inventories are high and sell when inventories are low, as someone would likely need to be the other side of the trades – a trading approach that is not the most intuitive for the MM group. In Section 7.4, more information is given on which trade groups mostly trade with which other groups.

Figure 6.24 (Figure 6.25) show MML (MMS) DP Fundamental charts for natural gas, with each point shaded according to the YoY % difference in the level of EIA natural gas inventories. Unlike Figure 6.22 and Figure 6.23, these charts show opposite and intuitive relationships between the MML and MMS with larger YoY surpluses (deficits) associated with larger MML (MMS) positions.

CHAPTER 7

Decomposing Trading Flow and Quantifying Position Dynamics

Chapter objectives

To understand the explanatory power that changes in the positioning of individual long and short trader categories have on price, a Shapley–Owen decomposition of the regression of changes in price against changes in positioning can be used. This provides some indication of which trader groups have been determining prices on a commodity-specific basis over time. By extension, Shapley–Owen decomposition can also be used to understand the explanatory power that changes in the positioning of individual trader categories have on other trader categories. This provides an indication of the trading flows between groups.

A Shapley–Owen decomposition is needed to derive the explanatory power, or the contribution to R-squared for each variable in a regression, as this is not otherwise possible in a multiple regression due to the interaction effects between the variables. In a multiple regression, only the R-squared of the overall equation is calculated.

In combination with the betas from the multiple regression, the overall approach also provides meaningful insight into potential price changes, by factoring into account the trading flows and the price sensitivity. It is also possible to then back-out the possible length of time that specific changes in trader positioning could need to complete. This can dramatically enhance risk management, trading performance, and market analysis.

7.1 Decomposing Net Positioning – The Methodology

To model the relationship between changes in positioning across the different trader groups and price, a simple multiple regression of changes in price against changes in each of the four main trader groups (MM, PMPU, SD, OR) can be done.

The equation below shows the equation of the regression of changes in price (y) against changes in the net positioning of each trader group:

$$y = \beta_0 + \beta_1 MM + \beta_2 PMPU + \beta_3 SD + \beta_4 OR$$

where

y = change in price.

MM, PMPU, SD and OR are all changes in net open interest.

All changes are in levels.

See Table 2.2 for abbreviations.

The regression will generate a set of coefficients (betas) for each of the four independent variables (the trader groups) and an overall R-squared value representing the total explanatory power that changes in these variables collectively have on changes in price.[1]

Determining the extent to which changes in each of the variables in isolation explains changes in price (the contribution to R-squared) is very difficult to derive due to the interaction effects between the variables.[2] Being able to do this, however, would show the extent to which changes in each of the trader groups in isolation, for example MM positioning, explain the price changes.

To calculate the contribution to the total R-squared from each variable, a Shapley–Owen decomposition needs to be done. It is a complex calculation, where in a regression of only four independent variables, 15 different regressions need to be performed and then combined together to isolate the contribution from each variable. If there are k independent variables there will be ($2^k - 1$) equations.

The 15 equations that need to be done, including the full regression (shown in red) are shown in Table 7.1:

TABLE 7.1 The 15 different regression equations.

$Y = \beta_0 + \beta_1\ MM$	$Y = \beta_0 + \beta_1\ PMPU + \beta_2\ OR$
$Y = \beta_0 + \beta_1\ PMPU$	$Y = \beta_0 + \beta_1\ SD + \beta_2\ OR$
$Y = \beta_0 + \beta_1\ SD$	$Y = \beta_0 + \beta_1\ MM + \beta_2\ PMPU + \beta_3\ SD$
$Y = \beta_0 + \beta_1\ OR$	$Y = \beta_0 + \beta_1\ MM + \beta_2\ PMPU + \beta_3\ OR$
$Y = \beta_0 + \beta_1\ MM + \beta_2\ PMPU$	$Y = \beta_0 + \beta_1\ MM + \beta_2\ SD + \beta_3\ OR$
$Y = \beta_0 + \beta_1\ MM + \beta_2\ SD$	$Y = \beta_0 + \beta_1\ PMPU + \beta_2\ SD + \beta_3\ OR$
$Y = \beta_0 + \beta_1\ MM + \beta_2\ OR$	$Y = \beta_0 + \beta_1\ MM + \beta_2\ PMPU + \beta_3\ SD + \beta_4\ OR$
$Y = \beta_0 + \beta_1\ PMPU + \beta_2\ SD$	

Where Y = change in price in levels.
The equation in red is the full regression equation.

---

[1] R-squared is a statistical measure of how close the data is to the fitted regression line. For example, an R-squared value of 1 or 100% indicates that the model explains all the variability of the dependent variable(s).
[2] The R-squared value generated from four separate regressions of changes in prices against changes in each of the trader groups will not equal the R-squared of a single multiple regression of changes in prices against changes in all four of the variables.

7.1.1 The Shapley–Owen Decomposition

Regressing changes in price (in levels) of the second-month crude oil (WTI) futures contract against changes in net positioning (in levels) using weekly data on a rolling 52-week basis, the following R-squared values for each of the 15 different regressions were generated at the end of 2018.[3]

TABLE 7.2   The R-Squared of each equation.

Equation	Regression	R- Squared
1	$Y = \beta 0 + \beta 1\ MM$	0.39
2	$Y = \beta 0 + \beta 1\ PMPU$	0.05
3	$Y = \beta 0 + \beta 1\ SD$	0.23
4	$Y = \beta 0 + \beta 1\ OR$	0.10
5	$Y = \beta 0 + \beta 1\ MM + \beta 2\ PMPU$	0.40
6	$Y = \beta 0 + \beta 1\ MM + \beta 2\ SD$	0.41
7	$Y = \beta 0 + \beta 1\ MM + \beta 2\ OR$	0.39
8	$Y = \beta 0 + \beta 1\ PMPU + \beta 2\ SD$	0.28
9	$Y = \beta 0 + \beta 1\ PMPU + \beta 2\ OR$	0.16
10	$Y = \beta 0 + \beta 1\ SD + \beta 2\ OR$	0.34
11	$Y = \beta 0 + \beta 1\ MM + \beta 2\ PMPU + \beta 3\ SD$	0.41
12	$Y = \beta 0 + \beta 1\ MM + \beta 2\ PMPU + \beta 3\ OR$	0.41
13	$Y = \beta 0 + \beta 1\ MM + \beta 2\ SD+ \beta 3\ OR$	0.41
14	$Y = \beta 0 + \beta 1\ PMPU + \beta 2\ SD + \beta 3\ OR$	0.41
15	$Y = \beta 0 + \beta 1\ MM + \beta 2\ PMPU+ \beta 3\ SD + \beta 4\ OR$	0.41

These 15 regression equations are then combined as shown in Table 7.3, where the R-squared values for the equations in the second column are subtracted from the R-squared values in the first column.

For example, the second row of the table shows equation 1 as 'MM PMPU' and equation 2 as 'PMPU'. These correspond to equation 5 and equation 2 in Table 7.2. The R-squared difference is 0.35 (0.40 − 0.05). The weights in the final column needed to combine the results are calculated using the formula:

$$weight_i = \frac{1}{n * C(n-1,k-1)}$$

where

n = *total number of independent variable in the full equation*

k = *number of independent variables in model i*

$C(n-1, k-1)$ = *number of ways of choosing (k − 1) items from (n − 1) items*

$$= \frac{(n-1)!}{(n-k)!(k-1)!}$$

[3]As noted previously in Section 2.1.2.1, the positioning data used was as of 25 December 2018 – the last release of the 2018. This was as of 24 December due to the holiday.

By way of an example, the weight (8.33%) in the blue row of Table 7.3 is calculated using the equation above, where $n = 4$ and $k = 2$ as follows:

$$weight_i = \frac{1}{4 * C(n-1, k-1)}$$

where

$$C(n-1, k-1) = \frac{(4-1)!}{(4-2)!(2-1)!} = \frac{6}{2*1} = 3$$

$$weight_i = \frac{1}{4*3} = \frac{1}{12} = 0.0833$$

TABLE 7.3 Combining the equations.

Variables in First Equation	Variables in Second Equation	R-Squared Difference	Weight
MM	None	0.39	25.00%
MM PMPU	PMPU	0.35	8.33%
MM SD	SD	0.18	8.33%
MM OR	OR	0.29	8.33%
MM PMPU SD	PMPU SD	0.13	8.33%
MM PMPU OR	PMPU OR	0.25	8.33%
MM SD OR	SD OR	0.07	8.33%
MM PMPU SD OR	PMPU SD OR	0.01	25.00%
		MM Contribution	0.21
PMPU	None	0.05	25.00%
MM PMPU	MM	0.01	8.33%
PMPU SD	SD	0.05	8.33%
PMPU OR	OR	0.06	8.33%
MM PMPU SD	MM SD	0.00	8.33%
MM PMPU OR	MM OR	0.01	8.33%
PMPU SD OR	SD OR	0.06	8.33%
MM PMPU SD OR	MM SD OR	0.00	25.00%
		PMPU Contribution	0.03
SD	None	0.23	25.00%
MM SD	MM	0.02	8.33%
PMPU SD	PMPU	0.23	8.33%
SD OR	SD	0.24	8.33%
MM PMPU SD	MM PMPU	0.01	8.33%
MM SD OR	MM OR	0.01	8.33%
PMPU SD OR	PMPU OR	0.24	8.33%
MM PMPU SD OR	PMPU SD OR	0.00	25.00%
		SD Contribution	0.12

Variables in First Equation	Variables in Second Equation	R-Squared Difference	Weight
OR	None	0.10	25.00%
MM OR	MM	0.00	8.33%
PMPU OR	PMPU	0.11	8.33%
SD OR	SD	0.11	8.33%
MM PMPU OR	MM PMPU	0.01	8.33%
MM SD OR	MM SD	0.00	8.33%
PMPU SD OR	PMPU SD	0.12	8.33%
MM PMPU SD OR	MM PMPU SD	0.00	25.00%
		OR Contribution	0.05

TABLE 7.3 (*Continued*)

The contribution to R-squared for each group (in red) are calculated as the SUMPRODUCT of the R-squared differences for each group and the weights.

The R-squared of the full equation (Equation 15 in Table 7.2) is 0.41. The contributions to R-squared for each trader group is shown in red in Table 7.3 is: MM (0.21), PMPU (0.03), SD (0.12), and OR (0.05), which all sum to 0.41! To be clear, the contributions to R-squared in this chapter refer to breaking down or decomposing the overall R-squared value between each variable, such that the contributions to R-squared all sum to the total R-squared value, rather than to 100%.

From the decomposition and for crude oil (WTI) at the end of 2018, based on 52 weeks of data, MMs explained more price movement than any other group, the explanatory power of the PMPU and OR groups was minimal, and for SDs about half that of the MM group.

7.2 Decomposing Long and Short Positioning – The Methodology

In Section 7.1, the changes in positioning were all based on net positioning. This means that only changes in open interest due to trading activity between different trader categories will be registered. If, for example, an MML trader, increased (decreased) its position with an MMS trader, who was decreasing (increasing) its position, the net change in MM positioning would be zero. The trade would still likely cause prices to change, but with the change in positioning being zero, the equation would not be able to explain the price change with no change in positioning. Only changes in positioning that occur between categories and that affect the net positioning are therefore registered, and only changes in price that occur because of these changes can be explained by the equation.

A solution is to expand the full regression to include all eight independent variables (MML, MMS, PMPUL, PMPUS, SDL, SDS ORL, and ORS), which is a significant increase in the number of calculations. The new equation would require 255 ($2^8 - 1$) different regressions, followed by 40,320 (8 factorial) combinations to isolate the contribution to R-squared of each of the eight variables. Using all eight variables is a significant improvement, but it is important to note that in a similar way to trades between the MML and MMS group not being captured when using net positioning and four variables as described above, trades within a single group, for example the MML group, would still not be captured. This would occur if an MML trader sold its long position to another MML trader, for example.

The equation below represents the regression of changes in price (y) against changes in long and short positioning of each trader group:

$$y = \beta_0 + \beta_1 MML + \beta_2 PMPUL + \beta_3 SDL + \beta_4 ORL$$
$$+ \beta_5 MMS + \beta_6 PMPUS + \beta_7 SDS + \beta_8 ORS$$

where

y = change in price.

MML, MMS, PMPUL, PMPUS, SDL, SDS ORL and ORS are all changes in open interest. All changes are in levels.

7.3 Who Has Been Driving Prices?

7.3.1 Decomposing Positioning in Crude Oil (WTI), Natural Gas, and Corn

By way of some examples, the Shapley–Owen decomposition is done on three different commodities (WTI, natural gas, and corn) on a rolling 52-week basis using weekly data since 2007.

For each commodity, the contribution to R-squared from each trader group is plotted as a stacked bar chart. Periods when the full regression is not statistically significant (p-value > 0.05) are not plotted and these periods appear as gaps.

Figure 7.1, Figure 7.2, and Figure 7.3 show the rolling 52-week contribution to R-squared for crude oil (WTI), natural gas, and corn respectively.

The regression was not statistically significant in parts of 2009 and 2015. Based on the total R-squared over the period, changes in positioning collectively explained 58% of price variance

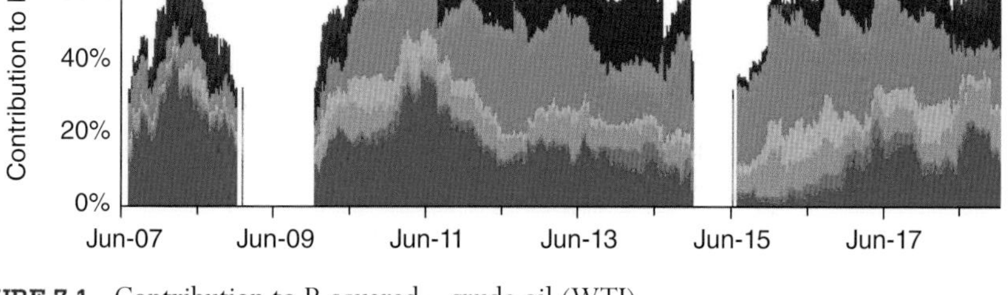

Shapley–Owen Decomposition: Contribution to R-Squared

■ MML ■ PMPUL ■ SDL ▫ ORL ■ MMS ■ PMPUS ■ SDS ■ ORS

FIGURE 7.1 Contribution to R-squared – crude oil (WTI).
COT symbols: As listed in Table 2.2.
This chart is not shown on the website.
Source: Based on data from Bloomberg.

in crude oil (WTI), with the highest contribution on average coming from the MML and MMS groups. This makes sense, as crude oil (WTI) is a highly speculated commodity.

By extension, 42% (the residual) of price variance in crude oil (WTI) was not explained by changes in the positioning variables. This might appear counter-intuitive, as logically, changes in positioning should explain most of the price movement, with little to no residual.

The most likely reason is that the equations use weekly COT data. Since the model only looks at changes in price from Tuesday to Tuesday, to be aligned with the COT release schedule, changes in positioning and prices outside this period are not captured.

Another reason for the residual possibly being high could be due to changes in spreading open interest – which has not been included in the regression – spread-related trading can have a significant impact on prices, especially in markets like natural gas where spread trading can be significant. The solution would be to expand the regression to include the MM, OR, and SD spreading categories, but this would significantly increase the number of regressions, as shown above.[4]

Different trading styles between trader groups can also increase the residual. For example, a large limit buy-order of 1,000 contracts, placed by a MM trader to work over an extended period of time, would likely have a limited impact on price, other than to provide support at that price level. This would invariably cause the residual to increase.

Finally, as mentioned in Section 7.2, trades within a single group, for example the MML group, would also not be captured.

Figure 7.2 shows the same analysis for natural gas. On average, changes in positioning explain only 37% of price variance, with the OR and MM categories on average being the most important. As described above, this could be due to the sizeable proportion of spread-related trading in natural gas.

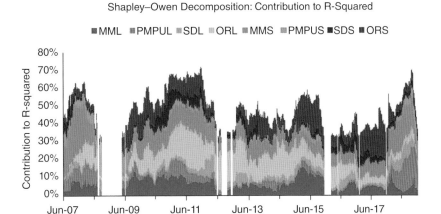

FIGURE 7.2 Contribution to R-squared – natural gas.
COT symbols: As listed in Table 2.2.
This chart is not shown on the website.
Source: Based on data from Bloomberg.

---

[4]For completeness, the Non-Reportable (NR) category should also be included (not part of the Disaggregated COT report). It is part of the legacy (full COT) report.

Shapley–Owen Decomposition: Contribution to R-Squared

■ MML   ■ PMPUL   ■ SDL   ▫ ORL   ■ MMS   ▫ PMPUS   ■ SDS   ■ ORS

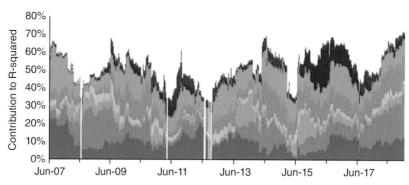

FIGURE 7.3   Contribution to R-squared – corn.
COT symbols: As listed in Table 2.2.
This chart is not shown on the website.
Source: Based on data from Bloomberg.

Figure 7.3 shows the same analysis for corn. On average, changes in positioning explain 72% of price variance, with the PMPU and MM categories on average being the most important.

This analysis can be done for any commodity, and similar profiles generated. In general, the explanatory power of each trader group is quite similar within a commodity over time, but sudden shifts can occur. The profiles can, however, be very different across different commodities – highlighting their idiosyncratic nature. This analysis is mostly useful in combination with other analyses, to provide context on which groups are the most important to focus on.

7.4 Who is Trading With Whom?

In Section 7.3, changes in price were regressed against changes in the positioning of each long and short trader group, with a Shapley–Owen decomposition then used to calculate the contribution to R-squared for each group. The objective was to identify which trader groups had the greatest explanatory power on price.

By regressing changes in the open interest of a specific trader group such as the PMPULs against the seven other long and short trader groups (MML, SDL, ORL, MMS, PMPUS, SDS, ORS), on the basis that different groups trade with each other, and calculating the contribution to R-squared from each group using a Shapley–Owen decomposition, the explanatory power of each group on each other group can be derived. This gives an idea of which trader groups have been trading with which other groups and a sense of the trading flow can be established. This approach does however omit trade flows within the same group, for example PMPUL traders trading with other PMPUL traders, as this is difficult to include in the regression. The NR category has also been excluded.

To be clear, the logic of the approach is as follows: if, for example, the only trading in a market was between MML traders and PMPUS traders, a regression of changes in MML open interest against changes in the open interest of all the other groups, followed by a Shapley–Owen decomposition, would show that changes in PMPUS open interest have the greatest explanatory power on MML open interest changes. This would therefore indicate that the trading flow was between the two groups.

Shapley–Owen Decomposition: Contribution to R-Squared

■ MML ■ SDL ■ ORL ■ MMS ■ PMPUS ■ SDS ■ ORS

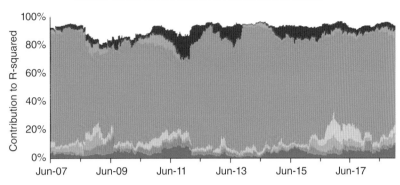

FIGURE 7.4 Contribution to R-squared – crude oil (WTI) PMPUL.
COT symbols: As listed in Table 2.2.
This chart is not shown on the website.
Source: Based on data from Bloomberg.

Figure 7.4 shows the contribution to R-squared for crude oil (WTI) in a regression of the PMPUL group against the seven remaining groups that could each, or in various combinations, be the other side of the trade.

The chart shows that a large proportion of the R-squared (an average of 70%) is explained by the PMPUS group, suggesting that PMPULs trade mostly with PMPUS. This is counter-intuitive as consumers (a large proportion of the PMPUL group) and producers (a large proportion of the PMPUS group) typically trade on different areas of the curve – consumers generally in the 3- to 9-month region, and producers mostly in the 9- to 24-month region.

One explanation could lie in how the PMPU group is classified. The group includes 'Users' and 'Merchants', and for the oil markets in particular, merchants can be a large proportion of the market. Their primary function is in the transport of crude oil globally, which carries significant price risks during the lifetime of the journey. Consequently, the buyers and sellers of physical cargoes (merchants) will frequently hedge these risks, and, according to this analysis, mostly between each other.[5]

Figure 7.5 shows a more intuitive profile for corn where the same regression has been performed – the PMPUL group against the seven other long and short trader groups. In this example, the most significant contributor to R-squared comes from the MMS group, but still with a large proportion from the PMPUS group.

7.4.1 Trading Flows

To identify the primary relationships or 'trading flows' in a commodity, Table 7.4 shows a matrix of the contributions to R-squared (top half) and also a matrix of betas (bottom half) for all the different trading combinations at the end of 2018 for crude oil (WTI). The most significant contributions to R-squared show the relationships with the most significant explanatory power and the sign of the beta, the direction of the relationship. The beta also gives some idea of the magnitude of the relationship.

---

[5]Another potential factor behind this relationship is described in Section 6.4.4.

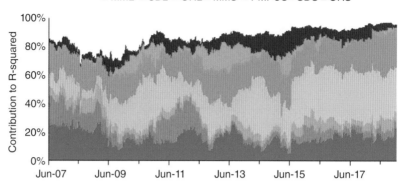

Shapley–Owen Decomposition: Contribution to R-Squared

■ MML ■ SDL ■ ORL ■ MMS ■ PMPUS ■ SDS ■ ORS

FIGURE 7.5 Contribution to R-squared – corn PMPUL.
COT symbols: As listed in Table 2.2.
This chart is not shown on the website.
Source: Based on data from Bloomberg.

The matrix is organised with the dependent variables on the left and the independent variables along the top. The R-squared matrix shows that the relationship between PMPUL and PMPUS has the highest R-squared (62%), consistent with Figure 7.4, followed by the relationship between PMPUS and PMPUL (60%). The similarity between these numbers indicates the extent of trading flow within the PMPU group and is also a good indication of the robustness of the approach.[6]

The beta of 1.0 between the PMPUL and PMPUS in the Beta matrix shows that as open interest for PMPUL rises (falls) by 1 contract, the open interest for the PMPUS rises (falls) by 1 contract. This indicates that as PMPULs buy more contracts, PMPUSs are taking the other side of the trade and going equally short.

TABLE 7.4   Matrices showing the contribution to R-squared and betas for crude oil (WTI).

WTI – R-Squared

	MML	PMPUL	SDL	ORL	MMS	PMPUS	SDS	ORS
MML		2%	2%	3%	7%	2%	31%	23%
PMPUL	9%		1%	7%	5%	62%	5%	4%
SDL	3%	1%		1%	1%	4%	15%	10%
ORL	14%	11%	2%		15%	22%	14%	4%
MMS	11%	11%	3%	17%		7%	12%	11%
PMPUS	10%	60%	1%	14%	2%		5%	3%
SDS	42%	7%	11%	9%	8%	8%		7%
ORS	35%	8%	8%	4%	10%	7%	11%	

---

[6]The R-squared values are not the same, as might be expected, as the underlying regressions are not the same. Whilst PMPULs trade predominately with PMPUSs, PMPUSs also have good trade with ORLs.

TABLE 7.4	(Continued)						

WTI Beta

	MML	PMPUL	SDL	ORL	MMS	PMPUS	SDS	ORS
MML		-0.2	-1.0	-0.4	0.2	-0.1	0.8	1.2
PMPUL	-0.8		-0.9	-0.9	0.7	1.0	0.8	1.0
SDL	-0.1	0.0		-0.1	0.1	0.1	0.2	0.3
ORL	-0.7	-0.7	-0.8		0.6	0.8	0.7	0.8
MMS	0.7	0.8	0.9	0.9		-0.8	-0.7	-0.9
PMPUS	0.8	0.9	0.9	0.9	-0.7		-0.8	-1.0
SDS	1.0	1.0	1.2	1.0	-0.8	-1.0		-1.2
ORS	0.7	0.7	0.8	0.6	-0.5	-0.7	-0.6	

COT symbols: As listed in Table 2.2.
Source: Based on data from Bloomberg.

To better visualise the flows, Figure 7.6 shows a trading flow radial chart for the ORL group in crude oil (WTI). Each of the eight trader groups is plotted around the edge of the chart (including the ORL group), with the axis showing the contribution of R-squared. From the chart, the highest R-squared of 22% with the PMPUS group is clearly identified.

This particular chart is for the last Report date of 2018 and based on 52 weeks of data. As each new week of data is released, the chart can be updated to reflect any change in trading flow.

Figure 7.7 shows a more cluttered chart with all the trader groups represented. The strong relationship between the PMPUL and PMPUS as mentioned above is very clear. Another useful way of showing trading flow is to use a Sankey diagram.

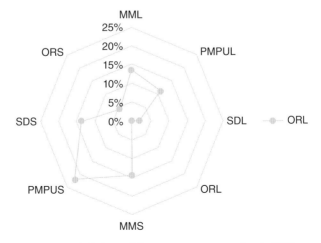

FIGURE 7.6 Trading flow radial chart of the ORL group in crude oil (WTI).
COT symbols: As listed in Table 2.2.
This chart is not shown on the website.
Source: Based on data from Bloomberg.

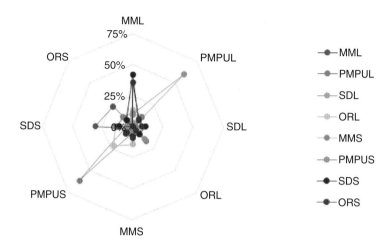

FIGURE 7.7 Trading flow radial chart for all crude oil (WTI) trader groups.
COT symbols: As listed in Table 2.2.
This chart is not shown on the website.
Source: Based on data from Bloomberg.

7.5 The Impact on Prices

For an indication of the sensitivity of price changes to changes in the positioning in each group, the betas of each variable (MML, MMS, PMPUL, PMPUS, SDL, SDS, ORL, and ORS) of the full regression of price (*y*) against changes in long and short positioning of each group are shown for crude oil (WTI) in Figure 7.8. No Shapley–Owen decomposition is required, as this is a simple multiple regression.

A positive beta means that an increase (decrease) in the open interest of a trader category has a positive (negative) impact on prices. A negative beta means that an increase (decrease) in the open interest of a trader category has a negative (positive) impact on prices.

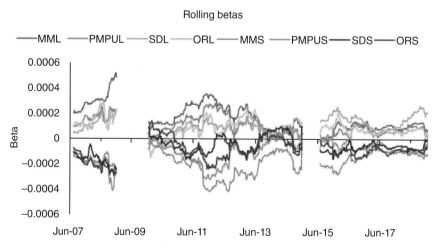

FIGURE 7.8 Rolling betas – crude oil (WTI).
COT symbols: As listed in Table 2.2.
This chart is not shown on the website.
Source: Based on data from Bloomberg.

The full regression equation defined in Section 7.2, of changes in price (y) against changes in long and short positioning of each group, with each beta, is shown below:

$$y = 0.201681 + 0.000056\,MML + 0.000009\,PMPUL$$
$$+ 0.000205\,SDL + 0.000019\,ORL - 0.000111\,MMS$$
$$- 0.000021\,PMPU + 0.000004\,SDS - 0.000050\,ORS$$

See Table 2.2 for abbreviations.

The beta for the MML category is 0.000056. This means that an increase (decrease) in the MML position of one contract will move the price of crude oil (WTI) up (down) by \$0.000056. For a price move of \$1 per barrel, the MM net positions would therefore need to change by 17,789 (1/0.000056) contracts.

In combination with Dry Powder analysis, these betas make it possible to better assess the impact a change in positioning could have on price. Figure 7.9 shows the same DP indicator chart for crude oil (WTI) shown in Figure 5.1.

The most recent week (black dot) has an MML open interest of +196,962 contracts and the highest exposure held by MMLs has been +519,545 on 30 January 2018 (highest point towards the top right of the cluster). For MMLs to therefore increase their long position to that level again, an increase of 322,583 contracts would need to occur. Based on the regression and the beta mentioned above, this would lead to a rise in the price of crude oil (WTI) of \$18.13 (322,583/17,789).

This is however *ceteris paribus*, meaning that the MML would have to change in isolation. Depending on which group(s) the MML trades with and depending on the beta of that group(s), the effect on price will either increase or decrease accordingly. In this respect, the analysis in Section 7.4 is helpful in identifying primary trading relationships.

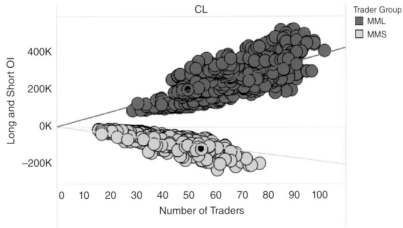

Dry Powder Indicator – 25/12/2018
Colour: Trader Group. Black Dot = Most Recent Week.

FIGURE 7.9 Dry Powder Net indicator – MM in crude oil (WTI).
This chart has been plotted using the application Tableau. The chart is on the companion website, where it can be plotted for any commodity on any date. It can also be customised according to trader group. Multiple groups and commodities can also be plotted together. It is updated regularly.
Source: Based on data from Bloomberg.

From Table 7.4, the MML group has the largest R-squared values with the SDS and ORS groups. The betas for these groups on price are 0.000004 and -0.000050 respectively. Assuming for example that the MML trades 50% of the 322,583 (161,291) contracts with each group, the trade with the SDS group will have a negligible impact on price as the beta is extremely low (161,291 × 0.000004 = $0.65). It is also positive, meaning that prices will rise by $0.65. The trade with the ORS group will have the following impact on the price (161,291 * 0.000050 = $8.09). It is negative, meaning that prices will fall with an increase in the shorts.

The likely overall impact on prices will then be: $18.13 + $0.65 − $8.09 = $10.69.

7.6 Speed of Positioning Changes

It is also useful to get an understanding of how long it could take for a position to change. For example, for the MML position to increase by 322,583, based on historical patterns, what would be the smallest number of weeks this could happen in?

There are a few ways to do this, and these are not exhaustive:

1. Look at the shortest period over the history of the data (June 2006 to December 2018), where the open interest has changed by a minimum of 322,583 contracts. This was the 46-week period between 18 December 2018 and 30 January 2018. Based on previous actual changes in open interest, the fastest period is therefore 46 weeks.

2. Look at the maximum weekly increase in open interest and assume this can happen multiple times. The largest weekly increase in MML open interest has been 51,380 contracts, so technically a position of 322,583 contracts could be built up over 7 weeks.

3. Look at the average weekly increases in open interest. The average weekly increase in MML open interest has been 10,179 contracts, so a position of 322,583 contracts could be built up over 32 weeks.

4. Look at the top largest actual increases in open interest that have occurred and assume they can happen consecutively. The top seven largest increases (51,380, 49,295, 48,223, 47,854, 47,742, 44,255, 36,580) sum to 325,329, so 7 weeks would be required.

5. Technically of course, a change of 322,583 contracts could also happen in a week, although this is very unlikely.

Starting for example with DP analysis to define a particular scenario, this combination of analytics can provide meaningful insight into potential price changes and the likely timeframe over which it could happen.

Based on the example above, the following statement is possible to make.

For MML to re-establish their record position of 519,545 contracts on 30 January 2018, they would need to buy 322,583 contracts, based on their position on 25 December 2018. Based on the recent trading patterns and dynamics over the last year, this could increase oil prices by $10.69/barrel and based, for example, on the average weekly increase in MM open interest, this could take 32 weeks.

This is a compelling statement and is particularly useful in risk management and scenario analysis. Collectively, these analytics can wrap sensible price forecasts and provide new insights into risk management for all commodities based on a variety of different scenarios.

Reference

Mark Keenan, Michael Haigh, David Schenck, and Malavika Dinaker (2018), 'Commodity Compass – Who's driving commodity prices – our new PVD model'. Société Générale (SG) Cross Asset Research – Commodities Group. www.sgmarkets.com/.

CHAPTER 8

Overbought/ Oversold (OBOS) Analysis – The Intersection of Extremes

Chapter objectives

In this chapter, the Overbought/Oversold (OBOS) framework is introduced as a way of generating trading signals in commodities that lie at the intersection of extremes in their long and short speculative positioning, and extremes in their price. Extremes in speculative positioning can provide useful trading insights in isolation, but it is mostly also in the context of price extremes that these they become particularly powerful.

The OBOS framework uses a combination of speculative positioning data and pricing data over specific timeframes. Specific thresholds are used to define whether a commodity becomes 'Overbought' or 'Oversold', within the framework, and it is during these points that trading signals are generated.

The framework is also useful in the analysis of behavioural patterns to help manage risk more effectively, and in combination with numerous other positioning models and analytics, to produce more sophisticated and refined trading signals.

8.1 The Overbought/Oversold (OBOS) Philosophy

Part of the core philosophy behind the OBOS framework is that speculative positions need to be unwound before expiry. All positions in the MM trader and many in the OR category are therefore aligned in this respect. This is because speculators do not typically access the physical markets and are therefore unable to make or take delivery of commodities.[1] In general, it is mostly only the PMPU, SD, and, to some degree, the OR categories are that able to access the physical markets.[2]

The larger the size of the speculative position, the greater the potential market impact when the position is unwound. Naturally a position can also be rolled over to another month before expiry, which normally has a greater impact on curve structure than on outright prices. Nonetheless, the expiring position still needs to be exited.

The rest of the philosophy lies in the fact that extremes in general, whether in price, in positioning, or otherwise, can often have a pronounced effect on behaviour, frequently driving shifts in sentiment and moves in price.

The OBOS framework cannot predict when positions will be unwound based on positioning alone, but its use of price and curve structure as inputs are helpful in this respect. Extreme long (short) positions that occur when prices are also at an extreme high (low) are often unwound faster, as extremes in price tend to be associated with increased nervousness among participants. This can have a disproportionate effect on prices. At the same time, depending on the shape of the underlying curve structure, this effect can be increased or dampened. For example, a long (short) position when the market is in backwardation (contango) tends to be less prone to unwind due to roll yield considerations, discussed further in Sections 8.2.3 and 8.5. The interplay between all these dynamics provides insight into the market and gives rise to numerous trading opportunities.

The framework, based on specific thresholds, defines commodities at the intersection of extreme long (short) speculative positioning, calculated using long (short) MM futures open interest (excluding options) as a percentage of the total open interest in the market, and extreme price strength (weakness), calculated using futures daily settlement prices, as Overbought (Oversold). When a commodity becomes Overbought (Oversold), within the framework, short (long) trading signals are generated for that commodity.

8.2 Constructing the Framework

The core OBOS framework consists of four components; a long Positioning Component, a short Positioning Component, a Pricing Component, and a Curve Component. These are calculated for each commodity within the framework.

---

[1] Some commodity funds can make and take delivery of physical commodities, but this is uncommon.

[2] Technically, it is uncommon for SD to access the physical market as they are mostly swap providers which mostly include banks. Many of the SD clients trading swaps are involved in hedging and do mostly have access to the physical market.

8.2.1 The Positioning Components

The long (short) Positioning Component is the current long (short) MM position (OI) calculated as a percentage of the current total open interest (OI) and expressed as a percentage of its historical range. As defined in Section 4.1.1.1, long (short) MM OI calculated as a percentage of the current total open interest (OI) is the same as Concentration. A useful range to use is a one-year rolling window for both Positioning Components.[3]

The formula for the long and short Positioning Components is as follows:

For long (short) positions:

$$long\left(short\right)Positioning\ Component\left(\%\right)$$
$$=\frac{\left(current\ MML\left(S\right)\%-\min\left(MML\left(S\right)\%_{range}\right)\right)}{\left(\max\left(MML\left(S\right)\%_{range}\right)-\min\left(MML\left(S\right)\%_{range}\right)\right)}$$

where

$$MML\left(S\right)\%=\frac{MML\left(S\right)\left(futures\ only\right)}{TOI\left(futures\ only\right)}$$

$$range=one\text{-}year\ rolling$$

See Table 2.2 for abbreviations.

8.2.2 The Pricing Component

The Pricing Component is the current price of the commodity expressed as a percentage of its historical range. To mitigate against any liquidity or expiry-related effects, the price of the second listed (second nearby) futures contract is used – any contract can, however, be used, depending on the objective. The second nearby futures contract may or may not be the second calendar listed month, as this depends on the listing schedule of the futures contracts.

The Pricing Component is calculated as follows:

$$Pricing\ Component\left(\%\right)=\frac{\left(current\ price-\min\left(price_{range}\right)\right)}{\left(\max\left(price_{range}\right)-\min\left(price_{range}\right)\right)}$$

where

$$range=one\text{-}year\ rolling$$

---

[3]Other rolling windows can also be used. The benefit of a one-year window is that sensitivity is increased. A two-year rolling window is also useful as it can offset seasonal variation for the more seasonally driven commodities. Ranges are discussed further in Section 8.2.4.

8.2.3 The Curve Component

The objective is to factor into account potential roll yield.[4] As this is most critical at the front of the curve for most investors, the difference between the second and third nearby contracts are taken. The shape of the curve at this point is then colour coded within the OBOS framework. Backwardated commodities are shown as green circles and commodities in contango are shown as blue circles.

$$If \left(Price \left(2nd\, Nearby \right) - Price \left(3rd\, Nearby \right) \right) < 0 = Contango$$

$$If \left(Price \left(2nd\, Nearby \right) - Price \left(3rd\, Nearby \right) \right) > 0 = Backwardation$$

8.2.4 Defining the Range

The price and positioning ranges can be calculated in one of two ways: using an anchored walk forward methodology, where the range is defined between a fixed start date (for example, the inception of the data) and the most recent date; or by using a rolling window methodology where the range is defined by a rolling window over a fixed period (for example, one year). For both methods, the range moves forward to include new data as it is released. This means that the overall size of the range, when using an anchored walk forward methodology, increases, whereas when using a rolling window methodology, it is constant.

As commodity markets evolve and market participants change with new trading patterns emerging, it makes sense to be able to accommodate and adapt to these shifts by using a rolling methodology. Furthermore, changes in regulation, such as the introduction and proliferation of speculative position limits, make an adaptive approach beneficial. Position limits are referred to frequently throughout the book, but in most detail in Sections 1.3.3.3, 4.1.1.3, and 5.1.2.1.

Both anchored and rolling window methodologies will include new data, and both will therefore be able to adapt to any structural or fundamental changes in the market that can permanently impact prices. A rolling approach, however, has the advantage of being able to adapt to changes, whilst not being constrained by historical price or positioning extremes that may no longer be relevant. By extension, one disadvantage is that potentially valuable historical information can be lost.

It is also particularly important to understand that when using a rolling window, it is possible for the Positioning and Pricing Components to change with no actual change in the price or speculative positioning of the commodity. This can occur because as the range rolls forward, earlier data drops out of the range and affects the calculation. This cannot happen with an anchored methodology.

There are advantages to both anchored and rolling window methodologies and, in practice, a combination of both is often helpful.

---

[4]See footnote 5 in Chapter 6.

8.2.5 Aligning the Data

The COT data is published weekly every Friday after the market close (with the Report date being the previous Tuesday). The Positioning Component is therefore calculated each Friday. In the event of a holiday, the published date will typically be deferred by a day. The release schedule of COT data is covered more in Sections 2.1.1.1. and 3.3.

To align the price of the commodity used to calculate the Pricing Component with the speculative positioning data, the price on the Friday, using the official closing price (settlement price) of the commodity, is used. One variation would be to use the price on the Report date, but with the market typically interpreting the latest positioning data in the context of current prices, the price closest to the Release date is more sensible. Another variation would be to use an average of prices over the week to mitigate any price spikes.

8.2.6 The Indicator Layout

The y-axis shows the Pricing Component and the left (right) hand side of the axis, the short (long) Positioning Component. The top right box (Overbought box) represents the intersection of extreme price strength and extreme long positioning and the bottom left box (Oversold box) the intersection of extreme price weakness and extreme short positioning. The indicator updates each week with each new data release and the commodities consequently move around their respective halves as a function of changes in price and/or changes in positioning data. As explained in Section 8.2.4, when using a rolling window, the commodities can move around as the range shifts.

Long (short) positions are shown in the right (left) hand side for each commodity, and every commodity is therefore represented twice, as there is both a long and short position.[5]

8.2.7 Generating Trading Signals

For the OBOS framework to generate trading signals, the Overbought and Oversold thresholds need to be clearly specified as defined in Section 8.1.

The 'default' thresholds used in the framework are the top and bottom quartiles of both the Price and the Positioning Component ranges as defined in Section 8.2.4. Naturally different thresholds, for example decile (10%), can be also be used for either or both components. The higher the threshold, the fewer trading signals are generated, but the reliability of the signal typically increases.

These thresholds are shown in Figure 8.1 as shaded grey boxes in the top right (Overbought box) and bottom left (Oversold box) of the chart. If a commodity is Overbought (Oversold), it will be in the Overbought (Oversold) box and an Overbought (Oversold) signal is generated. Overbought signals are 'sell signals'. Oversold signals are 'buy signals'. Trading signals can be directional or relative value (spread related), as changes in positioning extremes can often have a very pronounced effect on curve structure. A relative value trading approach can also be an effective way of capturing positioning dynamics, whilst insulating the trade from wider adverse market fluctuations.

---

[5]It is technically possible for a commodity not to have both a long and short position if the long or short position either does not meet the COT reporting threshold, or if there is simply no position – this would be extremely unusual in the MM category. Occasionally this can happen in some of the more illiquid commodities. In categories like the SD group this is also more likely.

8.3 The OBOS Concentration Indicator

Figure 8.1 shows the overall framework for the OBOS Concentration indicator for the MM group (data as of 25 December 2018). This indicator is also referred to as the classic OBOS indicator. The word Concentration is used to differentiate it from some of the other variations discussed below.

Long (short) positions are shown in the right (left)-hand side for each commodity, and every commodity is therefore represented twice, as there is both a long and short position.[6] The symbols of each commodity are shown in Table 2.1.

By way of an example, on the left-hand side of the framework, SM (soymeal) is in the Oversold Box as the price is 9.3% of its one-year range (bottom quartile) and the MMS position is 88.87% of the one-year range (top quartile). On the right-hand side, SM (soymeal) is not in the Oversold Box as the price is the same at 9.3% of its one-year range (bottom quartile) and the MML position is 6.22% of the one-year range (bottom quartile).

Two other boxes are also shown in the framework – one in the top left-hand corner and one in the bottom right-hand corner. These are discussed in Section 8.5.4.

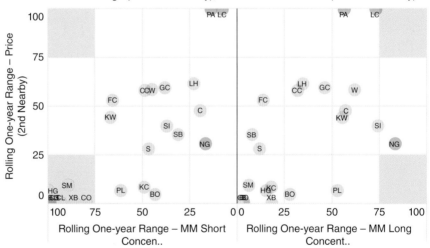

OBOS Concentration Indicator – 25/12/2018
Colour: Blue = Contango (2nd – 3rd Nearby), Green = Backwardation (2nd – 3rd Nearby).

FIGURE 8.1 The OBOS Concentration indicator using one-year rolling ranges.
This chart has been plotted using the application Tableau. The chart is on the companion website, where it can be plotted with any commodities on any date. It is updated regularly.
Commodity symbols: As listed in Table 2.1.
Source: Based on data from Bloomberg.

---

[6]It is technically possible for a commodity not to have both a long and short position if the long or short position either does not meet the COT reporting threshold, or if there is simply no position – this would be extremely unusual in the MM category. Occasionally this can happen in some of the more illiquid commodities. In categories like the SD group this is also more likely.

8.4 Key Attributes of the OBOS Approach

The OBOS framework, like the Dry Powder (DP) analysis in Chapter 5, looks at long and short speculative positions individually, but importantly also in the context of a second variable. In DP analysis, the second variable is the number of traders; in the OBOS framework, the second variable is the price of the commodity.[7]

Speculative positions are typically referred to on a net basis – typically the difference in long and short MM positions. Analysing individual long and short speculative positions is unusual, and analysing individual long and short speculative positions alongside a second variable is rare. As explained in Section 5.3.1, looking at individual long and short positioning provides information on the magnitude of each position, something that is often lost with net positioning analysis, but by including another variable such as price, more robust behavioural patterns can often be better isolated and understood.

The construction of the OBOS framework and the way in which the data is organised within it provides numerous insights into positioning dynamics. It also controls for some of a number of risks in Positioning Analysis:

- By normalising the long and short positions by open interest, broader market dynamics such as long-term trends and seasonal variations are absorbed. Comparisons between other commodities are also more meaningful. This is particularly important and is why the use of historical ranges is an integral part of the OBOS framework.

- Quantifying the long and short positions as a function of their respective historical ranges provides context and gives an idea of how much bigger the position could become. This is related to the discussion on the limitations to positions in Section 5.1.2.

- Quantifying the price level in the context of its historical range, using certain thresholds, helps align the framework with changes in price that could drive a fundamental response or change. Furthermore, in using more conventional range and threshold parameters, such as a one-year range and quartiles or deciles, familiarity is enhanced with some degree of potential self-reinforcement often likely. Commodity prices, for example, are frequently referred to as being in the top or bottom quartile/decile of their price range – a statement that is easily rationalised and put into context with a higher likelihood of it affecting behaviour. For example, from a fundamental and/or sentiment perspective, if copper is trading in its bottom price quartile, this might be a level where a mine could start considering supply cutbacks (bullish for prices) or where a financing bank might initiate a credit review of the viability of the mine, also leading to cutbacks.

- By focusing on extremes within the framework, price responses are often more significant as associated newsflow also typically increases, acting to magnify price moves and maximise trading opportunities. Newsflow in the context of positioning is discussed in Chapter 11.

- Certain assumptions about the profitability of the positions can be inferred by looking at Oversold and Overbought commodities. It would be unusual for speculators to initiate a new

---

[7]The OBOS framework also includes data on curve structure, which could be viewed as a third variable.

extreme position in terms of size at an extreme in price. This means that the extreme short (long) positions at extreme lows (highs) in prices should logically include traders holding a large unrealised profit. If the market looks like it might be changing direction, traders holding profitable shorts (longs) tend to start covering (liquidating) their positions as they are typically overly sensitive to early signs of any price reversal for fear their profits should evaporate. This action can lead to a self-reinforcing behavioural effect as more traders start to do the same thing, leading to potentially significant moves in prices.

8.5 Behavioural Patterns within the Boxes

The Overbought and Oversold boxes within the framework are used to define the extremes and to generate short (sell) and long (buy) trading signals, but it is important to remember that the act of being Overbought (Oversold) does not automatically lead to immediate long liquidation (short covering).[8] Typically, a fundamental, macroeconomic, or technical catalyst is still needed. The purpose of all these indicators in this chapter and also for many in Chapter 9 is to identify and flag commodities where the likelihood of positioning being closed out is high and the resultant move in prices likely to be significant.

In the absence of a catalyst, it is possible for a commodity to remain Oversold or Overbought for considerable periods of time. In this respect the OBOS charts in Figure 8.2 and Figure 8.3 are helpful.

8.5.1 Specific Properties of Oversold Commodities

Commodities in the Oversold Box are vulnerable to short covering and can lead to higher prices. Due to the following general properties of short positions and characteristics of the framework, these moves can be sudden and significant:

- Open profit: As explained in Section 8.4, short positions in the Oversold box are invariably associated with large unrealised profits. This sharpens behavioural dynamics due to the heightened risk of traders giving back profit if the market rises.

- Price shocks: Supply shocks tend to occur more frequently when prices are low as production becomes unprofitable, which can lead to upside price spikes or shocks.[9,10]

- Asymmetry in participants: As explained in Section 5.3.1, the composition of long and short speculative traders also tends to be different, which can add asymmetry in behaviour. Commodity investors, also classified as speculators, tend not to employ leverage, have long holding

---

[8]A general exception to this is for extreme positions that occur around expiry. If most of the short (long) position is in the expiry month, short covering (long liquidation) will be forced to occur. If the position is rolled over to another month, the resultant price effects often have a greater impact on curve structure than on outright prices.

[9]Demand destruction at high prices tends to be more gradual, meaning that demand-driven downside price shocks are less likely.

[10]An equivalent driver of downside price spikes is macroeconomic shocks. These are, however, usually agnostic to commodity prices and positioning profiles as they can occur at any time.

periods and are less sensitive to price swings. Long/short speculators, including hedge funds, normally use leverage and often have a more dynamic trading style. Large short speculative positions are therefore often less diversified and can often be more volatile.

■ The zero effect: There is a well-established argument that a commodity's price cannot fall to zero, but its rise could be unlimited – this often shapes the behaviour of traders and can have a profound impact on how risk is managed. Anecdotally, and from a behavioural perspective, this and many of the factors above combine such that speculators holding large short positions are more 'nervous' than those holding long positions.

8.5.2 Specific Properties of Overbought Commodities

Commodities in the Overbought Box are vulnerable to long liquidation and can lead to lower prices. Due to the following factors relating to the general properties of long positions and characteristics of the framework, these moves can, however, be muted, and in some cases lead to moves higher:

■ Sentiment factors: As prices rise, positive investor sentiment improves, and price momentum, driven by new participants entering the market, can take prices higher. This can lead to the formation of price bubbles where prices typically ultimately collapse, but the moves higher can become very protracted. This is often more apparent in commodities like oil, gold, and copper, where market familiarity is high and there are many access instruments (including ETFs, long-only funds, and structured products) available to facilitate this.

■ Roll yield: When a commodity's forward curve is in backwardation, a profile typically driven by short-term demand strength and associated with rising prices (and therefore quite common for overbought commodities), commodity investors seek to capitalise on the positive roll yield earned by rolling and rebalancing the futures position.[11] This can make long positions less prone to liquidation and can even drive new inflows. Naturally, the reverse applies to short positions when the market is in contango, but with long-only commodity investors, traditionally the most sensitive group to roll yield, this is primarily a consideration with long positions.

■ Position sizing effects: These often quite subtle factors can have a meaningful impact on price. Typically, as prices start to trend, speculators will often add to the positions as part of a momentum strategy, and many computerised trading algorithms employ strategies to do this. Increasing the size of a long position is more efficient in terms of margin requirements than a short position due to the difference in notional values. Position sizing is often done to ensure that exposure increases linearly, resulting in fewer contracts needing to be bought as the notional value increases, resulting in fewer position and exposure limit issues. These effects can lead to more exaggerated price moves in a rising market than in falling markets.[12]

---

[11]See footnote 5 in Chapter 6.

[12]Assume a trader goes short 100 contracts of crude oil at $100/b (notional exposure = 10 contracts * 1,000 barrels/contract * $100/b = $10,000,000) and the price then falls to $50/b (notional exposure = $5,000,000, with an open profit of $5,000,000). To scale into the position, and increase it by 10%, the trader will need to sell $1,000,000 of crude oil at $50/b. This equates to 20 contracts – double the amount for the long position. This can be a key factor in terms of margin requirements and can have an impact on position and exposure limits.

■ Rebalancing effects: while rebalancing by notional exposure causes a long position to decrease in size and a short position to increase, rebalancing or equalising by volatility is more common. At higher (lower) notional values, the same price move will have a greater (lesser) impact on volatility, which when equalising, will entail reducing a short position but increasing a long position.

8.5.3   OBOS Charts – 'Backtesting' the OBOS

The OBOS Overbought (Oversold) chart in Figure 8.2 (Figure 8.3) shows the periods when corn has been Overbought (Oversold) over the last five years. Weeks when corn was in the Overbought (Oversold) Box in Figure 8.1 are show as green (red) points on the chart. In many cases corn prices moved significantly lower (higher) shortly afterwards.

It is interesting to note how long a commodity remains in one of the boxes by the duration of the sequences in the charts. As mentioned in Section 8.5, it is important to remember that the act of being Overbought (Oversold) does not automatically lead to immediate short covering (long liquidation) and a catalyst is still needed. It is also important to understand that the OBOS framework is based on dynamic positioning and pricing ranges which can expand. This is a weakness of the approach, as identifying potential maxima and minima when markets are trending is difficult. One solution is to refer to other Positioning analytics, such as DP analysis, to help identify positioning extremes. This is discussed further in Section 9.1.1.3 and Section 9.1.1.4.

Further improvements and refinements to the OBOS framework are provided in the rest of this chapter, Chapter 9, and Chapter 11.

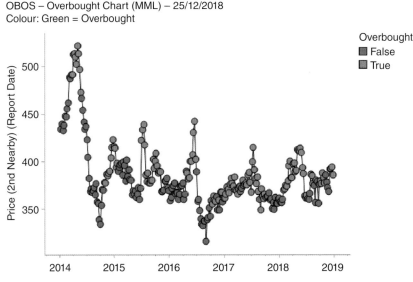

FIGURE 8.2   OBOS Overbought chart – MML in corn.
This chart has been plotted using the application Tableau. The chart is on the companion website, where it can be plotted for any commodity on any date. It is updated regularly.
Source: Based on data from Bloomberg.

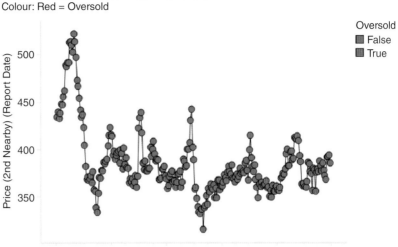

OBOS – Oversold Chart (MMS) – 25/12/2018
Colour: Red = Oversold

FIGURE 8.3 OBOS Oversold chart – MMS in corn.
This chart has been plotted using the application Tableau. The chart is on the companion website, where it can be plotted for any commodity on any date. It is updated regularly.
Source: Based on data from Bloomberg.

8.5.4 The Other Boxes

The OBOS framework in Figure 8.1 also includes two other boxes.

The top left-hand box is the same as the Oversold Box except that instead of prices being in the bottom quartile of their range, they are in the top quartile. The bottom right-hand box is the same as the Overbought Box except instead of prices being in the top quartile of their range, they are in the bottom quartile. Instances when commodities are in these boxes are infrequent, but when they do occur, they are worth highlighting and could indicate the following:

- They could be large short (long) positions that have been quickly established at the high (low) of the price range. If the trades are correct, they could indicate that prices are about to fall (rise).

- They could be large short (long) positions that have been ignored and are losing money as prices are now at the high (low) of the price range. These positions could be vulnerable to being closed or stopped out, leading to price strength (weakness). One reason for this is that the positions could be part of a relative value trade, where the other leg of the trade is in profit.

One way to differentiate between the two scenarios is to be aware of the history of the position and how it has developed over time. In the case of the first point, the swift appearance of the commodity in these boxes would suggest it to be true, whereas if the second factor was true, the move into the box would invariably be slower. One way to track the evolution of a commodity within the framework over time is to use the OBOS Time indicator discussed in Section 8.5.5.

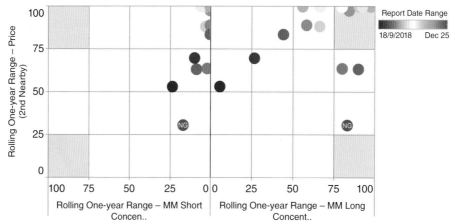

FIGURE 8.4 The OBOS Time indicator for natural gas using one-year rolling ranges.
This chart has been plotted using the application Tableau. The chart is on the companion website, where it can be plotted for any commodity on any date. It is updated regularly.
Source: Based on data from Bloomberg.

8.5.5 The OBOS Time Indicator

The OBOS framework is well placed in being able to track the recent evolution of a commodities positioning profile within the framework by including historical data. Figure 8.4 shows an OBOS Time indicator with the evolution of the natural gas OBOS profile over a 15-week period up into the Overbought Box and then back out.

Focusing on the MML positions on the right-hand side only, the move up into the Overbought Box and its subsequent fall out of the box is clear, starting with when the points were red before ending up green. These charts are useful in providing the history behind a move, especially when trying to understand behaviour around the other boxes mentioned in Section 8.5.4. The most recent week is labelled with the commodity symbol.

8.6 OBOS Variations

The OBOS framework allows for significant modification, such as the use of different trader groups and/or different measures of price. An extreme long (short) PMPU position in the context of low (high) prices could for example suggest that consumers (producers) see value in hedging. Naturally, when using PMPU data, the boxes within the framework would need to change position, with the producer (PMPUS) (consumer (PMPUL)) hedging box being in the top left (bottom right). This approach could be further refined by using prices towards the front (back) of the curve for PMPU longs (shorts), where their respective hedging activity is typically more pronounced. Chapter 9 covers many other more complex variations. One basic modification, which has an interesting degree of self-regulation within it, involves using net positioning data instead of separate long and short positioning data. The OBOS Net Concentration indicator is described in Section 8.6.1.

Another interesting variation involves looking at seasonal patterns. The OBOS Seasonal indicator, described in Section 8.6.2, shows whether certain commodities have an increased likelihood of being Oversold (Overbought) at certain times of the year.

8.6.1 The OBOS Net Concentration Indicator

Using net positioning data does, however, go against many of the key points in the core philosophy behind both the OBOS framework and also Dry Powder analysis. Many of these points are mostly defined in Section 5.3.1. It does, though, provide one interesting attribute that can be useful. An extreme net position can only occur when the other position is small.[13] This means that if an extreme net long (short) position starts to unwind, there is always capacity for the short (long) position to increase. This effect can add extra impetus to a price that may not necessarily be the case in the OBOS indicator, where only extreme long and extreme short positions are identified.

This approach adds a degree of self-regulation by eliminating instances where positioning is mixed within a market. The OBOS Net Concentration indicator only identifies markets at extremes in price that have an extreme long or short position *relative* to a small opposite position. Note also that the long or short position does not have to be extreme in isolation. The disadvantage of this approach is that the identification of extreme long and short individual positions can be lost.[14]

It can also be argued that the OBOS Net Concentration indicator gives an extra level of insight from a behavioural perspective. As discussed in Section 5.3.1, net positioning is more widely followed and more natural to put into context for many market participants, and by extension can often shape market sentiment. The OBOS framework represents the intersection of extremes in long and short positioning against extremes in price, while the OBOS Net Concentration indicator represents the intersection of extremes in net positioning, and by extension also extremes in sentiment, against extremes in price.

Another interesting dynamic on the OBOS net indicator compared to the OBOS indicator is that covering (liquidating) a net short (long) position, is different from covering a short (liquidating a long) position. This means that if a commodity is in the Oversold (Overbought) box, for example, in the OBOS indicator, the only way for the commodity to get out of the box is to reduce the short (long) position. If a commodity is in the Oversold (Overbought) box in the OBOS Net indicator, the commodity can get out of the box by both reducing the short (long) position, or increasing the long (short) position. This can add an extra dimension to how trading signals develop between the two indicators.

In practice, a combination of both the OBOS and OBOS Net Concentration indicators are often helpful.

---

[13]In the standard OBOS framework, it is technically possible for both Positioning Components to be extreme.

[14]By way of a simple example and using futures OI data without dividing by total OI; a record short position of 100,000 contracts at the low of the price rage would be identified in the OBOS framework irrespective of the size of the long position. It would, however, only be identified within the Net OBOS framework if the long position was small. Assume it is long 30,000 lots, making the position net short -70,000 lots. Assume this is extreme on a net basis. The position here would be Oversold on both an individual basis and on a net basis.

In contrast, a short position of 80,000 contracts, which is not extreme in isolation, against a long position of 10,000 contracts would also have a net position of -70,000 and would be identified in the Net OBOS framework as extreme on a net basis. The position here would only be Oversold on a net basis.

To produce the OBOS Net Concentration indicator, the Pricing Component stays the same as defined as in Section 8.2.2, but the formula for the Positioning Component changes to the following:[15]

$$Net\,Positioning\,Component(\%)$$

$$= \frac{\left(current\,MMnet\,\%_{} - \min\left(MMnet\,\%_{range}\right)\right)}{\left(\max\left(MMnet\,\%_{range}\right) - \min\left(MMnet\,\%_{range}\right)\right)}$$

where

$$MMnet\,\% = \frac{\left(MML\,open\,interest\left(\,futures\,only\,\right) - MMS\,open\,interest\left(\,futures\,only\,\right)\right)}{TOI\left(\,futures\,only\,\right)}$$

$$range = one\text{-}year\,rolling$$

See Table 2.2 for abbreviations.

Figure 8.5 shows the OBOS Net Concentration indicator on the same day as the OBOS indicator in Figure 8.1. Both charts are similar on this occasion, except gasoline is not in the Oversold box in the OBOS Net indicator.

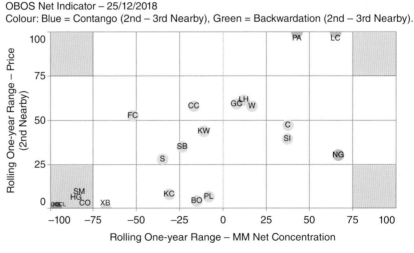

OBOS Net Indicator – 25/12/2018
Colour: Blue = Contango (2nd – 3rd Nearby), Green = Backwardation (2nd – 3rd Nearby).

FIGURE 8.5 The OBOS Net Concentration indicator using one-year rolling ranges.
This chart has been plotted using the application Tableau. The chart is on the companion website, where it can be plotted with any commodities on any date. It is updated regularly.
Commodity symbols: As listed in Table 2.1.
Source: Based on data from Bloomberg.

[15]Dividing the net exposure by the total open interest creates a net Concentration metric. There is an argument to say that just a net position would suffice, in a similar way to the DP Net indicator in Section 6.1.1, but when comparing multiple commodities within the same framework, dividing by total OI is a good way to normalise the data.

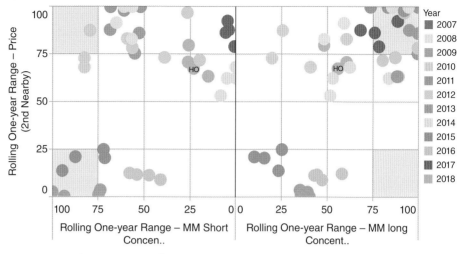

OBOS Seasonal Indicator – February
Colour: Red = oldest, Green = most recent.

FIGURE 8.6 The OBOS seasonal indicator for heating oil in February using one-year rolling ranges. This chart has been plotted using the application Tableau. The chart is on the companion website, where it can be plotted for any commodities for any month. It is updated regularly.
Source: Based on data from Bloomberg.

8.6.2 The OBOS Seasonal Indicator

Figure 8.6 shows the OBOS Seasonal indicator for heating oil in the month of March for all years going back to 2007. The colours refer to the years with the most recent data point labelled with the commodity symbol.

The indicator intuitively shows the northern hemisphere cold winter month of February as a month where heating oil has been repeatedly either in, or very close to, the Overbought Box. Prices are also shown to be generally elevated at this time of the year, with notable exceptions being 2009, 2015, and 2016.

Incorporating seasonal patterns into the OBOS framework is useful in isolating seasonal positioning profiles that can be considered 'normal' at certain times of the year. Seasonal positioning profiles are discussed in more depth in Section 5.2.4.

8.7 The DP/OBOS Hybrid Indicator

8.7.1 Limitations in DP Analysis and the OBOS Framework

In Chapter 5, Dry Powder (DP) analysis was introduced as a way of visualising positioning in commodity markets by reconciling historical long and short open interest, with the number of traders holding the position. One of the uses of DP indicator charts is as a trading indicator to help assess the likelihood of an existing position becoming bigger, or whether a position might be nearing a positioning extreme and vulnerable to liquidation.

A fundamental weakness in the DP approach, however, is the subjectivity of the trading signal generation. In Section 5.3, optimal locations within each cluster were indicated for generating reliable trading signals, but to define these locations precisely to generate clear trading signals, specific thresholds or specific levels need ideally to be set. Naturally this is challenging, with the clusters being dynamic and different in profile on the long and short sides and also between commodities.

Trading signals in the OBOS framework, by virtue of its construction, are objective. A weakness in the OBOS approach lies in the fact that, because the ranges are dynamic, the positioning of Overbought (Oversold) commodities can continue to increase, making them more extreme. Filtering out trading signals that have a greater risk of becoming more extreme is one solution.

By applying aspects of the OBOS framework to DP Analysis, the signal objectivity of the OBOS framework can be combined with DP Analysis to assess the likelihood of the positioning of already Oversold (Overbought) commodities becoming even more extreme.

8.7.2 Hybrid Approaches

Weaknesses in both DP analysis and the OBOS framework can therefore be addressed by partly blending them together within the same framework.

The DP/OBOS Hybrid framework brings together a standard DP indicator chart, that includes all positioning data, with the more structural aspects of the OBOS framework – specifically, the use of ranges and defined thresholds. The result is a DP/OBOS Hybrid model, where DP positioning data is used in a more structured and formulaic way and trading signals become more objective.

8.7.2.1 The DP/OBOS Hybrid Indicator Charts Figure 8.7 and Figure 8.8 show DP/OBOS hybrid indicator charts for crude oil (WTI) MML and MMS positions respectively. Each of the axes are one-year rolling ranges of Clustering on the *x*-axis and Concentration on the *y*-axis expressed as percentages of the range. Concentration defined in Section 4.1.1.1, and the number of traders plotted as Clustering, as defined in Section 4.1.1.2.[16]

By using Concentration and Clustering together, historical analysis is more meaningful as any long-term changes in open interest and/or changes in the number of traders over time are absorbed.[17] Historical trading signals are also more robust.

In Figure 8.7 and Figure 8.8, several lines are drawn and specific boxes defined. In Figure 8.7, the top right (blue) and bottom left (green) boxes are the intersections of the top and bottom quartiles (25%) of the long Concentration range with the top and bottom quartiles (25%) of the long Clustering range. In Figure 8.8 the boxes are reversed, the bottom right (green) and top left (blue) boxes are the intersections of the top and bottom quartiles (25%) of the short Concentration range with the top and bottom quartiles (25%) of the long Clustering range.

■ If the long position in Figure 8.7 is in the top right blue box, this means it is at the top of the range historically and can be defined as 'extreme'. If the short position in Figure 8.8 is also in its blue box (top left), this means it is at the bottom of the range historically and can also be defined as 'extreme'. This opposite extreme blue positioning is vulnerable to long liquidation and fresh short positions, as explained in Section 5.3.3, as a 'Strong Sell' signal.

---

[16]A rolling range of the Concentration is also used to calculate the Positioning Component in Section 8.2.1.
[17]The DP/OBOS Hybrid indicator is very similar to the DP Concentration/Clustering indicator charts covered in Section 6.1.2.2, but the emphasis here is more on defining trading signals.

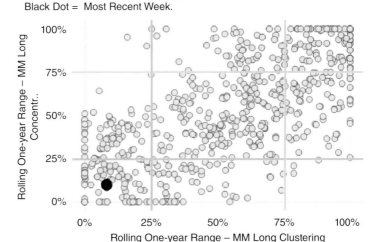

FIGURE 8.7 DP/OBOS hybrid indicator using one-year rolling ranges – MML in crude oil (WTI). This chart has been plotted using the application Tableau. The chart is on the companion website, where it can be plotted for any commodity on any date. It is updated regularly.
Source: Based on data from Bloomberg.

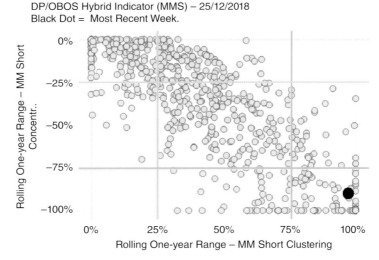

FIGURE 8.8 DP/OBOS hybrid indicator using one-year rolling ranges – MMS in crude oil (WTI). This chart has been plotted using the application Tableau. The chart is on the companion website, where it can be plotted for any commodity on any date. It is updated regularly.
Source: Based on data from Bloomberg.

■ If the long position in Figure 8.7 is in the bottom left green box, this means it is at the bottom of the range historically and can be defined as 'extreme'. If the short position in Figure 8.8 is also in its green box (bottom right), this means it is at the top of the range historically and can also be defined as 'extreme'. This opposite extreme green positioning is vulnerable to short covering and fresh long positions as explained in Section 5.3.3, as a 'Strong Buy' signal.

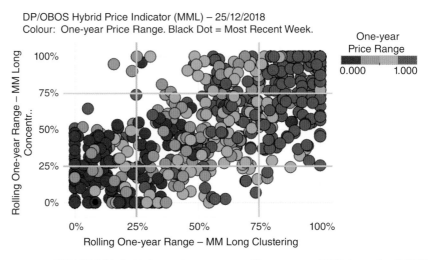

FIGURE 8.9 DP/OBOS hybrid chart using one-year rolling ranges – MML in crude oil (WTI). This chart has been plotted using the application Tableau. The chart is on the companion website, where it can be plotted for any commodity on any date. It is updated regularly.
Source: Based on data from Bloomberg.

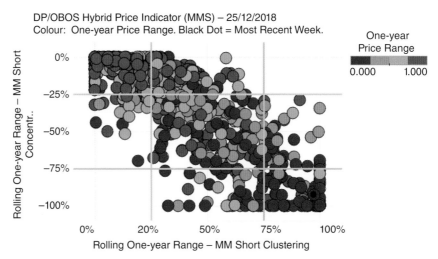

FIGURE 8.10 DP/OBOS Hybrid chart using one-year rolling ranges – MMS in crude oil (WTI). This chart has been plotted using the application Tableau. The chart is on the companion website, where it can be plotted for any commodity on any date. It is updated regularly.
Source: Based on data from Bloomberg.

The other regions of the indicator, for example the central box, can be used to define other types of signal as indicated in Figure 5.10.

DP indicator charts do not, however, include pricing data as only the structural aspects of the OBOS framework are used. All price information is lost in a hybrid approach. To enhance the DP/OBOS Hybrid indicator by including price data, specifically the OBOS Pricing Component, a DP/OBOS Hybrid Price indicator is generated.

8.7.2.2 The DP/OBOS Hybrid Indicator Price Charts

To include price, each point in a DP/OBOS Hybrid Price indicator is shaded as a function of the one-year price range – the same as the Pricing Component defined in Section 8.2.2.

Figure 8.9 and Figure 8.10 show the same data as Figure 8.7 and Figure 8.8 with each point shaded from dark red to dark green as a function of the one-year price range being at the bottom or top of the range.

The colours have been stepped to show four price levels to mimic the quartile ranges used in the OBOS framework. The darkest green (red) shaded therefore correspond to the top (bottom) quartiles of the price range in an OBOS chart and this extra information can refine the signals further. Finding a point in the top right (bottom right) hand box of Figure 8.9 (Figure 8.10), for example, that was not dark green (dark red), would potentially be a warning sign.

The development of these hybrid indicators and the blending of DP and OBOS analysis highlights some of the flexibility of Positioning Analysis and the range and depth of information that can be isolated. Furthermore, each of the analyses discussed so far are intuitive, visual, and they can be easily replicated. This makes patterns easier to isolate, signals easier to define, and analysis clearer in both presentation and communication.

CHAPTER 9

Advanced OBOS Analysis – Extremes in Sentiment and Risk

Chapter objectives

In Chapter 8, the Overbought/Oversold (OBOS) framework was introduced.

In this chapter, the framework is extended to include different positioning metrics such as Clustering and Position Size and also to make use of a wider set of variables like the VIX, Financial Conditions Indices (FCIs), and the dollar index (DXY) within the framework, to better understand positioning dynamics.

The use of Positioning Analysis in the risk management of commodity risk premia strategies is also covered.

9.1 The OBOS Framework – Clustering and Position Sizes

In Section 8.2.1, long and short Concentration were used in calculation of the Positioning Components in the OBOS framework.[1] The flexibility of the OBOS framework allows for different positioning metrics such as Clustering to be used in the calculation of the Positioning Components. This can add an extra dimension to the framework, provide further insight into positioning profiles, and refine trading signals.

---

[1]Concentration is defined in Section 4.1.1.1.

9.1.1 OBOS Clustering Indicator

In the OBOS Clustering indicator, the Pricing and Curve Components remain unchanged, but long and short Clustering is used in the Positioning Components calculation as follows:[2]

For long (short) positions:

$$long\left(short\right)Positioning\ Component\left(\%\right)$$

$$=\frac{\left(current\ MML\left(S\right)T\% \ -\ \min\left(MML\left(S\right)T\%_{range}\right)\right)}{\left(\max\left(MML\left(S\right)T\%_{range}\right)\ -\ \min\left(MML\left(S\right)T\%_{range}\right)\right)}$$

where

$$MML\left(S\right)T\%=\frac{MML\left(S\right)T\ number\left(futures\ only\right)}{TTF\left(futures\ only\right)}$$

$$range = one\text{-}year\ rolling$$

See Table 2.2 for abbreviations.

Figure 9.1 shows the OBOS Clustering indicator on the same day as the OBOS Concentration indicator in Figure 8.1 (data as of 25 December 2018). Compared to the OBOS indicator in Section 8.3, that uses Concentration, the main differences are as follows:

■ Live cattle and palladium being in the Overbought box (top right) from an extreme Clustering perspective, but not from an extreme Concentration perspective;

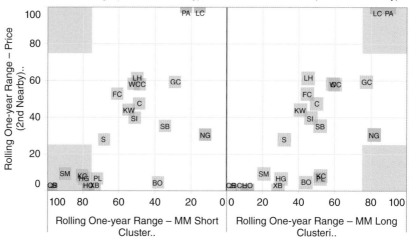

OBOS Clustering Indicator – 25/12/2018
Colour: Blue = Contango (2nd – 3rd Nearby), Green = Backwardation (2nd – 3rd Nearby).

FIGURE 9.1 The OBOS Clustering indicator using one-year rolling ranges.
This chart has been plotted using the application Tableau. The chart is on the companion website, where it can be plotted with any commodities on any date. It is updated regularly.
Commodity symbols: As listed in Table 2.1.
Source: Based on data from Bloomberg.

---

[2]Clustering is defined in Section 4.1.1.2

■ The same eight commodities are in the Oversold box on both indicators, except for coffee that is Oversold from a Clustering perspective and gasoline that is Oversold from a Concentration perspective only. Crude oil (WTI), Brent, cotton, copper, heating oil, gasoil, and soymeal are all Oversold from both a Concentration and Clustering perspective.

9.1.1.1 When Only Concentration is Extreme

For the commodities where Concentration is extreme (either Overbought or Oversold) but Clustering is not (live cattle, palladium, and gasoline), a likely reason could be due to differences in individual position sizes. This could arise if a small number of traders collectively have a large position, elevating the Concentration, but keeping Clustering low. This profile should not affect price behaviour and the core philosophy of the OBOS framework as explained in Section 8.5, as a few large traders exiting a position can also have a meaningful impact on prices. If Concentration and Clustering were previously both extreme, a fall in Clustering, with Concentration remaining high, suggests that sentiment could be changing.

9.1.1.2 When Only Clustering is Extreme

For the commodities where Clustering is extreme (either Overbought or Oversold), but Concentration is not (coffee), a likely reason could be due to timing differences. With Clustering being a measure of crowding or herding, but also of sentiment, such a profile could suggest that whilst the underlying traders' views may be aligned, their actual position sizes are still low, and Concentration is still in the process of increasing. Looking at the Position Size, as shown in Section 9.1.2, is helpful in this respect. Dry Powder analysis, discussed below in Section 9.1.1.4, is an effective way of assessing the likelihood of a position becoming bigger.

If Concentration and Clustering were previously both extreme, a fall in Concentration, with Clustering remaining high, suggests that positions are still being liquidated.

9.1.1.3 When Concentration and Clustering are Extreme

The commodities that are extreme (either Overbought or Oversold) in terms of both Concentration and Clustering (crude oil (WTI), Brent, cotton, copper, heating oil, gasoil, and soymeal) indicate that both positioning risk and crowding are extreme. The interpretation of Clustering becomes helpful in assessing how prices might evolve.

Clustering can be a measure of crowding or herding, but also of sentiment. As a measure of crowding or herding, extremes in both Concentration and Clustering suggest that the liquidation of a position could be more violent than if Concentration were just extreme. As a measure of sentiment, and by extension a measure of the alignment in the underlying market view, the likelihood of the position being liquidated could in fact be lower. This would occur if the market views the extreme position as 'justified' and believes that it could still grow and/or that prices still have further to move.

As the OBOS framework is based on dynamic positioning and pricing ranges, they can expand. This is a weakness in the framework, as identifying potential maxima and minima when markets are trending is challenging. One way of disentangling these conflicting dynamics is to incorporate other Positioning analytics and price metrics into the framework.

9.1.1.4 Disentangling Clustering Dynamics Using DP Analysis and the RSI

Dry Powder analysis, introduced in Chapter 5, is a way of assessing the likelihood of a position becoming bigger, and can be a very useful indicator in combination with OBOS analysis, as shown in Section 8.7.

Assessing whether sentiment is positive and hence the likelihood of prices continuing to move further is, however, significantly more challenging. In such cases, insights from fundamental analysis and technical analysis can be very helpful and including technical analysis-based signals into the framework can be useful.

One approach is to convert the Pricing Component in the OBOS framework to a simple RSI (relative strength index). The RSI is a powerful and widely followed measure of how overbought or oversold prices are from momentum or oscillator perspective. It is also excellent at identifying short-term price extremes.

Using an RSI approach is also an effective way of controlling for trend related issues in the Pricing Component calculation, where if prices steadily move in one direction for an extended period, the Pricing Component will always be at an extreme, but price momentum may not be high. If this is the case, the RSI will not register prices as oversold or overbought, and the OBOS framework will not define the commodity as Oversold or Overbought.[3]

9.1.2 OBOS Position Size Indicator

In the OBOS Position Size indicator, the Pricing and Curve Components remain unchanged, but long and short Position Sizes are used in the Positioning Components calculation as follows:[4]

For long positions:

$$Long\ Positioning\ Component(\%) = \frac{\left(current\ MMLPS\ -\ \min\left(MMLPS_{range}\right)\right)}{\left(\max\left(MMLPS_{range}\right)\ -\ \min\left(MMLPS_{range}\right)\right)}$$

where

$$MMLPS = \frac{MML\ open\ interest\left(futures\ only\right)}{MMLT\ number\ of\ traders\left(futures\ only\right)}$$

$$range = one\text{-}year\ rolling$$

See Table 2.2 for abbreviations.

For short positions:

$$Short\ Positioning\ Component(\%) = \frac{\left(current\ MMSPS\ -\ \min\left(MMSPS_{range}\right)\right)}{\left(\max\left(MMSPS_{range}\right)\ -\ \min\left(MMSPS_{range}\right)\right)}$$

[3]Incorporating macroeconomic and fundamental factors into the OBOS framework can also be helpful, as discussed with the OBOS Factor (VIX) indicator in Section 9.2.3. Newsflow analysis, discussed in Chapter 11, is also useful in identifying prices extremes as it tends to increase when prices start provoking a media response.
[4]Position size is defined in Section 4.1.1.3.

where

$$MMSPS = \frac{MMS \, open \, interest \left(futures \, only \right)}{MMST \, number \, o \, traders \left(futures \, only \right)}$$

$$range = one\text{-}year \, rolling$$

See Table 2.2 for abbreviations.

Figure 9.2 shows the OBOS Position Size indicator on the same day as the OBOS Concentration and OBOS Clustering indicators in Figure 8.1 and Figure 9.1 respectively (data as of 25 December 2018). Key differences between the indicators are as follows:

- No commodities are in the Overbought box, meaning that long Position Sizes are on average not extreme.

- There are four commodities in the Oversold box, meaning that the average size of these short positions is extreme.

- Gasoline is Oversold from a Position Size perspective and from a Concentration perspective, but not from a Clustering perspective, suggesting that a few traders have a large position.

- Gasoil, crude oil (WTI), soymeal, and gasoline are Oversold on all three metrics: Position Size, Concentration, and Clustering.

One of the differences between the OBOS Concentration in Figure 8.1 and the OBOS Clustering indicator in Figure 9.1 is that coffee is Oversold only from a Clustering perspective, which in combination with the low Position Size at around 40% of the maximum, suggests that the short position has room to increase.

OBOS Position Size Indicator – 25/12/2018
Colour: Blue = Contango (2nd – 3rd Nearby), Green = Backwardation (2nd – 3rd Nearby).

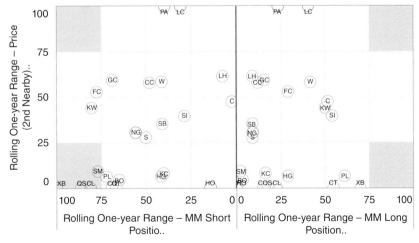

FIGURE 9.2 The OBOS Position Size indicator using one-year rolling ranges.
This chart has been plotted using the application Tableau. The chart is on the companion website, where it can be plotted with any commodities on any date. It is updated regularly.
Commodity symbols: As listed in Table 2.1.
Source: Based on data from Bloomberg.

In blending all the OBOS signals together and isolating commodities where all three factors are extreme, signals become more refined, and price behaviour becomes more predictable. By way of illustration, in the first week of January 2019, the week following the release of the positioning data (25 December 2018) for the three OBOS (Concentration, Clustering, and Position Size) indicators above, gasoil, crude oil (WTI), soymeal, and gasoline, the only three commodities Oversold on all three metrics, were up approximately 3%, 6%, 4%, and 1% respectively.

As discussed in in Section 8.5, it always important to remember, that for all these models either in combination or in isolation, the act of being Oversold (Overbought) in does not automatically lead to short covering (long liquidation). A fundamental, macroeconomic, or technical catalyst is still needed.

9.1.3 OBOS Hybrid Indicators

OBOS Hybrid indicators are different from the DP/OBOS Hybrid indicator in Section 8.7. They are a way of blending different OBOS indicators to show various relationships.

9.1.3.1 OBOS Hybrid Concentration/Clustering Indicator Figure 9.3 shows an OBOS Hybrid Concentration/Clustering indicator with long Clustering on the *y*-axis, long Concentration on the *x*-axis and the shading a function of the price range. The short side of the framework is shown in Figure 9.4 in the interest of space. All variables are one-year rolling.

Natural gas is not Overbought in either the OBOS Concentration and Clustering indicators in Figure 8.1 and Figure 9.1, although Concentration and Clustering are high. Within the OBOS Hybrid framework it is clearly Overbought in terms of both Concentration and Clustering together (the grey box) as shown Figure 9.3. Its price is, however, low (30% of its one-year range) as indicated by the red shading. This suggests that traders could be seeing potential value in the prices, making this indicator particularly useful in identifying value, even despite positioning already being elevated and sentiment strong.

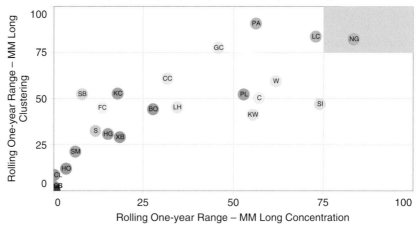

OBOS Hybrid Concentration/Clustering Indicator (MML) – 25/12/2018
Colour: Darker Green (Red) = Higher (Lower) Price Range (2nd Nearby).

FIGURE 9.3 Long OBOS Hybrid Concentration/Clustering indicator.
This chart has been plotted using the application Tableau. The chart is on the companion website, where it can be plotted with any commodities on any date. It is updated regularly.
Commodity symbols: As listed in Table 2.1.
Source: Based on data from Bloomberg.

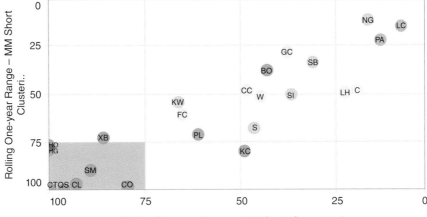

OBOS Hybrid Concentration/Clustering Indicator (MMS) – 25/12/2018
Colour: Darker Green (Red) = Higher (Lower) Price Range (2nd Nearby).

FIGURE 9.4   Short OBOS Hybrid Concentration/Clustering indicator.
This chart has been plotted using the application Tableau. The chart is on the companion website, where it can be plotted with any commodities on any date. It is updated regularly.
Commodity symbols: As listed in Table 2.1.
Source: Based on data from Bloomberg.

Figure 9.4 is the opposite of Figure 9.3 with short Clustering on the *y*-axis and short Concentration on the *x*-axis with shading a function of the price range. As explained above, the short side of the framework has been shown separately in to make the chart more visible. All variables are one-year rolling.

All the commodities (heating oil, copper, cotton, gasoil, crude oil (WTI), and Brent) with both extreme short Concentration and short Clustering (grey box) have already been identified as Oversold in Figure 8.1 and Figure 9.1, as their prices are also all low (as also shown by the red shading). If a commodity was in the grey box and shaded green, however, meaning that its price would be high, this would suggest that traders see it as overvalued, despite the elevated position and the sentiment being weak.

9.1.3.2 OBOS   Hybrid   Concentration/Clustering/Position   Size   Indicator

Figure 9.5 (Figure 9.6) shows long (short) Clustering on the *y*-axis and long (short) Concentration on the *x*-axis, with shading a function of the price range and bubble size a function of long (short) Position Size. All variables are one-year rolling.

The natural gas (NG) bubble in Figure 9.5 is tiny (10% of its one-year range), suggesting that there is also room to expand the Position Size. This also confirms the point in Section 9.1.3.1, where natural gas prices were shown to be only 30% of the historical range. By way of illustration, in the first week of January 2019, the week following the release of the positioning data (25 December 2018), natural gas was up approximately 4%.

The large bubbles in the Oversold box of Figure 9.6 also help show which commodities have the greatest average Position Sizes – providing an indication of how significant any short covering could be, the assumption being that commodities with the largest Position Size are likely to be vulnerable to generating the biggest price spikes.

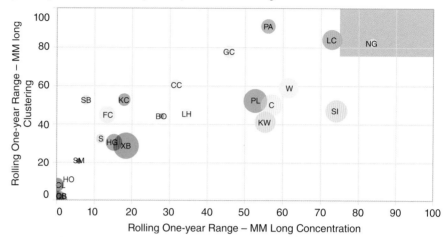

OBOS Hybrid Indicator (MML) – 25/12/2018
Colour: Darker Green (Red) = Higher (Lower) Price Range (2nd Nearby) Size: Larger
(Smaller) Bubbles = Greater (Smaller) Position Size Range

FIGURE 9.5 Long OBOS Hybrid Concentration/Clustering/Position Size indicator.
This chart has been plotted using the application Tableau. The chart is on the companion website, where it can be plotted with any commodities on any date. It is updated regularly.
Commodity symbols: As listed in Table 2.1.
Source: Based on data from Bloomberg.

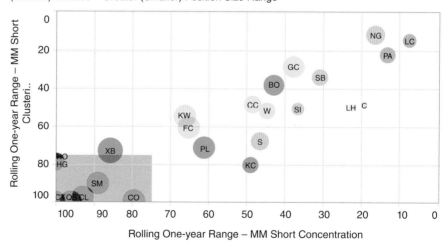

OBOS Hybrid Indicator (MMS) – 25/12/2018
Colour: Darker Green (Red) = Higher (Lower) Price Range (2nd Nearby) Size: Larger
(Smaller) Bubbles = Greater (Smaller) Position Size Range

FIGURE 9.6 Short OBOS Hybrid Concentration/Clustering/Position Size indicator.
This chart has been plotted using the application Tableau. The chart is on the companion website, where it can be plotted with any commodities on any date. It is updated regularly.
Commodity symbols: As listed in Table 2.1.
Source: Based on data from Bloomberg.

9.2 OBOS Factor Indicators

The OBOS Factor indicators are like OBOS indicators except the Pricing Component is substituted for a Factor Component, and the framework is expanded to accommodate four distinct types of extreme. Factors can include fundamental data, macroeconomic variables, and risk metrics. The Positioning Component and Curve Component remain the same.

Overbought High (Low) and Oversold High (Low) commodities are defined as those that lie at the intersections of both extremes in long (short) positioning and extremes in the factor level. Both extremes are always considered for the Factor Component, which is a difference to the OBOS framework. The factors can include variables such as the VIX, the VVIX, Financial Conditions Indices (FCIs), the dollar index (DXY), certain commodity currencies, and fundamental data such as inventories as listed in Section 9.2.5.

With the OBOS Factor indicator, the four possibilities are:

- extreme long positioning and extreme strength in the fundamental factor ('Overbought High');

- extreme long positioning and extreme weakness in the fundamental factor ('Overbought Low');

- extreme short positioning and extreme strength in the fundamental factor ('Oversold High');

- extreme short positioning and extreme weakness in the fundamental factor ('Oversold Low').

The formula for the Factor Component is calculated as follows:

$$Factor\ Component(\%) = \frac{\left(current\ factor\ level - \min\left(factor\ level_{range}\right)\right)}{\left(\max\left(factor\ level_{range}\right) - \min\left(factor\ level_{range}\right)\right)}$$

where

$$range = one\text{-}year\ rolling$$

9.2.1 Aligning the Data Between the Positioning and Factor Components

The Positioning Component is calculated weekly on Friday as described in Section 8.2.5. The Factor Component is also evaluated weekly on a Friday using the most recent piece of data.

- For OBOS Factor indicators where the fundamental data is released daily, such as the dollar index, the level on the close (settlement price) of the Friday is used.

- For OBOS Factor indicators where the fundamental data is released weekly, either intra-week or on a Friday, the most recent weekly value is used.

- For OBOS Factor indicators where the fundamental data is released monthly, the most recent value is used.

9.2.2 The OBOS Factor Framework Trading Signals

The OBOS Factor framework generates trading signals in the same way as the OBOS framework as described in Section 8.2.7. The same quartile thresholds are used for both the Positioning Component and the Factor Component to define the extremes.

- If the long Positioning Component is in the top quartile (25%) of its historical range and the Factor Component is in the top (bottom) quartile (25%) of its historical range, the commodity is defined as being Overbought High (Overbought Low); it will be in the Overbought High (Overbought Low) box and an Overbought High (Overbought Low) signal is generated.

- If the short Positioning Component is in the top quartile (25%) of its historical range and the Factor Component is in the top (bottom) quartile (25%) of its historical range, the commodity defined as being Oversold High (Oversold Low); it will be in the Oversold High (Oversold Low) box and an Oversold High (Oversold Low) signal is generated.

9.2.3 The OBOS VIX and OBOS VVIX Indicators

The OBOS VIX and OBOS VVIX indicators are OBOS Factor indicators that use extremes in MM positioning and extremes in the VIX or extremes in the VVIX to define commodities that are Overbought High (Low) and Oversold High (Low). Changes in the VIX and VVIX are reflective of changes in the level of fear and risk appetite in the markets which can have a significant impact on commodity prices through a variety of different sentiment channels.

The VIX and VVIX indices are discussed in Section 6.4.1 as variables in DP Factor indicators. In the context of the OBOS Factor framework, an increase in the VIX (VVIX) suggests an increase in financial risk (anticipation of financial risk). During these periods, investors often quickly reduce or cut exposure to risk assets, which can include commodities. This suggests long speculative commodity positions could be vulnerable to liquidation.

Figure 9.7 shows the OBOS Factor (VIX) indicator (data as of 25 December 2018) with the VIX near the top of its range. A critical difference between the OBOS indicators so far and the OBOS Factor indicator is that the same factor is used across all the commodities. This means that the individual commodities are only dispersed along the x-axis.

For clarity, only four commodities have been plotted, to avoid overcrowding. Copper, crude oil (WTI), and Brent are shown in the Oversold High box (top left) and natural gas in the Overbought High box (top right).[5]

For the VIX, the Overbought High box is probably the most interesting box, followed by the Oversold High box. This is because the VIX often, but not always, has an asymmetrical impact on prices – a spike in the VIX indicates fear and has a negative on many risk assets, but a fall in the VIX, indicating a decline in risk, often has less of an impact on commodity prices. Simply, if the VIX spikes, commodities like copper prices often fall, but if the VIX then collapses, copper might not necessarily rise. Overall, the sensitivity of the VIX to commodities is most pronounced for the more industrial commodities – particularly the industrial metal and energy sectors.

In Figure 9.7, the three commodities in the Oversold High box are generally all sensitive to changes in financial market risk and, by extension, with the VIX elevated, their extreme short speculative position in the framework would seem justified. Notwithstanding the asymmetry in the VIX

---

[5]Heating oil, gasoline, and gasoil are also in the Oversold High box but have been omitted to avoid overcrowding.

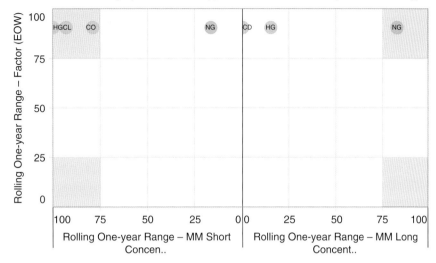

FIGURE 9.7 OBOS VIX Factor indicator.
This chart has been plotted using the application Tableau. The chart is on the companion website, where it can be plotted with any commodities on any date. It is updated regularly.
Commodity symbols: As listed in Table 2.1.
Source: Based on data from Bloomberg.

commodity price relationship discussed above, a fall in the VIX could be a catalyst to trigger short covering. The importance of a catalyst within the OBOS framework was discussed in Section 8.5.

Natural gas (NG) is a very fundamental commodity and its price behaviour is consequently very idiosyncratic. Its position in the Overbought High box is less significant, as natural gas is mostly agnostic to broader financial market dynamics. One factor worth considering is that natural gas is a large component in many commodity indices such as the Bloomberg Commodity index (approximately 8%). Any further increase in financial markets risk, could lead to the general liquidation of these types of products, which can impact all index constituents.

9.2.4 The OBOS FCI Indicators

> *Monetary policy works in the first instance by affecting financial conditions, including the levels of interest rates and asset prices. Changes in financial conditions in turn influence a variety of decisions by households and firms, including choices about how much to consume, to produce, and to invest.*

> *Federal Reserve Chairman Ben S. Bernanke, 2 March 2007*

Changes in Financial Conditions Indices indicate the overall stress in the money markets, bond markets, and equity markets. There are four major Bloomberg FCI indices: one for the US, one for the EU, one for GB, and one for Asia ex-Japan (AXJ).[6]

---

[6]FCI Indices also exist for individual countries, for example China and Hong Kong.

Financial conditions play a critical role in shaping the course of economic activity. For example, a negative shock to financial conditions can generate an adverse feedback loop in which deteriorating financial conditions make banks less willing to lend and households less willing to borrow. A sizeable decline in the willingness to borrow and lend can lead to a significant decline in economic activity, and that, in turn, can weaken financial conditions further and thus induce even greater caution on the part of lenders and borrowers.

In the context of the OBOS framework, a decrease in the Bloomberg FCIs points to a deterioration in financial conditions which can be bearish for commodity prices. This stands in contrast to the OBOS VIX Factor indicator as all the boxes in the framework are interesting – as both good and bad financial conditions can be powerful drivers of commodity prices, and the relationship is therefore more symmetrical. The OBOS FCI indicators use either one of the Bloomberg FCI US (BFCIUS), EU (BFCIEU), AXJ (BFCIAXJ), or GB (BFCIGB) indices as the Factor Component. These indices also lend themselves well to trading models as values are almost never revised.[7]

Figure 9.8 shows the OBOS Factor (FCI US) indicator (data as of 25 December 2018) with the FCI US index at the bottom of its range.

Again, for clarity, the same four commodities have been plotted to avoid overcrowding. Copper, crude oil (WTI), and Brent are shown in the Oversold Low box (bottom left) and natural gas (and almost silver) in the Overbought Low box (bottom right).[8] Their position in the Low boxes, reflecting weak US financial conditions, is also intuitive in the context of the VIX also being elevated during this period.

The position of the three commodities in the Overbought Low box, with their extreme short speculative position in the framework, would also seem justified. By extension, a rise in the FCI could also act as the catalyst to trigger the short covering, as discussed in Section 8.5.

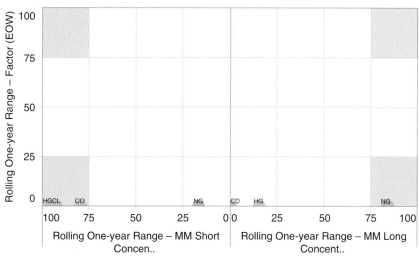

FIGURE 9.8 OBOS FCI Factor indicator.
This chart has been plotted using the application Tableau. The chart is on the companion website, where it can be plotted with any commodities on any date. It is updated regularly.
Commodity symbols: As listed in Table 2.1.
Source: Based on data from Bloomberg.

[7]The Bloomberg FCI US index has only been revised once on 26 July 2016 and involved the substitution of the Swaps/Treasury Spread index with a swaption volatility index. The other FCI indices have never been revised.
[8]Heating oil, gasoline, and gasoil are also in the Oversold Low box but have been omitted to avoid overcrowding.

9.2.5 Other OBOS Factor Indicators

A wide range of Factor Components can be used within the framework. The Positioning Component can also naturally be switched from using Concentration to Clustering or Position Size if required to isolate different positioning dynamics as discussed in Section 9.1.1 and Section 9.1.2.

Other factors could include:

Risk factors	VVIX index
	CVIX
	MOVE index
Newsflow/uncertainty indices	Economic Policy Uncertainty EPU Indices
	Newsflow indices
	Google Trends
Option data	Put/Call ratios
Macroeconomic data	US 10-year Treasure Yield
	S&P 500 index
Commodity currencies	Chilean peso (copper)
	Brazilian real (sugar, coffee)
	Russian rouble (Brent, nickel)
	South African Rand (gold, platinum)
	Australian dollar (gold)
	Canadian dollar (oil)
Commodity fundamentals	DOE Energy Inventories (WTI, gasoline, heating oil)
	DOE Days of supply (gasoline, heating oil)
	DOE natural gas stocks (natural gas)
	LME Stocks
	COMEX Stocks
Transport data	Baltic Dry Freight index
	Railcar data
	Export shipments/sales

In Section 11.3, the blending of newsflow factors into the OBOS framework is covered.

In Section 13.5.1, the OBOS Speculation ratio indicator is introduced as an alternative to the OBOS indicators when no positioning data is available.

9.3 Commodity Risk Premia – Positioning Analysis and Risk Management

Commodity risk premia are a new and developing area of commodity investment. Commodity risk premia strategies are commodity indices where the exposure to a specific commodity within the index is typically characterised by a short position at the front of the curve and a long position further down the curve. This is different from a plain vanilla investment in a commodity index, where the exposure is generally in the form of a long position at the front of the curve.

In a risk premia strategy, the overall exposure is dollar-neutral, meaning that the same notional exposure is held on both the short and long legs of the position. Individual commodity performance is generated as a function of the relative performance of the long and short position. The performance of the overall index is then a function of the aggregated performance of all the index components.

Commodity risk premia indices typically hold the same components and weights as either the BCOM or S&P GSCI index, depending on the investment mandate.

Most risk premia strategies involve going long either the F3 Bloomberg Commodity index (BCOM) index or S&P GSCI index, and short the Bloomberg Commodity index (BCOM) index or S&P GSCI index.[9]

■ The F3 nomenclature means that exposure in each commodity is held in the 'F3 position', three futures contracts down the curve, depending on the roll schedule in the index methodology for the index.

■ The F0 nomenclature means that the exposure is held in the 'F0 position', the first contract in the roll schedule. This position is the same as the benchmark index.

A risk premia index can be thought of as short the benchmark index and long the deferred index.

9.3.1 Risk Premia Performance

The following points highlight some common scenarios on how prices and curve structure can change and how risk premia strategies perform.

■ **Prices stay static with the curve in contango.** With most commodities being in contango, and the curvature being steeper at the front of the curve, the short F0 leg at the front of the curve tends to 'fall' more than the long F3 leg, located further down the curve, as the contracts move towards expiry and futures prices at the front of the curve converge towards the spot price. This means that if spot prices are static and the curve is in a contango structure, positive returns are generated simply by virtue of the structure of the curve and the mechanics of futures contracts.

■ **Prices stay static with the curve in backwardation.** When spot prices are static and the curve is in a backwardated market, the reverse is true and negative returns are generated as the short position moves up the steep front end of the curve. The losses are, however, partly reduced due to the difference in notional exposure. In a backwardated structure, there will be a reduced (increased) number of short (long) contracts at the F0 (F3) position, required to equalise the notional exposure, as prices are higher at the front. This means the long position offsets some of the loss.

■ **Prices falling and curve structure in either backwardation or contango.** When spot prices fall, positive returns are generated because the weakness in prices at the front of the curve is almost always greater than further down the curve, irrespective of the curve structure.

■ **Prices rising and curve structure in backwardation.** When spot prices are rising and the curve is backwardated, returns are also mostly positive. This is due to the overall curve shifting higher and the long bias generated by the increased number of futures contracts in the F3 position required to equalise the short exposure at the F0 position. If the backwardation

---

[9]Either the whole benchmark index, sector indices, or individual mono-indices can be traded. It is, for example, possible to just have a natural gas risk premia product. This could, for example, be short the BCOM (S&P GSCI) F0 natural gas mono index and long the BCOM (S&P GSCI) F3 natural gas mono index in equal notional amounts.

should, however, steepen at a rate faster than the overall curve shifts higher, losses will result. This is quite unusual, due to the proximity between the F0 and F3 legs and their co-movement being similar. In an F0, F6 structure there would be a greater risk, as the F6 contract would typically rise much less than the F0 contract.

- **Curve structure changing from backwardation to contango.** If the structure is in backwardation and the curve shifts into contango, the strategy will generate positive performance, as the movement at the front of the curve under such circumstances can be significant.

- **Curve structure changing from contango to backwardation.** If the curve structure moves from contango to backwardation, and particularly if the front of the curve spikes, significant negative performance is generated. Diversification across many different commodities can mitigate this risk but depending on the leverage in the strategy, a significant spike in a single commodity or commodity sector can result in large losses.

9.3.2 Risk Premia Risk Management

In general, the investment rationale of risk premia strategies is compelling, and the performance of many strategies have so far been positive.

In many of the scenarios discussed in Section 9.3.1, performance is positive, especially within a diversified index structure, as the likelihood of the key risks of either many commodities moving from contango to backwardation or of them spiking simultaneously is quite low. The risk of a single commodity moving from contango to backwardation or of spiking is significantly higher and this is perhaps the most significant risk for risk premia strategies, especially when the leverage is high.[10]

Positioning Analysis is particularly helpful in the risk management of risk premia strategies, specifically in identifying scenarios when the likelihood of prices rising (spiking) at the front of the curve is high.

The OBOS framework is most helpful in this respect as extremes in positioning can be quickly identified. As described in Section 8.5.1, Oversold commodities, as defined by the OBOS framework, are vulnerable to short covering and higher prices. Decreasing (or cutting completely) the exposure to Oversold commodities within a risk premia strategy is an effective way of controlling against the risk of price spikes and poor performance of the strategy. The more advanced OBOS indicators described in Section 9.1 can also be helpful in isolating different positioning risks.

Oversold commodities can also, however, be a major source of return in a risk premia strategy, especially if they keep falling in price. This can present a problem when managing risks, as simply decreasing or cutting the exposure can lead to missed opportunities in some cases. DP analysis, introduced in Chapter 5, can help in assessing the likelihood of further weakness for Oversold commodities, and provide a way to modify the extent to which the exposure is perhaps reduced. For example, if two commodities within a risk premia strategy were Oversold, but DP analysis for one suggested that further downside was possible, it may make sense to reduce exposure by less.

The use of the DP/OBOS Hybrid indicator, described in Section 8.7, is particularly useful within a risk premia strategy as both OBOS and DP positioning information is combined and trading signals are entirely objective and rule-based. This allows for the signals to be fully integrated into the index strategy.

---

[10]Returns are low for risk premia strategies, but with high Sharpe ratios and mostly low drawdowns. Consequently, many investments are leveraged considerably.

CHAPTER 10

Sentiment Analysis — Sentiment Indices and Positioning Mismatches

Chapter objectives

Changes in the number of COT long, short, and spreading traders can be a powerful measure of sentiment and an effective way of identifying behavioural patterns in commodities.

In this chapter, Sentiment indices based on changes in trader number positioning, a good proxy for sentiment, are developed to track the evolution of market sentiment. Two different indices are developed: Directional Sentiment (DS) indices, based on the number of long and short traders only; and Non-Directional Sentiment (NDS) indices, based on the number of traders holding a spreading position.

These indices can be applied to the whole commodity asset class, to specific commodity sectors or to individual commodities.

The chapter also introduces Mismatch indicators to provide a way of visualising and identifying positioning mismatches. These occur when the direction in the net number of traders (number of long traders − number of short traders) is different to the direction of their net position (long open interest − short open interest). Mismatches frequently intersect with price inflexion points and can be useful trading signals.

10.1 The Difference between Trader Numbers and Open Interest

The CFTC Commitments of Traders (COT) reports show the positioning in each of the trader categories in terms of both the aggregate long and short futures open interest and the number of long and short traders.[1,2]

Trends and changes in the numbers of long, short, and spreading traders can be a powerful measure of sentiment and an effective way of identifying behavioural patterns in commodities.

A major difference between trader numbers and open interest is that the number of long and short traders does not have to be equal. In contrast, the long and short open interest across all trader groups in the market must be equal.[3] This attribute increases the level of directionality in trader number and net trader number data, which can add additional insight to similar analytics based only on open interest. This is also explained in Section 4.1 in the context of Clustering and Concentration.

The reason why statements like (a) and (b) in Box 10.1 and not statements like (c) and (d) are more likely to be reported is in large part convention – typically the net position (based on open interest) is reported, and if that is at a record, the newsworthiness is increased. This is certainly because large positions can move prices when they are liquidated, which is indeed part of the philosophy in Chapter 8. The more tenuous linkage lies in the view that large or record positions are synonymous with the overall market positioning and a direct function of the overall market view.

Box 10.1 Hypothetical example highlighting the difference between trader numbers and open interest

Consider a total universe of 10 different MM crude oil (WTI) traders where 9 are long 100 contracts each, and 1 is short 3,000 contracts. Assume the following:

- The objective of each trader is to make a profit out of their position, as distinct from the position being a hedge, or part of a relative value trade, or a relative value position.
- The individual 3,000-lot short position is a record short position, in terms of its size.
- The number of long traders (9) is also a record.

Following the release of the weekly CFTC COT report, statements similar to the following would be likely to appear in market analysis or research reports and media channels:

(a) MMs ('funds') are net short crude oil.
(b) The size of the short position in crude oil has reached a record level.

Equally accurate, though unlikely to be reported, are the following alternative statements:

(c) The number of individual funds that are long crude is at record levels.
(d) 90% of funds are long crude oil.

---

[1] Spreading positions are also given for many of the categories.
[2] Combined futures and options positions, with the options component determined on a delta-adjusted basis, is also shown. This allows the number of option market participants to be determined.
[3] This assumes that the NR groups are also included. Trader numbers are not, however, included in the NR category. This is shown in Section 2.1.2.1.

Logically, however, the number or proportion of traders with the same directional view on price, rather than the thinking of a one or more large traders – albeit with a significantly bigger position – should be more indicative of the overall positioning profile in the market.

In the example in Box 10.1 the market is net short 2,100 contracts of crude oil (900 contracts long − 3,000 contracts short), but net long 8 traders (9 long traders – 1 short trader). Despite an overall net short position of 2,100 contracts, only 1 of the 10 traders is short – this is a strong statement about the underlying view or sentiment on the market.

Based on this example, the following potential scenarios behind this positioning profile each have specific price and/or behavioural implications:

1. **Conviction differences.** The short trader could simply have greater conviction than the long traders. However, given that 90% of the traders are long, this could also suggest that overall sentiment is positive, and prices are likely to move higher if the smaller long positions increase in size.

2. **Timing differences.** It could have been the case that the nine long traders were all short the week before, having just closed out their short positions, and are now building long positions. This possibility could also have significant implications on price, with sentiment quickly reversing when the positions become big enough to flip into a net long position.

3. **Regulatory differences.** It could be the case that all the long traders are operating within a framework, region, or are under some regulatory constraint that might force certain diversification requirements or exposure limits. This can have significant implications when trying to interpret market sentiment and direction, as the nine long traders are simply not able to hold a larger position.

4. **Style differences.** The short trader could be running a discretionary mandate, whereas the long traders with smaller positions could be driven by systematic or algorithmic trading approach. In this example, the short trader may have a value approach to trading, believing the market is overvalued, whereas the long traders could all be trend-following models with the trend still in place. This could also have significant implications on price direction, with the former being a function of human insight and sentiment, and the latter a function of computer modelling.

5. **Size differences.** The short trader could be managing a bigger fund than the long traders. Bigger funds are perceived to be better informed than smaller funds as they typically have more resources available for research. They have also presumably performed well historically and are therefore often expected to continue to do so. Conversely, the short trader could be running the same size fund as the long traders, but could simply be running bigger position sizes, be less diversified, or be operating with greater leverage than each of the smaller long traders.

6. **Information differences.** The short trader might know something that the rest of the market does not. This would perhaps be the most interesting scenario and is also not that uncommon in commodity markets. This could have important price implications.

By incorporating information on trader positioning and hence information on how many traders are behind a position, new questions, insights, and opportunities develop. A deeper understanding of market positioning is possible and more informed decisions can be made. Conversely, by not considering the number of traders, valuable information about the structure and sentiment of the market is lost. The benefits of using trader number data are also covered extensively in Chapter 4 in the context of Clustering and Position Size and in Chapter 5 as a critical component in Dry Powder analysis.

Tracking the evolution of individual trader positioning as an indicator of sentiment can be a good indicator of price direction and the Trader Sentiment (TS) indices have been designed to capture and track these dynamics.

Identifying mismatches between trader positioning and futures positioning with the Mismatch indicator can have meaningful price implications, as explained in several of the points above.

10.2 Trader Sentiment (TS) Indices

Trader Sentiment indices measure and track the evolution of commodity market sentiment through changes in the number of long, short, and spreading traders. They are based entirely on the number of traders and include no open interest data. The motivation is to isolate behavioural dynamics and proxy sentiment in the market. This is difficult to capture with open interest data due to traders having different position sizes, as explained in Box 10.1. By looking only at trader numbers, each trader is treated equally.

TS indices can be constructed using different COT categories of trader but are most effective when based on either Non-Commercial (NC) or Money Manager (MM) speculative categories as their trading activity is unconstrained by commercially driven trading or hedging activity. The Trader Sentiment indices in this chapter are based on the NC category, which includes both the MM and OR categories in the Disaggregated COT report. This encapsulates the broadest range of speculative activity in the market.

The CFTC and ICE COT reports show the number of long, short, and spreading traders. Trends and changes in the number of long and short traders are associated with bullish and bearish sentiment, which, together with trends and changes in the number of spreading traders, can also give an indication of the proportion of traders expressing a view on the structure of the forward curve via relative-value positions. Traders in the spreading category could also, however, be expressing a directional view on prices that might be better executed via a relative-value position to manage risk.

Collectively, the interplays between the number of long, short, and spreading traders are a powerful set of indicators in tracking various aspects of market sentiment.

10.2.1 Non-Directional Sentiment (NDS) Indices

NDS indices focus on the number of NC spreading traders. The CFTC defines 'spreading' in the COT report as:

> For the futures-only report, spreading measures the extent to which each non-commercial trader holds equal long and short futures positions.

The number of NC traders holding a spreading position is a function of one of two things:

- The number of traders expressing a relative-value view, likely speculating on how the shape (structure) of the forward curve might change.

- The number of traders expressing a directional view using a relative-value position.

The proportion of speculative spreading activity relative to directional activity provides information on the underlying view and the activity of speculators. Whilst a high proportion of spreading activity suggests traders are trading changes in curve structure rather than market direction, it might also be that market conditions may not support a pure directional view due to volatility being too high, liquidity low, or market uncertainty being elevated. Under these circumstances, the proportion of speculative spreading activity to directional activity offers some insight into the directional conviction of traders.

As movements in relative-value (spread) positions are typically less volatile than directional positions, it is common for traders to shunt exposure between directional and relative-value positions to manage risk as uncertainty or volatility shifts. After an extended price move higher, uncertainty often increases as the likelihood of a pullback or retracement in prices increases. To mitigate against this, a long trader might either reduce exposure or shift some of the directional exposure to a relative-value position by establishing short positions further down the curve. This can also happen at the beginning of a potential trend, where a trader might initiate a long position via a relative-value position. As confidence then increases, or as a price breakout becomes more evident, the position is shifted into a more directional position.

By measuring the number of traders holding spreading positions relative to the number of traders holding directional positions, insight into the strength of directional sentiment can also be gauged. These dynamics are captured in the NDS index.

10.2.1.1 The NDS Construction Methodology NDS indices track the evolution of the Non-Commercial (NC) Spreading Score. The NC Spreading Score is calculated for each commodity from the weekly COT report by dividing the number of spreading traders by the sum of the long, short, and spreading NC futures traders in the market.

It is important to remember that the NDS index is non-directional as spreading data is non-directional. The NDX simply measures the proportion of spreading activity in the market.[4] The Spreading Score is expressed as a percentage of its one-year range, with the highest score having a value of 100%, and the smallest, a value of 0%. Different ranges can be used as described in Section 8.2.4.

The NDS index is calculated each week as follows:

Spreading Score:

$$Spreading\ Score_i = \frac{spreading\ NC\ traders_i}{\left(long\ NC\ traders_i + short\ NC\ traders_i + spreading\ NC\ traders_i\right)}$$

Normalised Spreading Score:

$$norm\ Spreading\ Score_i$$
$$= 100 \times \left(\frac{\left(Spreading\ Score_i - \min\left(Spreading\ Score_{i,range}\right)\right)}{\left(\max\left(Spreading\ Score_{i,range}\right) - \min\left(Spreading\ Score_{i,range}\right)\right)} \right)$$

---

[4]If a trader holds a long position and a spread position, that trader will be recorded as both a long trader and a spreading trader in the COT report.

NDS index:

$$NDS\ Index = \frac{\sum_{i=1}^{n} norm\ Spreading\ Score_i}{n}$$

where

$$i = each\ commodity$$

$$range = rolling\ one\text{-}year$$

$$n = number\ of\ commodities\ in\ the\ index$$

See Table 2.2 for abbreviations.

10.2.1.2 The NDX Index and Crude Oil (WTI) Prices

Figure 10.1 shows the NDS index for crude oil (WTI) between 2006 and 2011. The NDS index is shown in two colours: red when spreading activity is high (index > 50%) and green when it is low (index < 50%). The commodity price data in the bottom pane is based on the 2nd nearby futures contract (as at the end of week EOW, or the Release date of the COT report).

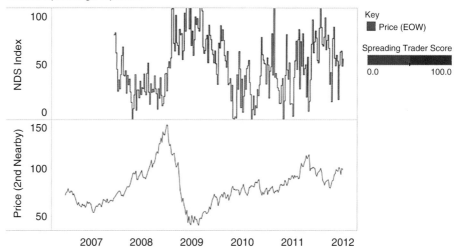

FIGURE 10.1 NDS index for crude oil (WTI).
This chart has been plotted using the application Tableau. The chart is on the companion website, where it can be plotted with any commodities (when multiple commodities are selected the sentiment index is averaged) (the price sub-chart is also, however, then averaged, so should be ignored) on any date. It is updated regularly.
Source: Based on data from Bloomberg.

In the lead-up to the collapse in oil prices and beginning of the Global Financial Crisis (GFC) in 2008, the NDS index indicated a low proportion of spreading activity, with directional positioning being the more dominant trading activity.

In mid-2008, as the GFC unfolded, the level of spreading activity increased as uncertainty increased, and macroeconomic concerns became more widespread. The jump in the NDX towards the end of oil price rally was driven by a shift in the underlying positioning profile, as the proportion of directional positioning decreased as sentiment became more cautious in the context of record oil prices.

The rise in the NDS index could have been a function of directional oil speculators exiting the market altogether, traders expressing a view on curve structure rather than price direction, or, as explained in Section 10.2.1, directional speculators shifting their exposure from a more directional profile to a more spread-driven profile.

It is important to note that this index is entirely based on the number of traders and not the size of their positions and is therefore sensitive to individual trader decisions. By way of illustration, if all the long traders in a commodity cut their exposure in half, this index would register no change. It is only when the traders close out positions entirely and cease to be reported, that the index will change. By extension, the index is agnostic to positioning changes relating to rebalancing, investment flows, volatility adjustments, or any portfolio related activity. The index is a pure reflection of the binary decision making of traders.

NDS indices can be applied to individual commodities, commodity sectors, or the entire asset class by averaging the normalised Spreading Scores of multiple commodities.

10.2.1.3 The NDX Index and Curve Structure Spreading data is often ignored in COT analysis despite spread positions often being larger than directional positions. One explanation is that because it is directionless as there are no long and short spreading categories – only a single spreading category – it is therefore difficult to interpret.

The shape of the forward curve can change for two reasons, which can occur either in isolation or in combination:

1. localised directional trading at certain regions on the curve – for example, producer selling depressing the back of the curve; or

2. actual spread trading – for example, buying the calendar spreads on the view that backwardation will increase.

NDS indices can also help clarify which of these might be behind changes in curve structure.

■ Changes in the shape of the curve when the NDS index is low (indicating a high (low) proportion of directional (spread) positioning) suggest that the structure might be shifting due to directional positions being taken at different points of the curve.

■ Changes in the shape of the curve when the NDS index is high (indicating a high (low) proportion of spread (directional) positioning) suggest that the structure might be shifting due to spread-related trading activity.

10.2.2 Directional Sentiment (DS) Indices

10.2.2.1 The DS Construction Methodology DS indices track the evolution of the Non-Commercial (NC) net Trader Score. The NC net Trader Score is calculated for each commodity from the weekly COT report as the difference between the Long and Short Trader Scores. The Trader Scores are the number of long (short) traders expressed as a one-year range, with the highest score having a value of 1 and the lowest a value of -1.

In contrast to the NDS index in Section 10.2.1, the DS index is a directional indicator with positive (negative) values associated with positive (negative) sentiment. The DS index is calculated each week as follows:

Long Trader Score:

$$long\,Trader\;Score_i = \left(\frac{\Big(long\,NC\,traders_i - \min\big(long\,NC\,traders_{i,range} \big) \Big)}{\Big(\max\big(long\,NC\,traders_{i,range} \big) - \min\big(long\,NC\,traders_{i,range} \big) \Big)} \right)$$

Short Trader Score:

$$short\,Trader\;Score_i = \left(\frac{\Big(short\,NC\,traders_i - \min\big(short\,NC\,traders_{i,range} \big) \Big)}{\Big(\max\big(short\,NC\,traders_{i,range} \big) - \min\big(short\,NC\,traders_{i,range} \big) \Big)} \right)$$

Net Trader Score:

$$net\,Trader\;Score_i = \Big(long\,Trader\;Score_i - short\,Trader\;Score_i \Big)$$

DS index:

$$DS\,Index = \frac{\sum_{j=1}^{n} net\,Trader\;Score_i}{n}$$

where

$$i = each\;commodity$$

$$range = rolling\,one\text{-}year$$

$$n = number\;of\;commodities\;in\;the\;index$$

See Table 2.2 for abbreviations.

Figure 10.2 illustrates the DS index for crude oil (WTI) over the last five years. The different colours are a function of the strength and direction of the DS index. Green represents positive

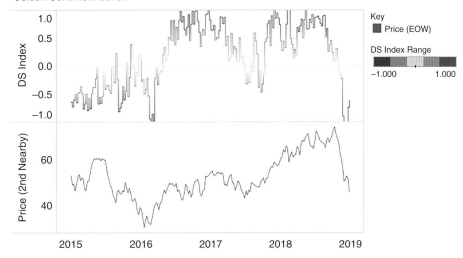

Directional Sentiment (DS) Index vs Price
Colour: Sentiment Level.

FIGURE 10.2   The DS index for crude oil (WTI).
This chart has been plotted using the application Tableau. The chart is on the companion website, where it can be plotted with any commodities (when multiple commodities are selected the sentiment index is averaged) (the price sub-chart is also, however, then averaged, so should be ignored) on any date. It is updated regularly.
Source: Based on data from Bloomberg.

sentiment, yellow neutral, and red negative sentiment. The commodity price data in the bottom pane is based on the second nearby futures contract.

In the same way as for NDS indices, the DS indices can be applied to individual commodities, commodity sectors, or the entire asset class by averaging the net Trader Scores of multiple commodities.

10.2.2.2 The DS Index Based on Open Interest   Figure 10.3 shows a comparison between the DS index and a variant of the DS index which uses changes in the net futures open interest instead of trader data for crude oil (WTI).

These two indices are broadly aligned, as changes in the net number of traders are often accompanied by similar changes in the net futures position. There are, however, frequent periods when these indices diverge, suggesting either a mismatch in sentiment (trader positioning) relative to changes in open interest (futures positioning), or periods when the market is in the process of changing direction and the trader positioning and futures positioning is misaligned.

In early 2016, for example, Figure 10.3 shows a divergence between the DS index (top panel) and the DS index using futures data (middle panel) just at the beginning of a turnaround in prices.

A cleaner way of identifying these mismatches is with the Positioning Mismatch indicator, explained in Section 10.3.

Directional Sentiment (DS) Index &
Directional Sentiment (DS) Index (Futures) vs Price
Colour: Sentiment Level.

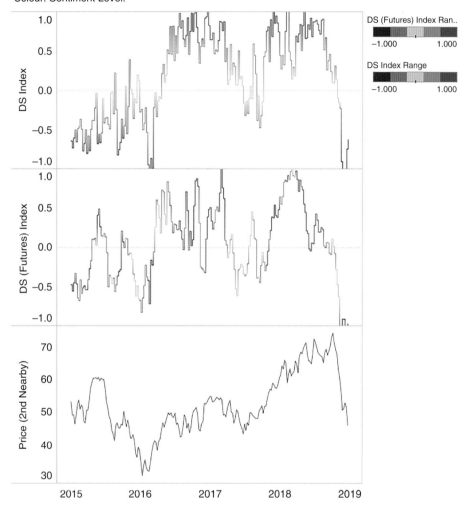

FIGURE 10.3 The DS index for crude oil (WTI) plotted against the DS index (futures).
This chart has been plotted using the application Tableau. The chart is on the companion website,
where it can be plotted with any commodities (when multiple commodities are selected the sentiment index is averaged) (the price sub-chart is also, however, then averaged, so should be ignored)
on any date. It is updated regularly.
Source: Based on data from Bloomberg.

10.3 Mismatches in Positioning and Price Inflexion Points

10.3.1 Mismatch Indicators

Mismatch indicators identify positioning mismatches between the net number of individual speculative traders and their net speculative futures position. These points frequently intersect with
price inflexion points and can be useful trading signals. They are also associated with periods of
heightened volatility and elevated newsflow in the market.

Figure 10.4 shows a Mismatch indicator chart for cotton for the MM group. Each point represents a week, with the net open interest plotted on the *y*-axis and the net number of traders plotted on the *x*-axis. The position of each point is a function of the net MM position (MM long futures position − MM short futures position), and the net number of MM traders (MM long number of traders − MM short number of traders). Mismatch charts are mostly the same as the DP net indicator charts discussed in Section 6.1.1.

In Mismatch indicator charts blue points are 'normal', meaning that a net long (short) futures position is associated with a net long (short) number of traders behind it – these points are termed 'aligned'.

The red points in the two Mismatch quadrants (top left and bottom right) are 'abnormal', meaning that the net futures position and the net trader position are associated with directionally opposite positions and are 'misaligned'. This could be a net long futures position and a net short number of traders, or the reverse, a net short futures position and a net long number of traders.

The black dot shows the most recent week with a mismatch.

Mismatches are not common and frequently intersect with price inflexion points as mentioned above. By tracking the historical occurrence of Mismatches these can quickly be identified. Figure 10.5 shows a chart of the evolution of Mismatches over time (red points) for palladium between 2013 and 2018, with Mismatch periods evident in 2015/2016 at the lows and ahead of a period of strength and then and also in 2018, ahead of another leg up in prices.

Figure 10.6 shows a Mismatch chart for live cattle between 2013 and 2018, with the most Mismatch periods preceding a turnaround in prices, except for an extended 2015 when prices continued to fall. Mismatches that occur during price trends in the absence of a turnaround often indicate that the trend has much further to go, and in some cases can suggest that the trend is continuing. One explanation of this could be a function of changes in type or proportion of market

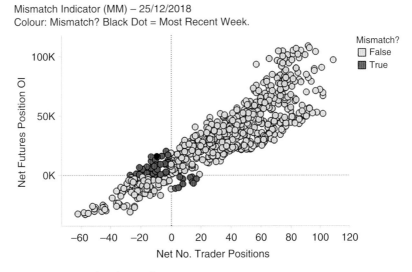

FIGURE 10.4 Mismatch indicator for cotton.
This chart has been plotted using the application Tableau. The chart is on the companion website, where it can be plotted for any commodity on any date. It is updated regularly.
Source: Based on data from Bloomberg.

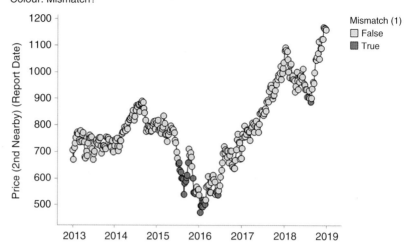

Mismatch Indicator Chart (MM) – 25/12/2018
Colour: Mismatch?

FIGURE 10.5 Historical occurrences of Mismatches in palladium.
This chart has been plotted using the application Tableau. The chart is on the companion website, where it can be plotted for any commodity over any timeframe. It is updated regularly.
Source: Based on data from Bloomberg.

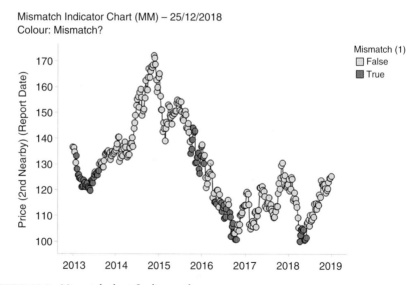

Mismatch Indicator Chart (MM) – 25/12/2018
Colour: Mismatch?

FIGURE 10.6 Mismatch chart for live cattle.
This chart has been plotted using the application Tableau. The chart is on the companion website, where it can be plotted for any commodity over any timeframe. It is updated regularly.
Source: Based on data from Bloomberg.

participants – more fundamentally driven traders or smaller traders exiting the market, but the larger trend following traders remaining. It may also be driven by rebalancing and/or volatility related trading activity.

Similar continuation patterns are seen with crude oil (WTI), as was evident during the falls in 2008 and 2014 as shown in Figure 10.7.[5]

Mismatches can be very difficult to interpret and ideally need to be viewed in the context of broader market dynamics, as it is often unclear how prices will behave when they occur. They are very sensitive and should be considered useful warning signs that are able to detect potential shifts in positioning and sentiment that many other indicators will fail to identify early enough.

Mismatch signals are also useful in combination with other positioning indicators such as the Dry Powder analysis in Chapter 5 and the OBOS framework in Chapter 6. Mismatches that occur at positioning extremes can add some reassurance that a price trend might be nearing completion and could be close to a reversal.

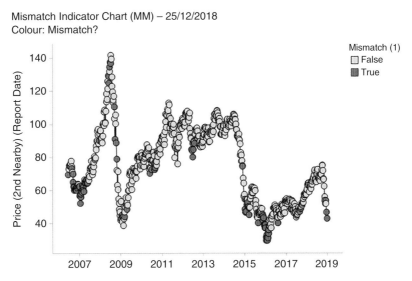

FIGURE 10.7 Historical occurrences of Mismatches in crude oil (WTI).
This chart has been plotted using the application Tableau. The chart is on the companion website, where it can be plotted for any commodity over any timeframe. It is updated regularly.
Source: Based on data from Bloomberg.

---

[5]It is also important to look at the level of Mismatch. A Mismatch of one trader or a few futures contracts would be negligible. To highlight only significant Mismatches a threshold – based on the size of the futures position and/or the number of traders in the Mismatch – could be implemented. A percentage approach, for example a Mismatch of 5% of the total traders or 5% of the total open interest, could also be sensible, as it could be better standardised across other commodities and would increase the robustness.

10.3.1.1 Who Wins?

By looking at the occurrence and behaviour of Mismatches when the net futures position is long but the net trader position is short, relative to a Mismatch when the net futures position is short but the net trader position is long, in the context of different price patterns, the indicator can be refined.

In this respect, the analysis in Chapter 3 can be useful in helping to decide how prices might behave when a Mismatch occurs. Figure 3.3 and Figure 3.5 show the difference in performance between net futures position and net trader positioning which can be helpful in identifying who usually 'wins' in a Mismatch. If, for example, a Mismatch occurs where traders are net long and the futures position is still net short, and the data in Figure 3.5, based on net trader positioning, has historically been better aligned with price direction, this could suggest that prices will rise.

CHAPTER 11

Newsflow in Positioning Analysis

Chapter objectives

Newsflow analysis is a relatively new area of research, made possible by the growth in computing power, the existence of sizeable electronic news databases, and the proliferation of algorithms that allow articles to be automatically 'read' and tagged according to specific criteria.

Incorporating commodity newsflow into certain areas of commodity, Positioning Analysis can be useful in the following ways:

■ Commodity positioning-related newsflow is important in helping to assess and track the current level of interest in positioning data. Like technical analysis, Positioning Analysis carries a degree of self-reinforcement, which can affect prices, shape sentiment, and influence behaviour. As positioning-related newsflow increases or decreases, the more or the less pronounced these positioning-related effects often become.

■ When positioning is extreme in a commodity, the absolute level of commodity trading-related newsflow in that commodity, and also the direction of newsflow in terms of whether it is bullish or bearish for prices, can significantly affect behaviour. A large long or short position and bullish or bearish price-related newsflow respectively suggests the position could become bigger, or, if positioning is already extreme, less vulnerable to liquidation. Similarly, if newsflow starts to wane, prices could start to become vulnerable as positions are no longer justified and positions begin to unwind.

This chapter covers the construction of different types of newsflow indices and ways of including them into Positioning Analysis to refine signals and provide more information.

11.1 Newsflow Data in Commodity Markets

Newsflow analysis is a relatively new area of research, made possible by the growth in computing power, the existence of sizeable electronic news databases, and the proliferation of algorithms that allow articles to be automatically 'read' and tagged according to specific criteria. These include sentiment, stance, and other attributes.

The majority research in this area has focused on the equity markets due to the volume of newsflow and the relative ease with which articles can be read. Most of the analysis centres on identifying bullish and bearish sentiment with the view that a high (low) proportion of bullish to bearish stories suggests sentiment is positive (negative) and the share price of that company should rise (fall). Defining sentiment as positive or negative is done by identifying patterns in the occurrence and order of specific words and phrases that are considered to be either positive or negative.

For commodity markets, the task is less straightforward as the context of the article is critically important. A report about higher wheat prices, for example, might be positive for a wheat producer, but negative for a wheat consumer. An algorithm designed to identify positive or negative sentiment based on word patterns within the article is likely to find this challenging to differentiate between. In contrast, a bullish report about a new company's product, suggesting the share price could move higher, is much clearer to identify as both consumers (the customers) and the producer (the company) benefit.

Another problem with commodities is that changes in many of the price drivers are opposite to their effect on price. Sentences like 'oil prices rose as exports fell' or 'copper prices rise as copper inventories decline' make up a large proportion of commodity-related newsflow. Algorithms that identify and associate words like 'rise' as being bullish, could then get confused with the word 'decline' in the same sentence. This stands in contrast to the sentence 'shares in company X rise as sales increase' where both verbs are aligned.

Newsflow in commodity markets often requires a slightly different approach and making commodity newsflow analysis meaningful needs careful management.

In this chapter, three different aspect of newsflow are considered and used in different ways:

- commodity positioning-related newsflow

- commodity trading-related newsflow

- directional commodity price newsflow.

11.1.1 Commodity Newsflow in Positioning and Sentiment Analysis

Incorporating commodity newsflow into commodity Positioning Analysis can be useful in several ways and by carefully blending specific types of newsflow with positioning data, some of the issues in Section Figure 11.1 can be managed.

1. *Commodity positioning-related newsflow*, discussed in Section 11.2.1, is important in helping to assess and track the current level of interest in positioning data. Like technical analysis, Positioning Analysis carries a degree of self-reinforcement, which can affect prices, shape sentiment, and influence behaviour. As positioning-related newsflow increases or decreases, the more or the less pronounced these positioning-related effects often become. Being able

to track trends in the newsworthiness of positioning data is therefore a useful way of assessing its relevance.

2. If positioning becomes extreme (either very high or very low) for a commodity in a particular group like the MM group, the absolute level of *commodity trading-related newsflow*, discussed in Section 11.2.2, in the commodity can affect behaviour.[1]

   a. High trading-related newsflow and large positioning suggests a high level of interest in the market, and by extension, that the positioning is likely justified. These periods are also often associated with increased volatility.

   b. Low trading-related newsflow and large positioning could suggest the positioning is not justified and instead may have been established through unusual or unconventional market activity. Such scenarios could include a large fund exiting a position, a large hedge being established or unwound, or a position being built up to influence or affect prices or fundamentals in some way. Price behaviour can often be unpredictable under these scenarios.

   c. High trading-related newsflow and low positioning could be driven by factors like market indecision, trading apathy, poor liquidity, or the fact that positions are yet to be established.

   d. Low newsflow and low positioning suggest little to no interest in the market.

3. If positioning becomes extreme for a commodity in a particular group like the MM group, the *direction of commodity price newsflow*, discussed in Section 11.2.3, in terms of whether it is bullish or bearish for prices, can significantly affect behaviour. A large long (short) position and bullish (bearish) price-related newsflow suggest the position could become bigger or, if already at an extreme, be less vulnerable to liquidation. If this newsflow starts to wane, however, prices could start to become vulnerable as positions unwind.

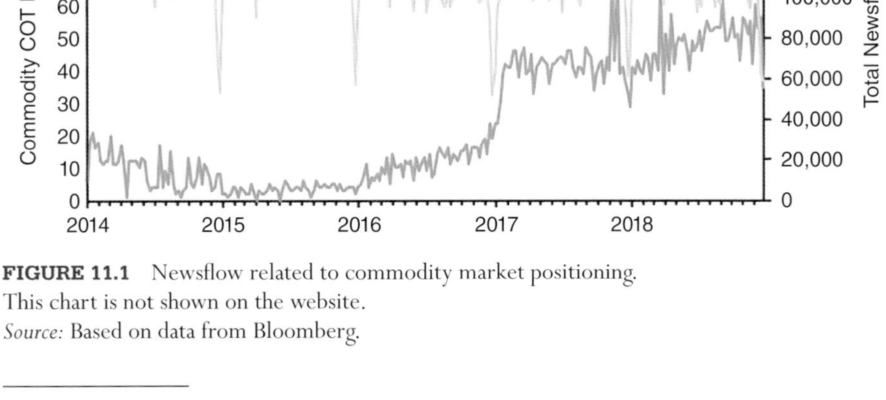

FIGURE 11.1 Newsflow related to commodity market positioning.
This chart is not shown on the website.
Source: Based on data from Bloomberg.

---

[1]Commodity trading-related newsflow is newsflow specifically related to the exchange-traded commodity, rather than stories mentioning the commodities in a wider context.

Addressing point 1 above, Figure 11.1 shows the evolution of positioning-related newsflow. The newsflow is in the form index, shown in green, and coded to count the number of stories published by Bloomberg that are related to commodity positioning. The construction of the index is detailed in Section 11.2.1. By way of a benchmark, the grey line shows the total number of stories published about everything on Bloomberg.

Based on the assumption that stories would not be written about commodity positioning if there was no interest in them, the most likely conclusion, based on the rise in the index, is that Positioning Analysis is growing in both interest and awareness. By extension, positioning dynamics are becoming an increasingly important factor in making trading decisions. As explained in point 1 above, tracking the evolution of this interest using newsflow is a way of quantifying the weight and emphasis placed on Positioning Analysis.

11.1.1.1 Reasons Why Commodity Positioning Newsflow Could be Rising?

The increase in positioning newsflow has been significant, especially against a backdrop of constant newsflow, as shown by the grey line in Figure 11.1. There could be several explanations for why this might be the case:

- Since the Global Financial Crisis (GFC) in 2008, commodity markets have been through extended periods where fundamental price drivers (supply/demand) have become less significant, and more macro-driven factors have become increasingly more important. This shift has also been supported by the fact that many commodities have become more financialised either directly or via sentiment channels.[2] When commodity prices decouple from fundamentals for extended periods of time, their price behaviour can become difficult to understand. Trying to disentangle fundamentals from non-fundamentals, to define these periods, can be equally challenging. Positioning Analysis and technical analysis often take on a greater degree of importance during these periods, as market participants tend to become increasingly more open to embracing other areas of analysis. The GFC also catalysed a general shift in thinking towards the realisation that a wide range of different analytical tools was prudent in helping to navigate different market regimes better. Consequently, Positioning Analysis appears to have become more established and more widespread.

- The growth in alternative data and data analytics has reshaped the fundamental analysis landscape by revealing vast new areas of data. In a comparable way to newsflow analysis, it has also come about through the growth in technology and computing power. Alternative data includes everything from various types of satellite imagery to various transport dynamics, where the location of ships throughout the world can be tracked, inventories in obscure locations measured, crop acreage counted, and crop yields evaluated by measuring chlorophyll levels from space. The coverage, accessibility, and proliferation of this data, previously only available to a limited number of market participants, has become more accessible. This has given rise to the argument that its value has been eroded. To maintain an edge, many of these market participants have started to embrace a wider range of analytical tools, including positioning.

- The growth in machine learning, sentiment analysis, and behavioural finance also made possible by the growth in computing power has contributed to new areas of analysis. With positioning and flow data often major components in these types of analytics, interest in the data has increased.

11.2 Building Basic Newsflow Indices

Section 11.2 describes some of the philosophy and logic behind building certain types of newsflow indices, with code examples that can be used directly in Bloomberg to create newsflow indices.

In Section 11.3 the use of these newsflow indices in Positioning Analysis and in a trading context is discussed.

11.2.1 Commodity Positioning Newsflow Indices

The newsflow index in Figure 11.1 was developed on a Bloomberg terminal, using some simple search codes with terminology based on the assumption that most commodity stories referring to positioning will include the term 'Commitment of Traders' or 'COT'. The index simply tracks the number of stories per week containing this terminology within commodities.[3]

To build the index the news search function on the Bloomberg terminal needs to be accessed by typing 'N <go>', followed by selecting 'more search options' and the search builder option. Using the 'manual editor' option, the code shown in Box 11.1 can be entered directly. An index of the results can then be viewed under the 'NT <go>' function after saving the code.

The 'TOPIC'-related terms in the code have been added to ensure that only commodity-related positioning stories are counted. By restricting the search to include only Bloomberg stories, a high-quality and reliable news database is used that does not change over time. One of the drawbacks about using web-based news archives is that they can be vulnerable to changes over time as content is moved or deleted. Naturally, many stories will be missed by only using Bloomberg, but it is the overall trend in newsflow that is most important rather than absolute numbers.

Box 11.1 Code for COT newsflow indicator

COT newsflow code:

```
KEYWORDS:("COT" OR "COMMITMENT* OF TRADER*") WITHIN (WIRE:BLOOMBERG
AND TOPIC:CMD AND NOT (TOPIC:FRX) AND NOT (TOPIC:BON) AND NOT
(TOPIC:FIALL) AND NOT (TOPIC:FINFUT) AND NOT (TOPIC:LAW))
```

Source: Based on data from Bloomberg.

---

[3]This can also be done on a daily basis.

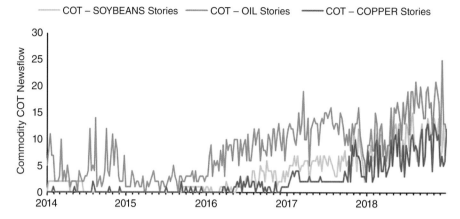

FIGURE 11.2 Newsflow related to oil, copper, and soybean market positioning.
This chart is not shown on the website.
Source: Based on data from Bloomberg.

By changing the code to include specific commodities like oil or soybeans or copper, commodity-specific COT newsflow indices can be created. Figure 11.2 shows the evolution of positioning news for oil, copper, and soybean with the respective codes shown in Box 11.2.

Box 11.2 Code for COT oil, copper, and soybean newsflow indicator

COT oil newsflow code:

```
KEYWORDS:(("COT" OR "COMMITMENTS* OF TRADER*") AND ("crude oil"
OR "brent" OR "wti")) WITHIN (WIRE:BLOOMBERG AND TOPIC:CMD AND
NOT (TOPIC:FRX) AND NOT (TOPIC:BON) AND NOT (TOPIC:FIALL) AND NOT
(TOPIC:FINFUT) AND NOT (TOPIC:LAW))
```

COT copper newsflow code:

```
KEYWORDS:(("COT" OR "COMMITMENTS* OF TRADER*") AND ("copper")) WITHIN
(WIRE:BLOOMBERG AND TOPIC:CMD AND NOT (TOPIC:FRX) AND NOT (TOPIC:BON)
AND NOT (TOPIC:FIALL) AND NOT (TOPIC:FINFUT) AND NOT (TOPIC:LAW))
```

COT soybean newsflow code:

```
KEYWORDS:(("COT" OR "COMMITMENTS* OF TRADER*") AND ("soybean*"))
WITHIN (WIRE:BLOOMBERG AND TOPIC:CMD AND NOT (TOPIC:FRX) AND NOT
(TOPIC:BON) AND NOT (TOPIC:FIALL) AND NOT (TOPIC:FINFUT) AND NOT
(TOPIC:LAW))
```

Source: Based on data from Bloomberg.

All the COT-based newsflow indices are useful in tracking the overall interest in positioning data over time as explained in point 1 in Section 11.1.1, either collectively or on a market-specific basis. Trends and levels in these indices are then an effective way of grading the direction and strength of the positioning newsflow, and, by extension, a way to rank or weight trading signals based on that interest, the assumption being: the stronger the newsflow, the greater the interest in positioning; and the greater the interest in positioning, the greater its relevance to price, sentiment, and behavioural dynamics.

By way of a simple example, if the speculative short position is at an extreme in both corn and soybeans, and the respective COT newsflow indices show that positioning-related newsflow in corn is significantly lower than in soybeans, it is likely that the short covering in soybeans could be more violent and exaggerated due to the increased awareness and interest in the position.

11.2.2 Commodity Trading Newsflow Indices

Separately, but nonetheless related to positioning newsflow, is commodity *trading* newsflow. A high (low) level of commodity trading newsflow in the context of large or extreme positioning can provide some insight into the justification of the position as explained in point 2 of Section 11.1.1.

Commodity trading newsflow indicators specifically track newsflow related to the trading activity in the *exchange-traded* commodity, rather than newsflow related to other aspects of the commodity. The intensity of trading-related newsflow for a specific commodity, in the context of certain positioning profiles, is important in helping to understand how risky a large position may be, as explained in Section 11.3.1.

To build a commodity trading newsflow index for oil, stories related to exchange-traded oil, rather than stories related to the physical oil market, would ideally only need to be captured. By way of a hypothetical example, the text 'Nymex crude oil prices closed at the highest level in one-year' would be counted as trading newsflow, whereas the text 'crude oil exports continue to drop in Venezuela' would not be counted.

To target trading-related news stories, and specifically those in relation to futures trading activity (because ultimately Positioning Analysis is only about futures contracts), the code should include words like 'NYMEX' or 'ICE' or 'price(s)' within close proximity (for example, a proximity of two words) to the commodity's name.

It is essential to understand that terminology like this is still very broad and stories about oil inventories, OPEC activity, oil volatility, and many different aspects of the physical oil business will be captured. Most of these stories will invariably be in the context of price or trading activity, so there is little point in filtering them out.

To help increase the likelihood of capturing only the most relevant newsflow, the Bloomberg database can also be curtailed to include only the 'key commodities' stories which addresses some of the issues mentioned above. Box 11.3 shows the code for an oil trading newsflow index.

It is also possible to extend the search to other databases like Twitter directly through the Bloomberg terminal.[4] The code for the twitter database is also shown in Box 11.3.

---

[4]Numerous different data sources can be referenced through Bloomberg either in isolation or in combination. The Twitter database on Bloomberg starts in early 2018.

Box 11.3 Code for an oil trading newsflow index

Oil trading newsflow code:

```
KEYWORDS:(("crude oil" OR "brent" OR "wti") N/2 ("nymex" OR "ICE" OR
"price*")) WITHIN (WIRE:BLOOMBERG AND TOPIC:CMDKEY)
```

Oil trading newsflow (Twitter) code:

```
KEYWORDS:(("crude oil" OR "brent" OR "wti") N/2 ("nymex" OR "ICE" OR
"price*")) WITHIN WIRE:TWT
```

The term N/2 means "near or within 2 words" of.

Source: Based on data from Bloomberg.

The code can easily be adapted for other commodities. To make an equivalent commodity-trading newsflow index for copper, for example, the code could be changed from:

```
KEYWORDS:(("crude oil" OR "brent" OR "wti") N/2 ("nymex" OR "ICE" OR
"price*"))
```

to:

```
KEYWORDS:(("copper") N/2 ("comex" OR "LME" OR "price*")).
```

It is important to note that this commodity-trading newsflow is directionless – the objective is to gauge the intensity of the newsflow, not whether the flow is bullish or bearish for prices.

11.2.3 Directional Commodity Price Newsflow Indices

The direction of commodity price newsflow, in terms of whether it is bullish or bearish for prices, adds insight into price behaviour when positions are extreme, as explained in point 3 of Section 11.1.1.

Naturally, developing robust code able to identify every story as either bullish or bearish would be challenging, and many of the issues in doing this for commodity markets have been addressed in Section 11.1. One way around this is focus directly on the newsflow related to price direction and search for bullish (bearish) verbs like 'rose', 'increased' and 'advanced' ('fell', 'decreased' and 'declined') near the name of the commodity.

The problem with many commodity markets is that changes in many of the key price drivers are opposite to their effect on price, which in text analytics can be difficult to capture accurately as mentioned in Section 11.1. The hypothetical line in an oil story: 'oil prices *rose* as oil inventories/exports/supply *fell*' or the opposite equivalent 'oil prices *fell* as oil inventories/exports/supply *rose*' are difficult to disentangle within a search string, as the verbs are common to both – just their order is different.

One solution is to remove words like 'inventory, inventories, stock(s), exports and supply' that work in reverse to their effect on prices. Words that do not work in the opposite way to their price effect like 'demand' would not need to be removed. The line 'oil prices *fell (rose)* as demand *fell (rose)*' is ok, as changes in demand are aligned with the changes in price.

Box 11.4 shows the code for a bullish oil price index and a bearish price index with many of the most commonly encountered words that work in reverse removed. By focusing the terminology on the price effect only, which is typically clear in commodity stories, as the effect of some price drivers is not always obvious and it is consequently often clarified, many different scenarios can be considered.[5]

Looking at a few hypothetical examples, stories like:

— 'oil prices rose as Iranian sanctions came into effect'; or
— 'freezing temperatures drove oil prices higher'; or
— 'oil prices jumped as violence erupted in Libya'; or
— 'the dollar index continued to rise, increasing oil prices, as the US economy recovered'

can each be successfully identified as bullish or bearish by just isolating the price effect and ignoring the actual price driver as the price effect is clearly explained.

Box 11.4 Code for oil price newsflow index

Bullish oil price newsflow code:

```
KEYWORDS:((("crude oil" OR "brent" OR "wti") N/2 ("RISE*" OR "ROSE"
OR "UP" OR "HIGH*" OR "ABOVE*" OR "ADVANCE*" OR "JUMP*" OR "CLIMB*" OR
"SURGE*" OR "UPTURN*")) AND NOT ("export*" OR "supply" OR "inventor*"
OR "stock*")) WITHIN WIRE:BLOOMBERG)
```

Bearish oil price newsflow code:

```
KEYWORDS:((("crude oil" OR "brent" OR "wti") N/2 ("fall*" OR "fell"
OR "down" OR "low*" OR "below" OR "decline*" OR "drop*" OR "decrease*"
OR "plunge*" OR "downturn*" OR "collapse*")) AND NOT ("export*" OR
"supply" OR "inventor*" OR "stock*")) WITHIN WIRE:BLOOMBERG
```

The term N/2 means near or within 2 words of.

The "*" represent wild characters.

Source: Based on data from Bloomberg.

---

[5]Examples of price drivers that can be difficult to interpret, or whose price effects change in different environments, include: geopolitical events, changes in certain types of transport data such as shipping data (can be an indication of current demand or future supply), and macroeconomic variables including currency movements and interest rate dynamics, which can all have variable effects on prices over time depending on the environment.

11.3 Combining Newsflow with Positioning

Commodity-trading newsflow as defined in Section 11.2.2, and Directional commodity price newsflow as defined in Section 11.2.3 can both be combined with Positioning Analysis in a variety of ways, depending on the final objective. As a tool to enhance trading signals, an effective way to do this is within a framework similar to that used for the OBOS factor indicators described in Section 9.2. OBOS Factor indicators are like OBOS indicators except the Pricing Component is substituted for a Factor Component, and the framework is expanded to accommodate four distinct types of extreme.

Figure 11.3 shows the evolution of the oil trading newsflow index, described in Section 11.2.2 and generated with the code in Box 11.3, with the price of crude oil (WTI) overlaid. The chart shows that periods where oil prices fall frequently coincide with increased newsflow. Newsflow is reasonably static when oil prices rise, and a few of the peaks in price also appear to coincide with increased newsflow.

Figure 11.4 shows an OBOS Newsflow indicator with crude oil (WTI) MMS (MML) positioning used in the Positioning Component calculation, and the oil trading newsflow index used as the Factor Component based on the same newsflow code used in Figure 11.3.

The MML and MMS positions are plotted here as open interest, instead of being converted to Concentration, as it is the level of open interest, in the context of newsflow, that is mostly of interest. In addition, only a single commodity is shown in the framework, so the requirement to normalise the data across other markets is not relevant.

The four black boxes in each of the four corners represent the intersections of extreme positioning with high and low newsflow, defined as the newsflow index being in the top (bottom) quartiles of its one-year range, in a similar way to many of OBOS Factor indicators described in Chapter 9. The extra new blue box (rectangle) in the top (bottom) centre shows the intersection of high (low) newsflow with extreme low positioning.

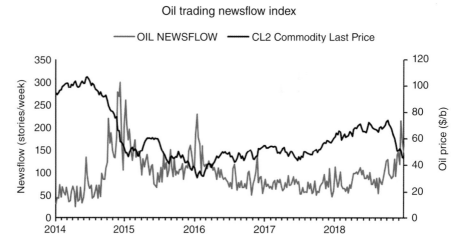

FIGURE 11.3 Oil trading newsflow index.
This chart is not shown on the website.
Source: Based on data from Bloomberg.

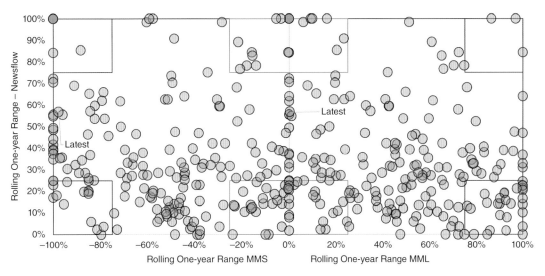

FIGURE 11.4 OBOS Newsflow Factor indicator – crude oil (WTI).
This chart is not shown on the website.
Source: Based on data from Bloomberg.

Each of the points in the chart is a different week for a single commodity (crude oil (WTI)) since January 2015. This has been done for illustrative purposes and is hence different to many of the other OBOS charts shown in the book, where only the most recent week is shown for a number of different commodities.[6,7]

This OBOS Newsflow indicator is a useful tool to quickly assess the level of newsflow in the context of positioning extremes as described in Section 11.1.1. The indicator can be used with other trader groups, for example the PMPU group, to visualise positioning (hedging) extremes in the context of high (low) newsflow. The main drawback of the approach, as with all OBOS Factor indicators, is that price data is not considered.

11.3.1 Integrating Commodity Trading Newsflow into a Classic OBOS Indicator

The core philosophy behind the OBOS framework is that extreme long (short) positions that occur when prices are also at an extreme high (low) are often unwound faster and more violently, which can have a disproportionate effect on prices. The level of newsflow and the direction of newsflow (bullish or bearish) surrounding these periods can be critical.

---

[6]Exceptions include the OBOS Time and OBOS Seasonal indicators described in Section 8.5.2 and Section 8.6.2.

[7]In contrast to the OBOS indicator charts shown throughout this book, Figure 11.7 has been plotted in Excel rather than Tableau. This is because the newsflow data is not a Bloomberg field and needs to be extracted from the Bloomberg terminal as values. All the Tableau analytics in this book are automatically driven from Bloomberg.

To include trading newsflow into a classic OBOS framework, as distinct from the OBOS Factor framework discussed in Section 11.3, where no price information is included, weeks are divided into those associated with high, low, and average levels of newsflow, using the same code used in Figure 11.3.

Figure 11.5 shows an OBOS indicator of MM positioning in crude oil (WTI) only, with historical weeks also shown. This is the same as the classic OBOS indicator in Figure 8.1, except the Positioning Component calculation is based on open interest instead of Concentration for the reasons explained in Section 11.3, and no curve structure information is included. Each of the points in the chart is again a different week for a single commodity for the purpose of clarity since January 2015. The red (green) box shows the Oversold (Overbought) box, as explained in Section 8.2.7. The newsflow has been incorporated by colouring the points according to the level of newsflow.

The blue weeks show when the trading newsflow was in the bottom quartile of is one-year range, the yellow weeks show when the trading newsflow was in the top quartile, and the small grey weeks when it was average – defined as being in the middle two quartiles.

Yellow (blue) weeks in the Oversold box are weeks lying at the intersection of extreme short MM positioning, extreme price weakness, and extreme high (low) newsflow. Similarly, yellow (blue) weeks in the Overbought box are weeks lying at the intersection of extreme long MM positioning, extreme price strength, and extreme high (low) newsflow. The yellow (blue) weeks outside the boxes showed when newsflow was extreme high (low), but the market was neither Overbought nor Oversold.

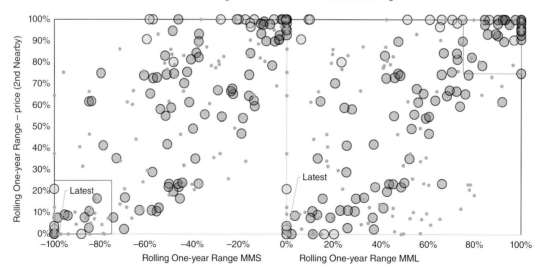

FIGURE 11.5 OBOS indicator with trading newsflow – WTI.
This chart is not shown on the website.
Source: Based on data from Bloomberg.

11.3.2 Integrating Direction Commodity Price Newsflow into a Classic OBOS Framework

In a similar way to the oil trading (non-directional) newsflow index in Section 11.3.1, the oil price (directional) newsflow indices can both be included in an OBOS framework in the same way. The key difference is that two different newsflow indices are needed: the bullish newsflow index and the bearish equivalent.

Figure 11.6 shows the evolution of the oil directional price newsflow indices, as described in Section 11.2.3, plotted as a stacked area chart for clarity with the price of crude oil (WTI) over-laid. Periods where oil prices rise (fall) coincide with higher levels of bullish (bearish) newsflow.

Figure 11.7 shows the same OBOS indicator for crude oil (WTI) as shown in Figure 11.5, with bullish and bearish price newsflow indices incorporated. The green (red) weeks where the bullish (bearish) oil price newsflow index was in the top quartile of its one-year range.

The green (red) weeks within the Oversold box in the bottom left of the chart indicate weeks lying at the intersection of extreme short MM positioning, extreme price weakness, and extreme high bullish (bearish) newsflow.

The green (red) points within the Overbought box in the top right of the chart indicate weeks lying at the intersection of extreme long MM positioning, extreme price strength, and extreme high bullish (bearish) newsflow.

The OBOS philosophy behind the OBOS framework is that extreme long (short) positions that occur when prices are also at an extreme high (low) are often unwound faster and more violently, which can have a disproportionate effect on prices; the inclusion of price-based bullish and bearish newsflow into the framework acts to refine these signals even further.

Short covering (long liquidation) is less likely to occur, or less likely to be as significant for an Oversold (Overbought) commodity, if the newsflow is bearish (bullish). In a similar way, short covering (long liquidation) is more likely to occur and is expected to be more significant for an Oversold (Overbought) commodity if the newsflow is very bullish (bearish).

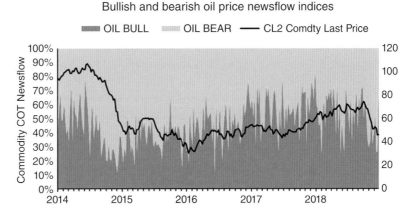

FIGURE 11.6   Oil price newsflow indices.
This chart is not shown on the website.
Source: Based on data from Bloomberg.

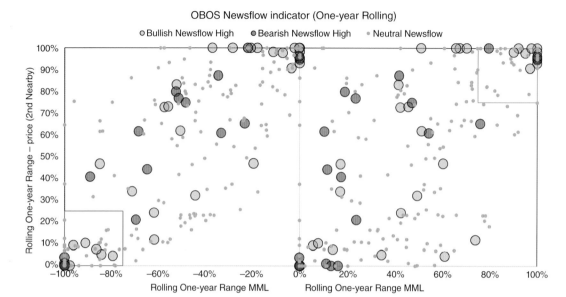

FIGURE 11.7 OBOS indicator with bullish and bearish price newsflow indices – crude oil (WTI). This chart is not shown on the website.
Source: Based on data from Bloomberg.

Another approach is to combine both bullish and bearish newsflow together into a ratio to avoid using two newsflow indices, but the drawback is that spikes in the range can dramatically alter the range for some time. This is because ratios can be very volatile.

11.4 Economic Policy Uncertainty

Economic Policy Uncertainty (EPU) indices, as developed and published by Baker, Bloom, and Davis, are newsflow indices based on various types of policy uncertainty.[8] They are published on their website and are also available on Bloomberg. Most of the indices are based on newsflow from newspaper articles and target specific EPU terminology. Numerous EPU indices have been developed to cover a wide range of regions and countries. More recently these indices have also been extended to cover specific topics – for example, the EPU Brexit index.

The relationship between commodity prices and changes in EPU can at times be strong, with increases in EPU indices like the Chinese Policy Uncertainty index frequently driving weakness in commodity markets. EPU indices can also be incorporated into Positioning Analysis in a comparable way to the indices described above with two small caveats.

Firstly, most of these indices are monthly, which can sometimes make the data difficult to blend with weekly positioning data; and secondly they are also subject to revision, which makes backtesting of signals difficult. Nonetheless, with the OBOS framework able to handle data at different data release frequencies and with the revisions often being minimal, they can be especially useful tools to help refine positioning signals.

---

[8]www.policyuncertainty.com/.

CHAPTER 12

Flow Analysis – The 'Flow Cube' and the 'Build Ratio' in Commodity Markets

Chapter objectives

The Flow Cube organises changes in price, open interest, and volume into a framework to define the type of trading that has recently occurred within a commodity futures markets; and the Build ratio is a way of quantifying how efficient the trading has been.

The Flow Cube is a clear way of visualising the trading activity over a certain period, with the trading activity organised into one of eight 'mini cubes' according to the eight different types of trading activity. This can be done for the whole commodity market by looking at changes in price, open interest, and volume for all futures contracts in aggregate, or it can be done with individual futures contracts to better understand the trading activity at specific points or in specific regions down the curve.

Figure 12.1 is a way of visualising the Flow Cube framework. This is also shown in more detail in Figure 12.2.

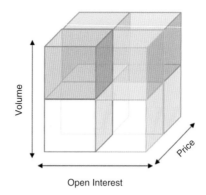

Volume

Open Interest

Price

FIGURE 12.1   The Flow Cube.
Source: Author.

12.1 The Flow Cube

The Flow Cube and Build ratio organise and quantify changes in price, open interest, and volume into a framework to define the type and efficiency of trading activity. This can be done over any timeframe (daily, weekly, monthly) and for any commodity on an aggregate or individual futures contract basis.

The approach means that the recent trading activity in a commodity, or the trading activity at specific points down its forward curve, can be defined and then, in combination with the Build ratio, defined in Section 12.1.3, quantified in terms of its efficiency.

This means that in combination with some knowledge of the type of trading activity down the curve, in terms of speculative or hedging, the efficiency of trading activity can be assessed and by extension the extent of more fuzzy types of trading such as the level of 'High-Frequency Trading (HFT)' observed.

12.1.1.1 The Relationships Between Changes in Price, Volume, and Open
Interest   In a futures market, volume refers to the number of futures contracts bought and sold between traders. The higher (lower) the volume, the higher (lower) the level of trading activity. The open interest is the number of open contracts held by traders. These are positions that have not yet been closed or have not expired.

Table 12.1 shows provides some background on the relationships between changes in volume and open interest in the form of a simple example on the potential evolution of volume and open interest on a hypothetical trading day:

TABLE 12.1   **Volume vs open interest.**

Day	Activity	Volume	Open Interest
1	Trader A buys 1 contract and Trader B sells 1 contract	1	1
2	Trader C buys 5 contracts and Trader D sells 5 contracts	5	6
3	Trader D buys 1 contract and Trader A sells 1 contract	1	5
4	Trader E buys 5 contracts and Trader C sells 5 contracts	5	5
	Total	**12**	**5**

- Open interest:

  - increases, when a buyer and seller initiate a new position between themselves;

  - decreases, when an existing buyer and existing seller close out an existing position;

  - remains constant, when an existing buyer (seller) sells (buys) an existing position to a new buyer (seller).

- Volume: All trading activities contribute to an increase in volume.

12.1.2 The Flow Cube Across Commodity Markets

The direction of price and change in open interest indicate the type of trading activity, while the direction of volume indicates the strength of the flow.

In the Flow Cube, eight trading activities are defined. All trading activity will fall into one of these definitions. Each is defined in Table 12.2.

While total long open interest is always equal to total short open interest, incorporating price direction into the framework allows the trading activity to be 'classified' according to the patterns in Table 12.2. If open interest is increasing, both long and short positions are being established, but when prices are also rising (falling), for example, the activity is defined as long (short) building.

The Flow Cube shown in Figure 12.2 is a visual representation of Table 12.2. It is divided into eight mini cubes depending on the type of activity. Strong (weak) flows, a function of the change in volume, are represented by the solid (hollow) cubes.

The solid blue cube, for example, lies at the intersection of higher average prices, higher open interest, and higher average volume, and therefore represents strong long building (SLB). The hollow red cube lies at the intersection of lower average prices, lower open interest, and lower average volume, and therefore represents weak long liquidation (WLL).

The averages are calculated over the period of one week, using daily data, and compared on a weekly basis to determine changes. The open interest data is taken at the end of each week and not averaged.

As open interest is released on a daily basis, the Flow Cube could be calculated daily using the daily changes in open interest, volume, and price to increase sensitivity. It could also be calculated

TABLE 12.2 The eight trading activities.			
Price	Open Interest	Volume	Trader Activity
Up	Up	Up	Strong Long Building (SLB)
Up	Up	Down	Weak Long Building (WLB)
Down	Down	Up	Strong Long Liquidation (SLL)
Down	Down	Down	Weak Long Liquidation (WLL)
Down	Up	Up	Strong Short Building (SSB)
Down	Up	Down	Weak Short Building (WSB)
Up	Down	Up	Strong Short Covering (SSC)
Up	Down	Down	Weak Short Covering (WSC)

Source: Based on data from Bloomberg.

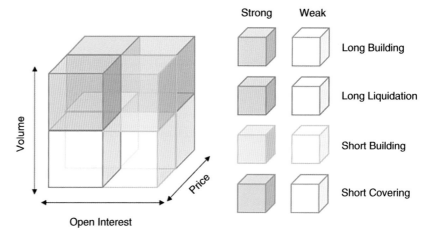

FIGURE 12.2 The Flow Cube.
Source: Author.

on a monthly basis using the average changes in volume and price over the month and the open interest at the end of the month, but the sensitivity would be reduced. Rolling periods can also be used to smooth the data and provide short- and long-term flow profiles, meaning that on a rolling 5-day basis the flow could be weak long building (WLB), but on a rolling 10-day basis the flow could be strong long building (SLB). This kind of profile could indicate a shift in trading activity.

A week is a good balance in being sensitive enough, but not too sensitive, such that idiosyncrasies in daily trading and any futures contract expiry-related activity would be maximised. Weekly periods can also be switched to run Tuesday to Tuesday to reconcile with weekly positioning data.

Figure 12.3 shows the historical flow profile for natural gas over 2018 on a weekly basis. The colours are based on the Flow Cube classifications defined in Figure 12.2.

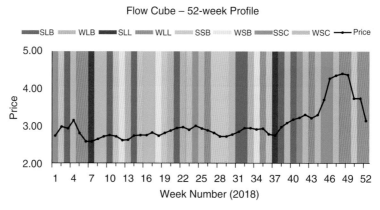

FIGURE 12.3 Historical flow profile for natural gas (2018).
Trading activity symbols: As listed in Table 12.2.
This chart is not shown on the website.
Source: Based on data from Bloomberg.

Focusing on the volatility in the natural gas market in late 2018, the beginning of the rise in prices in November 2018 (week 44) was characterised by a mix of weak short covering (WSC) and strong short covering (SSC). This activity took prices to the highest levels since early 2014. Weak long liquidation (WLL) put a ceiling on prices, before a period of strong short building (SSB) and continued weak long liquidation drove prices lower.

In combination with other positioning analytics such as Dry Powder analysis, introduced in Chapter 5, the likely persistence of these flow patterns can be estimated based on the level of dry powder. In combination with the Positional Variance Decomposition, described in Chapter 7, the potential impact on price can also be determined.

One of the main advantages of using Flow Analysis in combination with Positioning Analysis is that the analysis periods can be configured to run in parallel with the reporting of position data, to provide additional information.

In isolation, Flow Analysis is particularly useful as the lag in the data is minimal.

12.1.3 The Build Ratio

The Build ratio measures how much of the daily volume has been translated into open interest – a measure of trading efficiency. It is calculated by dividing the absolute daily change in open interest by the volume traded on that day. The ratio is then averaged over the week and expressed as a percentage.

The formula for the Build ratio is:

$$Build\ ratio\left(\%\right) = \frac{\left|aggregate\ open\ interest_t - aggregate\ open\ interest_{t-1}\right|}{aggregate\ volume_t}$$

where

$$Aggregate\ open\ interest = total\ open\ interest\ for\ all\ futures\ contracts$$
$$Aggregate\ volume\quad = total\ volume\ for\ all\ futures\ contracts$$

A Build ratio of 100% means that all volume on a given trading day has been translated into open interest and there was no intraday trading. Volume driven by intraday trading, which does not lead to a change in open interest, causes the Build ratio to decrease. This type of trading activity could be an indication of HFT activity.

To provide some context for the Build ratio, it can be compared to its one-year average. Figure 12.4 shows the flow profile for all commodities in the week ending 28 December 2018. The height of each column is a function of the Build ratio for the most recent week, with the horizontal black bar representing the average Build ratio calculated over the last year.

These flow patterns can also be analysed from a seasonal perspective, based on the assumption that at specific times of the year, hedges are established, and certain flow profiles will be more common. Deviations from 'normal' patterns can be useful in identifying and explaining changes in a market.

Focusing on cocoa, by way of an example, the flow has been strong long building (SLB) with a Build ratio of 5.1% over the week. Compared to its historical one-year average, the efficiency of position building is much higher (average Build ratio is 2.7%), suggesting a degree of purposefulness or urgency in establishing the length.

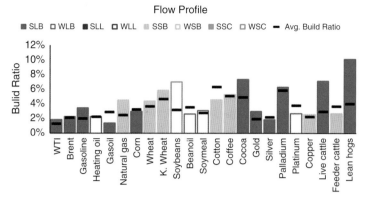

FIGURE 12.4 Commodity market flow profile with current and average Build ratio (week ending 28 December 2018).
Trading activity symbols: As listed in Table 12.2.
This chart is not shown on the website.
Source: Based on data from Bloomberg.

12.1.4 The Speculation Ratio

The Speculation ratio shows the volume traded every day as a proportion of open interest. It is a measure of trading activity and a good indication of speculative, specifically intraday, activity. The Speculation ratio is also a useful way of normalising volume for comparison purposes between commodities.

The Speculation ratio is calculated by dividing the daily volume by the daily open interest, averaged over the week and expressed as a percentage. In general, commodities with a higher (lower) Speculation ratio are those often associated with higher (lower) trading activity, which is then often anecdotally associated with higher (lower) intraday trading activity (and hence speculation), or lower (higher) hedging activity.

Technically, only a Speculation ratio in excess of 100%, as commonly seen in many of the Chinese commodity futures markets and as covered in Chapter 13, can be linked to intraday speculative trading activity.[1]

The formula for the Speculation ratio is:

$$Speculation\ ratio(\%) = \frac{aggregate\ volume_t}{aggregate\ open\ interest_t}$$

where

$Aggregate\ open\ interest$ = total open interest for all futures contracts
$Aggregate\ volume$ = total volume for all futures contracts

12.1.5 The Build Ratio vs the Speculation Ratio

The Build and Speculation ratios are related to each other but convey different information about commodity flow and trading activity.

Consider the following hypothetical examples for commodity A and commodity B:

---

[1]This linkage is made entirely on the basis that hedging activity is rarely undertaken on an intraday basis, although it is possible.

Commodity A has an open interest of 100,000 contracts at the end of day one, 125,000 contracts at the end of day two, and 150,000 contracts at the end of day three. On each of the days, the volume is 50,000 contracts.

- On day two, the Build ratio is 50% ((125,000 − 100,000)/50,000), as half the volume on day two was translated into a position. On day three the Build ratio is also 50% ((150,000 − 125,000)/50,000) as half the daily volume was again translated into a position. The Build ratio gives an idea of the efficiency at which positions are being built (or liquidated).

- On day two, the speculation ratio is 40% (50,000/125,000), as volume equivalent to 40% of the open interest was traded. On day three the speculation ratio is 33% (50,000/150,000) as volume equivalent to 33% of the open interest was traded. This shows that volume as a proportion of the open interest is decreasing and, in this context, trading activity is less.

Commodity B has an open interest of 10,000 contracts at the end of day one, 15,000 contracts at the end of day two, and 20,000 contracts at the end of day three. On each of the days, the volume is 50,000 contracts.

- On day two, the Build ratio is 10% ((15,000 − 10,000)/50,000), as 10% the volume of day two was translated into a position. On day three the Build ratio is also 10% ((20,000 − 15,000)/50,000) as 10% the daily volume was again translated into a position.

- On day two, the speculation ratio is 225% (50,000/15,000), as volume equivalent to 233% of the final open interest was traded. On day three the speculation ratio is 150% (50,000/20,000) as volume equivalent to 150% of the open interest was traded.

Looking at commodities A and B, and making the assumptions that volume not translated into open interest is all intraday speculation and volume translated into open interest will include all hedging activity and some non-intraday speculative activity, a few observations can be made.[2]

- The proportion of hedging activity is less in commodity B than commodity A as only a maximum of 10% of the volume can be hedged compared to a maximum of 50% in commodity A.

- The proportion of intraday speculative activity is higher for commodity B, with 233% and 150% of the open interest being traded over the two days, compared to 75% and 50% in commodity A.

- There is definitely intraday speculation in commodity B.

Both ratios can be useful in understanding flow dynamics and trading activity within a commodity market, and they are useful for comparing commodities. In general, however, commodities with a high Speculation ratio and a low Build ratio are likely to have a higher (lower) levels of intraday speculation (hedging).

In conjunction with price moves, these ratios can also provide an indication of the stability of the move. A price move supported by a higher Build ratio and lower Speculation ratio could suggest a more solid or a better structured move compared to a lower Build ratio and higher Speculation ratio, where the move could be more 'fragile'. Section 13.3 shows how the Build ratio and Speculation ratio can be used together to understand trading activity in the Chinese commodity futures market better.

---

[2]Naturally, all open interest is not hedging-related, as speculators can also take long-term speculative positions. It is, however, very unusual for a hedge to last less than a day. Generally, all intraday trading is assumed to be speculative in nature, driven mostly by day trades seeking to avoid paying initial margin overnight, or high-frequency traders (algorithmic) traders where the holding times are extremely short.

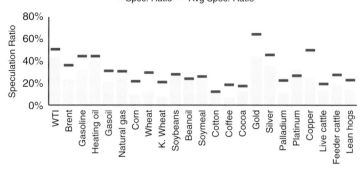

FIGURE 12.5 Commodity market Speculation ratios with average Speculation ratio (week ending 28 December 2018).
This chart is not shown on the website.
Source: Based on data from Bloomberg.

12.1.6 Relative Speculation Ratios

Figure 12.5 shows the Speculation ratios for all commodities in the week ending 28 December 2018. The height of each column is a function of the Speculation ratio for the week, with the horizontal red bar representing the average Speculation ratio calculated over the last year. The Speculation ratio for all commodities is below their one-year average for all markets – a likely reflection of the Christmas holiday period.

The top three most 'speculated' commodities in 2018, with the highest average Speculation ratio were gold (64%), crude oil (WTI) (51%), and copper (50%). Cotton (12%), cocoa (17%), and coffee and live cattle (both 19%) had the lowest Speculation ratios.

12.2 The Flow Cube down the Forward Curve

In Figure 12.4 the Flow Cube was applied to a commodity on an aggregate basis, meaning that changes in open interest and volume for all futures contracts were aggregated together. To better visualise flow dynamics down the forward curve of a commodity, the Flow Cube can also be applied to each individual futures contract as shown in Figure 12.6, where price is shown on the *y*-axis and the futures contract number on the *x*-axis.

For each contract, the change in open interest, the change in average price, and volume are compared against the previous period to define the primary trading activity for that contract over the month. A week is a sensible timeframe, being not too sensitive, but still able to identify trading activity at points further down the curve where liquidity can be low. As explained in Section 12.1.2, different periods can be used in the calculation, as well as rolling windows to smooth the data.

Figure 12.7 shows the flow profile down the curve for crude oil (WTI) on the week ending 21 December 2018. The pattern is characterised by weakness, in the form of either weak long liquidation (WLL), strong short building (SSB) and weak short building (WSB). These patterns provide insight into how the curve structure might evolve.

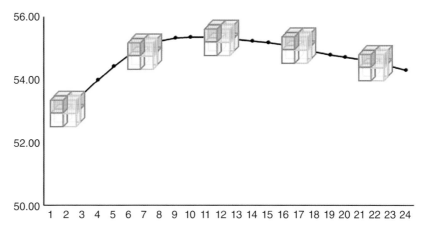

FIGURE 12.6 Flow Cubes down the curve.
Only a few flow cubes are drawn for clarity.
Source: Author.

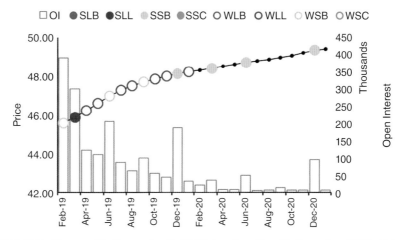

FIGURE 12.7 Flow profile for crude oil (WTI) (week ending 21 December 2018). Prices are shown on the left-hand *y*-axis and open interest on the right-hand *y*-axis.
Trading activity symbols: As listed in Table 12.2
This chart is not shown on the website.
Source: Based on data from Bloomberg.

In this example, the weakness down the curve continued in the week following, with the contango steepening. The black dots indicate when the change in open interest is less than 1% of the total are are ignored in the analysis.

Figure 12.8, Figure 12.9, and Figure 12.10 show the changing flow patterns down the crude oil (WTI) forward curve in October 2018. At the beginning of the month, on 5 October, flow was weak, characterised by weak long buying (WLB) over most of the contracts. One week later on 5 October, most contracts showed weak short building (WSB), marking the beginning of a potential shift in structure. At the end of the month, as the front segment started to move into heavy contango, most contracts showed weak long liquidation (WLL) with strong short building (SSB).

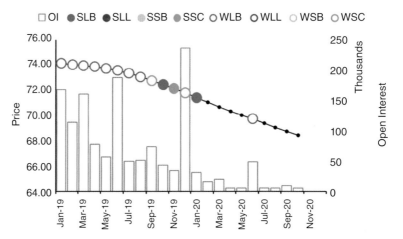

FIGURE 12.8 Flow profile for crude oil (WTI) (week ending 5 Oct 2018). Prices are shown on the left-hand *y*-axis and open interest on the right-hand *y*-axis.
Trading activity symbols: As listed in Table 12.2.
This chart is not shown on the website.
Source: Based on data from Bloomberg.

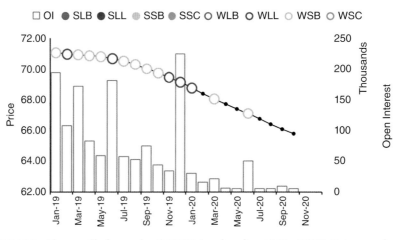

FIGURE 12.9 Flow profile for crude oil (WTI) (week ending 12 Oct 2018). Prices are shown on the left-hand *y*-axis and open interest on the right-hand *y*-axis.
Trading activity symbols: As listed in Table 12.2.
This chart is not shown on the website.
Source: Based on data from Bloomberg.

The bar chart in the background of each chart shows the contract open interest down the curve. This can be useful when the flow in that contract is either liquidation (SLL or WLL) or covering (SSC or WSC) as it gives an idea of the maximum number of contracts that can be closed out. For example, in Figure 12.10, the flow in the November 2019 contract is weak long liquidation (WLL). The open interest in that contract at the time was 36,979, meaning that if the WLL continues, the maximum number of contracts that can currently be liquidated is 36,979. It is improbable

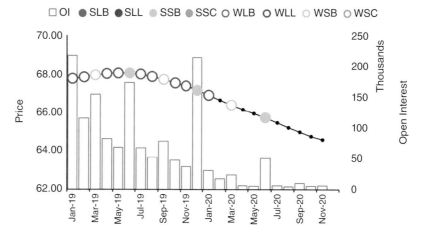

FIGURE 12.10 Flow profile for crude oil (WTI) (week ending 26 October 2018).
Trading activity symbols: As listed in Table 12.2.
This chart is not shown on the website.
Source: Based on data from Bloomberg.

that all the contracts will be closed out, with no other flow activity occurring, but an awareness of the underlying open interest provides some handle on what is possible for that point in the curve.

The Build ratio down the forward curve can also be calculated. In the same way that it has been shown to provide a measure of efficiency of trading activity for a whole commodity in Figure 12.4, it can also be applied to each contract individually to measure the efficiency of trading down the curve. In combination with the type of trading activity in and around a certain point on the curve, a Build ratio in excess of its average, or counter seasonally, could suggest the curve is behaving abnormally, with an increased likelihood of changing structure.

12.2.1 The Speculation Ratio down the Forward Curve

The Speculation ratio can also be extended down the curve, to provide more context to the trading activity. Figure 12.11 shows the Speculation ratio down the curve for crude oil (WTI).

The front-month February 2019 contract has the highest ratio (not shown as it distorts the chart) as it is approaching expiry. Volume is therefore high, with open interest falling as positions are being rolled over. The Speculation ratio at the front-month contract is therefore not particularly useful, other than to look at the rate that contracts are being closed out as expiry approaches, or for analysis on a comparative basis by looking at previous expiries.

Looking at the rest of the contracts, most contracts show a similar Speculation ratio, suggesting that the curve is stable with no contract or segment susceptible to excessive trading activity.

The April contract has the highest speculation ratio, suggesting that this is where the highest proportion of intraday trading activity could be occurring.

Collectively, and in combination with some knowledge of the type of trading activity at certain regions of the curve, in terms of speculative or hedging activity, the level of trading activity can be assessed. The type of trading activity down the curve is largely anecdotal but is generally characterised by speculative activity at the front of the curve, followed by consumer activity, and, lastly, producer activity, towards the back of the curve.

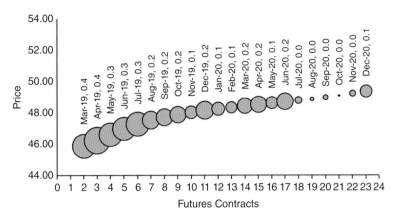

FIGURE 12.11 Speculation ratio profile for crude oil (WTI) (week ending 21 December 2018). Prices are shown on the left-hand *y*-axis.

This chart is not shown on the website.

Source: Based on data from Bloomberg.

12.3 The LBMA-i Trade Data

As explained in Section 2.3.1, the London Bullion Market Association (LBMA) started publishing a weekly report on market activity on the London gold and silver over-the-counter (OTC) market on 20 November 2018. The report provides data on the trading volumes and outstanding interest on the gold and silver OTC market.[3] These include trading volumes and outstanding interest on an array of different products including spot, forward and swaps, options and leased gold, and on different maturity buckets, spot, 1-week, 2w, 1-month, 3m, 6m, 9m, 12m, and beyond 12m.

Applying the Flow Cube to this data both in aggregate and/or down the curve, using LMBA forward rate prices at each maturity, and equating the LBMA-i volume and outstanding interest at each maturity buckets to the volume and open interest of futures contracts, it becomes possible to apply Flow Cubes down the OTC forward curve.

Insight into trading and hedging activity can then be better assessed in the OTC market and then also reconciled with the COMEX futures market to identify potential mismatches and shifts in trading activity.

As this data develops further, new insights into these markets will become possible.

The Flow Cube lends itself well to the analysis of flow data in OTC markets where this type of data is available.

References

Mark Keenan, Michael Haigh, David Schenck, and Malavika Dinaker (2018), 'Commodity Compass – The "Flow Cube" & the "Construction Ratio" – Understanding Flow Patterns'. Société Générale (SG) Cross Asset Research – Commodities Group. www.sgmarkets.com/.

Mark Keenan, Michael Haigh, David Schenck, and Malavika Dinaker (2019), 'Commodity Compass – Flow Cubes Along the Curve'. Société Générale (SG) Cross Asset Research – Commodities Group. www. sgmarkets.com/.

---

[3]Outstanding interest includes open interest in the swap, forward, options, and leasing market, as well as spot transactions that have yet to be settled.

CHAPTER 13

Chinese Commodity Markets — Analysing Flow

Chapter objectives

This chapter focuses exclusively on the Chinese commodity futures markets, with the primary objective of defining, assessing, and tracking the level of trading activity, and specifically speculative activity, that frequently dominates the newsflow on these exchanges.

As there is no equivalent CFTC Commitment of Traders (COT) report for Chinese exchanges, insight on trading activity for these exchanges can be approximated using the Speculation Ratio (SR) indicator and the Build Ratio (BR) indicator.

A new Overbought/Oversold OBOS model for Chinese commodities, based on extremes in price and the SR, is also developed.

13.1 The Chinese Commodity Exchanges

There are three main Chinese commodity futures exchanges, the Dalian Commodity Exchange (DCE), the Zhengzhou Commodity Exchange (ZCE), and the Shanghai Futures Exchange (SHFE), of which the Shanghai International Energy Exchange (INE) is a subsidiary.

13.1.1 The Shanghai Futures Exchange (SHFE)

The Shanghai Futures Exchange (SHFE) is under the uniform regulation of China Securities Regulatory Commission (CSRC) and organises the futures trading approved by CSRC in accordance with the principles of openness, impartiality, fairness, and integrity. Its ultimate goal is serving the real economy.

Currently there are 14 futures contracts available for trading on the SHFE. They include futures on copper, aluminium, zinc, lead, nickel, tin, gold, silver, steel rebar, steel wire rod, hot-rolled coil, fuel oil, bitumen, and natural rubber.[1]

13.1.1.1 The Shanghai International Energy Exchange (INE) Approved by the China Securities Regulatory Commission (the CSRC), the Shanghai International Energy Exchange Co., Ltd., or INE, is an international exchange, jointly initiated and established by relevant entities including the Shanghai Futures Exchange. It is open to global futures participants.

Registered in the China (Shanghai) Pilot Free Trade Zone on 6 November 2013, INE operates the listing, clearing and delivery of energy derivatives including, crude oil, natural gas, petrochemicals, etc., formulates business rules, implements self-regulation, publishes market information, and provides technology, venue, and facility services.

On 26 March 2018, the INE launched crude oil futures.[2]

13.1.2 The Dalian Commodity Exchange

Founded in 1993, the Dalian Commodity Exchange (DCE) is a futures exchange approved by the State Council and regulated by China Securities Regulatory Commission (CSRC). Over the years, through orderly operation and stable development, DCE has already become the world's largest agricultural futures market as well as the largest futures market for oils, plastics, coal, metallurgical coke, and iron ore.

A total of 17 futures contracts and 1 option contract have been listed for trading on DCE, which include No.1 soybean, soybean meal, corn, No.2 soybean, soybean oil, linear low density polyethylene (LLDPE), RBD palm olein, polyvinyl chloride (PVC), metallurgical coke, coking coal, iron ore, egg, fibreboard, blockboard, polypropylene (PP), corn starch futures, ethylene glycol, and soybean meal options.[3]

13.1.3 The Zhengzhou Commodity Exchange

Zhengzhou Commodity Exchange (ZCE) was founded on 12 October 1990. With the approval of the State Council, ZCE was established as China's first pilot futures market. After two years of the successful operation of a spot market, ZCE officially launched futures trading on 28 May 1993.

---

[1]Source: www.shfe.com.cn/en/.
[2]Source: www.ine.cn/en/about/simintro/.
[3]Source: www.dce.com.cn/DCE/.

To date, ZCE has listed 18 futures products and one options product, including common wheat, strong gluten wheat, early rice, late indica rice, japonica rice, cotton, cotton yarn, rapeseed, rapeseed oil, rapeseed meal, white sugar, apple, thermal coal, methanol, pure terephthalic acid (PTA), flat glass, manganese silicon, ferrosilicon futures, and white sugar options, covering crucial fields of national economy including agricultural, energy, chemical, construction materials, and metallurgical industries.[4]

13.2 The Size of the Chinese Commodity Exchanges

The total aggregate open interest for the exchange as shown in Figure 13.1, at the end of 2018, converted to USD is just under $200 billion.

Figure 13.1 shows the breakdown of aggregate open interest between the exchanges. Chinese exchanges double-count volume and open interest to reflect the long and short side of a trade. The China Futures Association counts only one side of the transaction, however, which is the convention with most international exchanges. All volume and open interest data from the exchanges have consequently been halved in the analysis in this chapter.

Volume and open interest figures for Chinese Commodity Futures compared to non-Chinese exchanges is often significantly higher. One of the reasons is due to the small contract sizes. For example, the sizes of copper contracts listed on the SHFE and the London Metal Exchange (LME) are 5mt and 25mt respectively. Comparisons between volume and open interest are therefore often done in terms of dollar values.

Table 13.1 is a list of the commodity futures and their symbols used in the analyses in this chapter. Wire steel (WRT) on the SHFE, late indica rice futures (IRL), wheat, strong gluten (VN), japonica rice futures (ZVB), cotton yarn future (QCY), regular wheat (VOO), early long grain non-glutinous rice (IRI) and rapeseed (ZRC) on the ZCE and corn (AC), polypropylene (PYL),

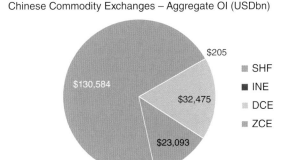

FIGURE 13.1 Aggregate open interest in USD by exchanges – end 2018. This chart is not shown on the website.
Source: Based on data from Bloomberg.

[4]Source: http://english.czce.com.cn/.

TABLE 13.1	List of the Chinese commodity symbols used in the chapter.		
RBT	Steel rebar	IRE	Zhengzhou ferrosilicon
AA	Aluminium	IRL	Zhengzhou late indica rice
SAI	Silver	VN	Zhengzhou wheat, strong gluten
BIT	Bitumen	ZVB	Zhengzhou japonica rice
ROC	Hot-rolled coil	QCY	Cotton yarn
CU	Copper	VOO	Zhengzhou regular wheat
RT	Rubber	IRI	Zhengzhou early 1. grain NG rice
ZNA	Zinc	ZRC	Zhengzhou rapeseed
XII	Nickel	AE	Soymeal
AUA	Gold	AC	Corn
FO	Fuel oil	IOE	Iron ore
KSP	Bleached softwood kraft pulp	SH	Soybean oil
PBL	Lead	PAL	Palm oil
XOO	Tin	PYL	Polypropylene
WRT	Wire steel	POL	Polyethylene
SCP	Crude oil	KEE	Coke
PT	Zhengzhou pure terephthalic acid	PVC	Polyvinyl chloride
ZME	Methanol	CKC	Coking coal
CB	Zhengzhou white sugar	LGE	Ethylene glycol
ZRR	Rapeseed meal	DCE	Egg
VV	Zhengzhou cotton	BP	No.2 soybean
TRC	Zhengzhou thermal coal	DCS	Corn starch
ZRO	Zhengzhou rapeseed oil	AK	Soybean, No.1
APW	Zhengzhou apple	FRE	Fibreboard
FGL	Zhengzhou glass	BLC	Blockboard
IMR	Zhengzhou silicon manganese		

Source: Based on data from Bloomberg.

polyethylene (POL), PVC (PVC), ethylene glycol (LGE), corn starch (DCS), fibreboard (FRE), and blockboard (BLC) on the DCE have been excluded from most the analysis in the chapter, as their open interest was less than 10,000 contracts at the end of 2018.[5]

Figure 13.2, Figure 13.3, and Figure 13.4 show the breakdown of notional value in USD, open interest in contracts, and volume in contracts respectively, for all commodity futures in China with an aggregate open interest of more than 10,000 contracts at the end of 2018.

Nickel, listed on the SHFE, has the greatest notional value in USD, followed by rubber and zinc, both on the SHFE.

In terms of open interest – a good measure of liquidity, steel rebar on the SHFE, followed by methanol and pure terephthalic acid on the ZCE, are the largest markets. In terms of volume, also a good measure of liquidity, steel rebar on the SHFE, followed by soymeal on the DCE and pure terephthalic acid on the ZCE, have the highest volume.

---

[5]The notional value for a commodity is calculated by multiplying the average open interest (halved) for the week ending 21 December 2018, by the tick value and the contract price on 21 December 2018.

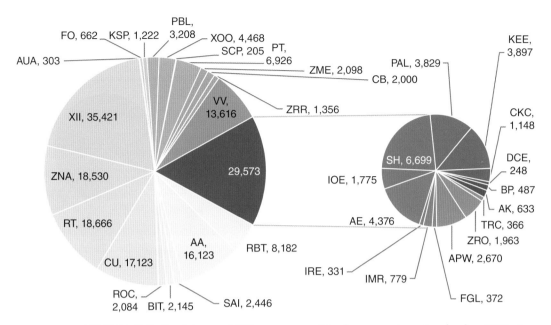

FIGURE 13.2 Breakdown of Chinese commodities by aggregate notional value (USDm) – end 2018.

Commodity symbols: As listed in Table 13.1.

This chart is not shown on the website.

Source: Based on data from Bloomberg.

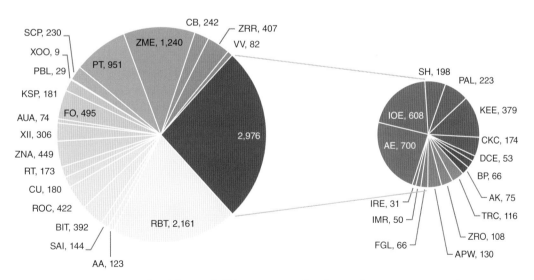

FIGURE 13.3 Breakdown of Chinese commodity futures by aggregate open interest (contracts) – end 2018.

Commodity symbols: As listed in Table 13.1.

This chart is not shown on the website.

Source: Based on data from Bloomberg.

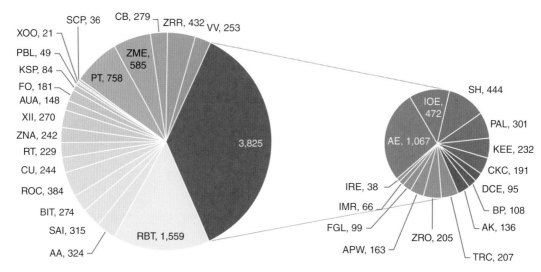

FIGURE 13.4 Breakdown of Chinese commodities by aggregate volume – end 2018.
Commodity symbols: As listed in Table 13.1.
This chart is not shown on the website.
Source: Based on data from Bloomberg.

13.3 Speculative vs Hedging Activity in Chinese Commodities

There is no equivalent CFTC Commitment of Traders (COT) report for Chinese exchanges, so to try and understand the level of speculative and hedging activity, alternative solutions are required.[6]

In Sections 12.1.3 and 12.1.4 the Build ratio and the Speculation ratio were defined as a way of better understanding flow patterns and trading activity in commodities. The Build ratio measures how much of the daily volume has been translated into open interest – a measure of trading efficiency. The Speculation ratio shows the volume traded every day as a proportion of open interest and is a way of normalising volume for cross-commodity comparisons. Markets with a higher (lower) Speculation ratio are those often associated with higher (lower) trading activity, which is then often anecdotally associated with higher (lower) intraday trading activity (and hence speculation), or lower (higher) hedging activity as discussed in Section 12.1.4 and Section 12.1.5.

Figure 13.5 shows the Speculation ratio (grey columns) for all the Chinese commodity markets relative to their 52-week average (red bar) at the end of 2018. The recently launched crude oil contract (SCP) on the INE has the highest ratio at approximately 640% – a little below its 52-week average. This means that the daily volume is on average 6.4 times greater than the open interest. No other commodity has a ratio similar to this. This suggests a very high proportion of intraday trading.

---

[6]The only positioning related data is the rankings data released by the SHFE. This is covered in Section 2.3.2.

The Speculation ratio for nearly all commodities is in line with their 52-week averages, except for fuel oil and bleached softwood kraft pulp on the SHF and apples on the ZCF that are well below their averages. Such a shift could be driven by a fall in trading volumes or simply the fact that positions are being held for longer periods of time – perhaps a function of increased hedging activity. The current Speculation ratio for methanol is above its 52-week average, indicating an elevated level of trading activity.

Commodities with a high Speculation ratio and a low Build ratio are likely to have higher (lower) levels of speculation (hedging). By plotting the Speculation ratio against the Build ratio in a bubble chart as shown in Figure 13.6, where the size of the bubble is a function of the notional value of the market in USD billions, these commodities can be easily identified. Data is based on the 52-week average up until 21 December 2018.

Due to the clustering of the blue bubbles, they have been expanded in Figure 13.7 for clarity.

Crude oil (SCP) is towards the top left of Figure 13.6 with the smallest bubble of all 40 commodities, indicating the relative size of the market relative to the other commodities. It has a Speculation ratio of 690%, a Build ratio of 1%, and a total notional value based on prices at the end of 2018 of $195m. These ratios mean that each day on average $1,345m (690% of $195m) trades, with only 1% of the volume being translated into open interest on average.

Silicon manganese (IMR) on the ZCE has the highest Build ratio and a low Speculation ratio, suggesting a relatively lower level of speculation and a higher level of hedging activity.

In Figure 13.7, Steel Rebar (RBT) in the SHFE is the largest market, with a notional value based on prices at the end of 2018 of $8.2bn. It has a Speculation ratio of 126% and a Build ratio of 2%. This means that each day on average $10.3bn (126% of $8.2bn) trades, with 2% of the volume being translated into open interest on average.

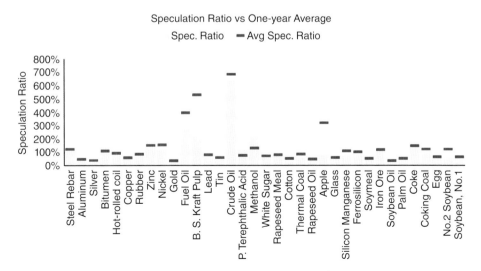

FIGURE 13.5 Speculation ratio vs One-year average – 21 December 2018.
This chart is not shown on the website.
Source: Based on data from Bloomberg.

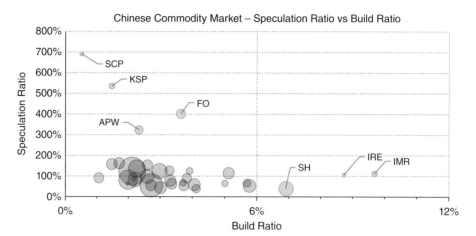

FIGURE 13.6 Speculation ratio vs Build ratio – 52-week average 2018.
Commodity symbols: As listed in Table 13.1.
This chart is not shown on the website.
Source: Based on data from Bloomberg.

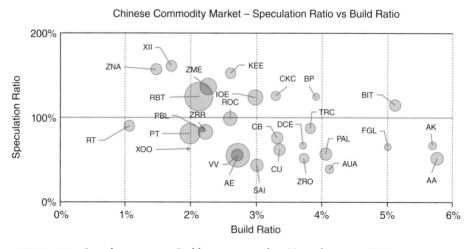

FIGURE 13.7 Speculation ratio vs Build ratio (zoomed) – 52-week average 2018.
Commodity symbols: As listed in Table 13.1.
This chart is not shown on the website.
Source: Based on data from Bloomberg.

13.4 The Flow Cube and Build Ratio in Chinese Commodities

The Flow Cube, introduced in Chapter 12, organises and quantifies changes in price, open interest, and volume into a framework to define the type of trading activity. This can be done over any timeframe (daily, weekly, monthly) and for any commodity on an aggregate or individual futures contract basis. The approach means that the recent trading activity in a commodity, or the trading activity at specific points down its forward curve, can be defined and then in combination with the Build ratio, defined in Section 12.1.3, quantified in terms of its efficiency.

For the Chinese commodities in particular, where there are no COT equivalent reports on positioning, the Flow Cube is a useful way to get some insight into trading activity and flow patterns.[7]

Figure 13.8 is the same as Figure 12.4 and shows the flow profile for all commodities in the week ending 21 December 2018. The height of each column is a function of the Build ratio for the week, with the horizontal black bar representing the average Build ratio calculated over the last year. The colours are based on the Flow Cube classifications defined in Figure 12.2.

The profile across the commodity landscape is highly differentiated, with no common profile across the asset class which could be an indication of lower speculation. When speculative flows are very high, differentiation between the commodities is lower and correlation tends to increase, as trading activity is similar in each market. This was particularly evident in 2016 with the run-up in speculative volumes and prices for many Chinese commodities.

Focusing on copper on the SHFE, trading is characterised by weak long liquidation (WLL) at a rate slightly more than its one-year average.

Applying the Flow Cube to the forward curve for copper, as shown in Figure 13.9, allows the aggregate flow profile to be disaggregated across contracts. The January 2019 month contract shows the weak long liquidation, invariably linked to expiry-related activity, but further down the curve in the April 2019 and June 2019 contracts there is strong short building (SSB).

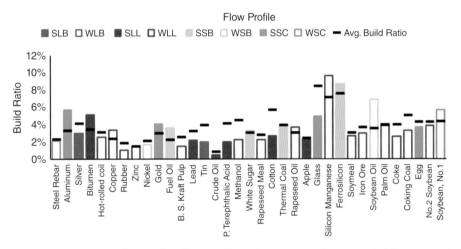

FIGURE 13.8 Commodity market flow profile with current and average Build ratio (week ending 21st December 2018).
Trading activity symbols: As listed in Table 12.2.
This chart is not shown on the website.
Source: Based on data from Bloomberg.

[7]See footnote 2 in Chapter 12.

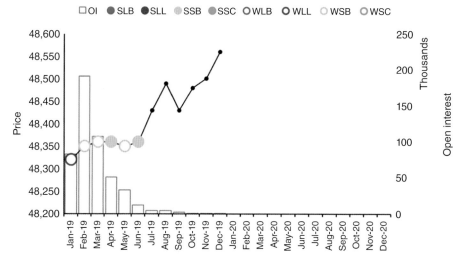

FIGURE 13.9 Flow profile for copper (SHFE) – week ending 21 December 2018.
Trading activity symbols: As listed in Table 12.2.
This chart is not shown on the website.
Source: Based on data from Bloomberg.

13.5 The OBOS Framework and the Speculation Ratio

The OBOS framework, introduced in Chapter 8, defines commodities at the intersection of extreme long (short) speculative positioning as Overbought (Oversold).

The core philosophy behind the OBOS framework is that all speculative positions need to be unwound before expiry, and whilst the framework cannot predict when these positions will be unwound, extreme long (short) positions that occur when prices are also at an extreme high (low) are often unwound faster, which can have a disproportionate effect on prices.

As explained in Section 13.3 there is no equivalent CFTC Commitment of Traders (COT) report for Chinese exchanges, so to make use of the OBOS framework and philosophy, an alternative measure is needed. By substituting the Positioning Component for the Speculative ratio, a proxy for speculation, commodities at the intersection of extremes in price and extremes in the Speculation ratio can be identified.

The philosophy behind this approach lies in the view that when commodity prices are at an extreme and the Speculation ratio is extreme, meaning that the volume traded every day as a proportion of open interest is extreme, and likely dominated by a high level of speculative activity, the vulnerability of prices retracing or reversing is higher, on the basis that there is little substance behind the move. This is a big assumption, but if the move was legitimate, or fundamentally driven, for example, it is likely that there would be more hedging activity and the Speculation ratio would be unlikely to be at such an extreme level.

13.5.1 The OBOS Speculation Ratio Indicator

The framework consists of two components: a Positioning Component and a Pricing Component. Each commodity is then plotted within the framework.

The Positioning Component, initially defined in Section 8.2.1, uses the Speculation ratio as defined in Section 12.1.4. There are no long and short components to the Speculation ratio, so only one Positioning Component is required. This is like the OBOS Net Concentration indicator in Section 8.6.1. The Pricing Component remains the same as defined in Section 8.2.2. A one-year rolling range is also used.

The formula for the Positioning Component is adapted as follows:

$$Positioning\ Component\ (\%) = \frac{\left(current\ SR - \min\left(SR_{range}\right)\right)}{\left(\max\left(SR_{range}\right) - \min\left(SR_{range)}\right)\right)}$$

where

$$SR = Speculation\ ratio$$

$$range = one\text{-}year\ rolling$$

Figure 13.10 shows the OBOS Speculative ratio indicator for the Chinese commodity landscape on 21 December 2018.

The red (green) box are the Overbought and Oversold boxes at the intersection of extreme price strength (weakness) and extreme levels in the Speculation ratio.

No commodities are in the Overbought (red) box, but palm oil (PAL) on the DCE is in the Oversold (green) box.

The two black boxes can also be useful. They indicate intersections of high (low) prices in the top (bottom) black box when the Speculation ratio is low. This suggests a lower level of speculative activity, which could indicate that positions are less vulnerable to price reversals.

This approach is similar to the OBOS framework in Chapter 8 and the advanced OBOS analysis in Chapter 9, but is clearly limited in the absence of comparable positioning data. The indicator is useful as a tool to identify potential price risks in a clear and intuitive way.

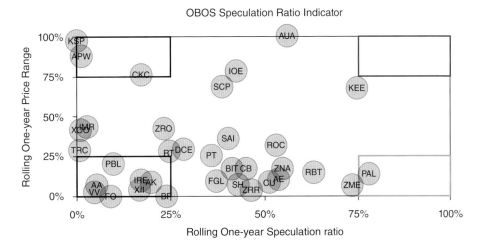

FIGURE 13.10 The OBOS Speculation ratio indicator using one-year rolling ranges. Commodity symbols: As listed in Table 13.1.
This chart is not shown on the website.
Source: Based on data from Bloomberg.

Reference

Mark Keenan, Michael Haigh, and Malavika Dinaker (2017), 'Commodity Compass – Chinese vs Western Commodity Markets – Key Questions and Insights'. Société Générale (SG) Cross Asset Research – Commodities Group. www.sgmarkets.com/.

CHAPTER 14

Machine Learning — A Machine's Perspective on Positioning

Chapter objectives

In this chapter, decision trees and random forests are introduced as ways of uncovering relationships between changes in positioning and changes in commodity prices.

Tree-based learning algorithms, which include decision trees and random forests, are amongst the most-used machine learning methods. The objective is to identify which aspects of positioning are the most useful in helping to understand commodity markets from a machine's perspective.

Machine learning applied to positioning data to predict prices is particularly useful in the analysis of positioning data, with 'feature importance' a powerful way of identifying new patterns and new relationships in positioning.

These are insights that can help improve how other positioning signals, indicators, and models are interpreted and used.

14.1 Introduction to Machine Learning (ML)

> Machine learning (ML) is the scientific study of algorithms and statistical models that computer systems use to effectively perform a specific task without using explicit instructions, relying on patterns and inference instead. It is seen as a subset of AI.
>
> Machine-learning algorithms build a mathematical model of sample data, known as 'training data', in order to make predictions or decisions without being explicitly programmed to perform the task.
>
> Machine-learning algorithms are used in the applications of email filtering, detection of network intruders, and computer vision, where it is infeasible to develop an algorithm of specific instructions for performing the task.
>
> Machine learning is closely related to computational statistics, which focuses on making predictions using computers. The study of mathematical optimisation delivers methods, theory, and application domains to the field of machine learning.
>
> Data mining is a field of study within machine learning and focuses on exploratory data analysis through unsupervised learning. In its application across business problems, machine learning is also referred to as predictive analytics.
>
> *Source:* https://en.wikipedia.org/wiki/Machine_learning.

The main objective of machine learning (ML) is to uncover predictive relationships within datasets. It is broadly divided into two areas: supervised learning and unsupervised learning. In supervised learning, an algorithm is first calibrated (or trained) on a dataset to identify relationships between a group of input variables (X) and an output variable (Y). In unsupervised learning, the algorithm seeks to identify patterns within the input variables.

In this chapter, decision trees (classification and regressions trees) and the random forest algorithm (classification and regression random forests) are introduced as ways of uncovering relationships between changes in positioning and changes in commodity prices – specifically to learn which aspects of positioning are the most useful in helping to better understand commodity markets from a machine-learning perspective.[1]

Tree-based learning algorithms – including decision trees and random forests – are amongst the most-used learning methods and can map non-linear relationships easily.[2] One advantage of ML is that the results are often easily interpreted and can easily be used alongside other signals, indicators, models, and analyses to provide additional/alternative insight in Positioning Analysis.

To generate the decision trees, to produce the random forest, and to do the feature importance analysis in this chapter, the application XLSTAT is used. XLSTAT was chosen due to its ease of use, its stability, and its detailed help files. Furthermore, to use XLSTAT, no programming knowledge is required, and it runs within the Excel application as an add-in. Python is an excellent alternative, and arguably one of the leading programming languages in ML, but it naturally requires some programming skill.[3]

---

[1]Decision trees where the target variable is discrete are called classification trees. Decision trees where the target variable can take continuous values are called regression trees.

[2]Non-linear relationships are where the change in one entity does not correspond with constant change in another entity.

[3]www.xlstat.com/en/.

14.2 Decision Trees

The objective of this section is to provide a full explanation, in a series of stages and examples, of how decision trees are constructed and how they can be used in Positioning Analysis.

A decision tree is a supervised learning algorithm designed to predict an output variable, for example the weekly return of crude oil (WTI). The output variable can also be called the target variable.

The function of a decision tree is to split the output dataset (the price returns) into two or more subsets, for example positive and negative returns, using specific decision rules derived from the input dataset, for example changes in positioning data. The variables contained in the input dataset are known as the features.

The decision tree identifies the most differentiating features in the input dataset, as well as the threshold values that best split the output dataset into the most homogeneous subsets.

14.2.1 Decision Trees Using Binary Data

Figure 14.1 gives a simple example of a binary decision tree set-up to predict whether prices of crude oil (WTI) increased or decreased over the week based on binary changes in MML and MMS positions over that week. The decision tree identifies the variable (either MML or MMS) that best separates the weeks where prices increased from those where prices decreased. The underlying algorithm used here only uses two binary features: whether MML or MMS increased or decreased their positions.

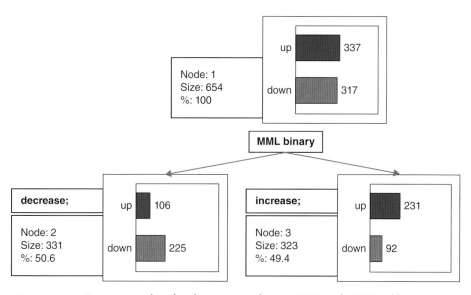

FIGURE 14.1 Decision tree based on binary input changes (MML and MMS) and binary output changes (WTI prices).
Source: Based on data from Bloomberg.
Output taken directly from XLSTAT.

The underlying data consists of 654 weeks (June 2006 to December 2018) of MM positioning data and price data. The weeks run from Tuesday to Tuesday, to be aligned with the COT release schedule, and prices are therefore contemporaneous to the positioning data.

The algorithm then identifies the 'best question to ask' to generate the most homologous (most uniform) child nodes. The question is: whether MMLs (as opposed to MMSs) changed their position. The underlying algorithm is explained fully in Section 14.2.2.

Observations from the decision tree diagram in Figure 14.1 include:

- Node 1 (also referred to as the root node) shows the 654 weeks divided into 337 weeks where crude oil (WTI) prices increased and 317 weeks where they decreased. It is therefore also called an up-node.

- Node 2 shows that out of the 654 weeks, MMLs decreased their position in 331 weeks. Out of those 331 weeks, crude oil (WTI) prices rose in 106 of the weeks (32%) and fell in 225 of the weeks (68%). It is therefore also called a down-node.

- Node 3 shows that out of the 654 weeks, MMLs increased their position in 323 weeks. Out of those 323 weeks, crude oil (WTI) prices rose in 231 of the weeks (72%) and fell in 92 of the weeks (28%).

Table 14.1 shows the confusion matrix, a table displaying the number of successful and unsuccessfully-classified observations for each of the categories, shows that 69.72% of points in the entire dataset of 654 weeks were correctly classified by this tree – a good percentage. Simply put, this means that increases (decreases) in MML position are associated with up (down) moves in crude oil (WTI) prices.

Figure 14.2 shows a similar decision tree, but for NG. Here the tree, set up in the same way as the tree in Figure 14.1, identifies the 'best question' to ask as to whether MMSs (as opposed to MMLs) changed their position.

14.2.2 The Decision Tree Algorithm – How Does It Work?

The decision tree in Figure 14.1 splits the tree according to whether MMLs changed their position, whereas for natural gas in Figure 14.2, it was the opposite, asking whether MMSs changed their position.

The criterion used here to split the tree is the Gini index. It is a measure of dispersion within a dataset and measures the degree of homogeneity. A value of 0 means the dataset is perfectly homogeneous, while values near 0.5 represent a heterogeneous dataset (0.5 is the highest value).

TABLE 14.1 Confusion matrix based on binary input changes (MML and MMS) and binary output changes (crude oil (WTI) prices).

Confusion matrix

from\to	up	down	Total	% correct
up	231	106	337	68.546
down	92	225	317	70.978
Total	323	331	654	69.72477

Source: Based on data from Bloomberg.
Output taken directly from XLSTAT.

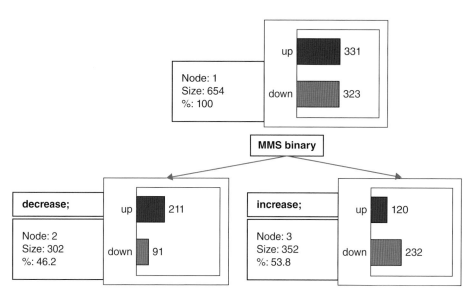

FIGURE 14.2 Decision tree based on binary input changes (MML and MMS) and binary output changes (natural gas prices).
Source: Based on data from Bloomberg.
Output taken directly from XLSTAT.

In this binary example, where prices either increased or decreased, a homogeneous sample would consist solely of price increases or price decreases, whereas a heterogeneous set would consist of a mix of price increases and price decreases.

The Gini index is calculated as follows:

$$Gini = 1 - \left(\left(\frac{number\ of\ price\ increases}{number\ of\ observations} \right)^2 + \left(\frac{number\ of\ price\ decreases}{number\ of\ observations} \right)^2 \right)$$

The Gini index for the root node in Figure 14.1 is calculated to be:

$$Gini = 1 - \left(\left(\frac{337}{654} \right)^2 + \left(\frac{317}{654} \right)^2 \right) = 0.500$$

To then split a branch into two, all the possible Gini scores of all the possible splits are calculated. In this example there are two possible splits, by changes in MMLs or by changes in MMSs. The split that yields the two branches with the highest degree of homogeneity on average, computed as the lowest weighted average Gini score, is chosen.

For example, after a split by changes in MMLs, two branches containing 331 and 323 observations are generated. The Gini score of the left branch is 0.435 while the Gini score of the right branch is 0.407. As a result, the weighted average Gini score is:

$$Weighted\ Average\ Gini = \frac{(331 * 0.435) + (323 * 0.407)}{(331 + 323)} = 0.421$$

Splitting by changes in MMS would have generated two branches (this is not shown, but can be calculated from the underlying data), each containing 333 (left branch) and 321 (right branch) observations. The Gini score of the left branch would be 0.444, while the Gini score for the right branch would be 0.460. Here the weighted average Gini score would be:

$$Weighted\ Average\ Gini = \frac{(333*0.444)+(321*0.460)}{(333+321)} = 0.452$$

As the weighted average Gini score is lower in the first case (0.421 is less than 0.452) and therefore more homogeneous, the algorithm decides to split the data by looking at MML positions.[4]

14.2.3 Validating the Tree

In the decision trees above, the entire dataset of 654 weeks has been used. To validate the robustness of the tree in Figure 14.1, it must be tested on unseen data.

The approach is to first 'train' the algorithm on some portion of the data and then 'test' it on another portion of data. The testing portion could, for example, be the last 52 weeks of the dataset and the training portion the 602 weeks before that.

Figure 14.3 shows a new decision tree trained only on the first 602 weeks of data (the training dataset).

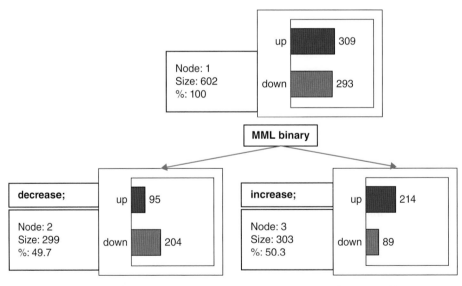

FIGURE 14.3 Decision tree based on binary input changes (MML and MMS) and binary output changes (WTI prices) – training dataset 602 weeks, testing dataset 52 weeks.
Source: Based on data from Bloomberg.
Output taken directly from XLSTAT.

---

[4]Besides the Gini index, other decision criteria exist, including some based on information theory (entropy) and intra-group variance. Only the Gini index is used in the chapter.

This tree identifies the same question to ask first as the tree in Figure 14.1 – whether MMLs increased or decreased their position.

Applying the decision tree to the last 52 weeks in the dataset (the testing dataset), there were 38 weeks (73%) where the algorithm correctly predicted price direction by asking whether MMLs increased or decreased their position.

When two datasets are used, two confusion matrices can now be generated; one for the training set (602 weeks) and one for the testing set (52 weeks). These are shown in Table 14.2. In the training set, 69.44% of the points were correctly classified, and in the testing set, 73.10% of the points were correctly predicted – an improvement of a few percentage points.

14.2.4 Decision Trees Using Non-binary Data

Only binary data has been used so far – either an increase or a decrease in MM positioning and whether prices were up or down. The algorithm also works with non-binary data, deciding not only which feature to best split the tree with, but also at what threshold.

With greater possibilities, non-binary trees can grow exponentially during training as they fit the data, and ultimately, without any constraints, they will fit all the data as every scenario would be captured. If they grow too big, however, they become overfitted, and they risk performing poorly when applied to testing samples. One solution is to cut the tree before it gets too big.

Figure 14.4 shows the non-binary decision tree to predict whether prices of crude oil (WTI) increased or decreased over the week based on changes in MML and MMS positions over that week. The tree is cut at three levels of depth. The data has again been divided into a training set (602 weeks) and a testing set (52 weeks), as explained in Section 14.2.3. The first question the decision tree asks now is whether MMs changes their position by more or less than -794 contracts.

TABLE 14.2 Confusion matrix based on binary input changes (MML and MMS) and binary output changes (WTI prices) – training dataset 602 weeks, testing dataset 52 weeks.

Confusion matrix (training)				
from\to	up	down	Total	% correct
up	214	95	309	69.256
down	89	204	293	69.625
Total	303	299	602	69.435

Confusion matrix (testing)				
from\to	up	down	Total	% correct
up	17	11	28	60.714
down	3	21	24	87.500
Total	20	32	52	73.077

Source: Based on data from Bloomberg.
Output taken directly from XLSTAT.

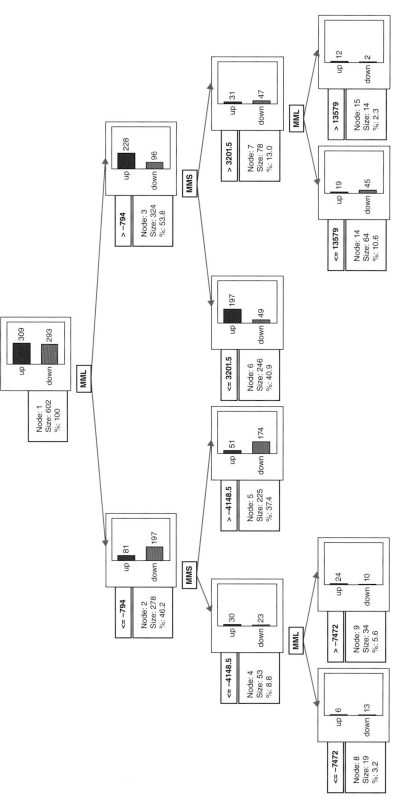

FIGURE 14.4 Decision tree based on non-binary input changes (MML and MMS) and binary output changes (WTI prices) – training dataset 602 weeks, testing dataset 52 weeks.

Source: Based on data from Bloomberg.
Output taken directly from XLSTAT.

Focusing on the first three nodes in the tree:

- Node 1 in Figure 14.4 shows the 602 weeks divided into 309 weeks where crude oil (WTI) prices increased and 293 weeks where they decreased (this is the same as Figure 14.3).

- Node 2 shows that out of the 602 weeks, MMLs changed their position by less than or equal to -794 contracts in 278 weeks. Out of those 278 weeks, crude oil (WTI) prices rose in 81 of the weeks and fell in 197 of the weeks.

- Node 3 shows that out of the 602 weeks, MMLs changed their position by more than -794 contracts in 324 weeks. Out of those 324 weeks, crude oil (WTI) prices rose in 228 of the weeks and fell in 96 of the weeks.

The complete tree structure for Figure 14.4 is shown in Table 14.3. This provides a detailed description of key statistics and actions at each node in the tree.

The tree rules for Figure 14.4 are shown in Table 14.4. This provides a description of the actions at each node.

The confusion matrices in Table 14.5 show that for the training set (602 weeks), 77.24% of the points were correctly classified, and in the testing set, 69.23% of the points were correctly predicted. For the training dataset, the results are higher than the binary tree in Table 14.2, but a little lower for the testing dataset. This could suggest that merely the direction of MM activity

TABLE 14.3 Tree structure based on non-binary input changes (MML and MMS) and binary output changes (WTI prices) – training dataset 602 weeks, testing dataset 52 weeks.

Tree structure

Nodes	Objects	%	Improvement	Purity	Split variable	Values	Predicted values
Node 1	602	100.00%	50.060	51.33%			up
Node 2	278	46.18%	9.225	70.86%	MML	<= -794	down
Node 3	324	53.82%	18.483	70.37%	MML	> -794	up
Node 4	53	8.80%	3.011	56.60%	MMS	<= -4,148.5	up
Node 5	225	37.38%	3.639	77.33%	MMS	> -4,148.5	down
Node 6	246	40.86%	4.094	80.08%	MMS	<= 3,201.5	up
Node 7	78	12.96%	6.178	60.26%	MMS	> 3,201.5	down
Node 8	19	3.16%		68.42%	MML	<= -7,472	down
Node 9	34	5.65%		70.59%	MML	> -7,472	up
Node 14	64	10.63%		70.31%	MML	<= 13,579	down
Node 15	14	2.33%		85.71%	MML	> 13,579	up

Source: Based on data from Bloomberg.
Output taken directly from XLSTAT.

TABLE 14.4 Decision rules based on non-binary input changes (MML and MMS) and binary output changes (WTI prices) – training dataset 602 weeks, testing dataset 52 weeks.

Tree rules

Nodes	Price binary (Pred.)	Rules
Node 1	up	
Node 2	down	If MML <= -794 then Price Tues binary = down in 46.2% of cases[a]
Node 3	up	If MML > -794 then Price Tues binary = up in 53.8% of cases
Node 4	up	If MML <= -794 and MMS <= -4,148.5 then Price Tues binary = up in 8.8% of cases
Node 5	down	If MML <= -794 and MMS > -4,148.5 then Price Tues binary = down in 37.4% of cases
Node 6	up	If MML > -794 and MMS <= 3,201.5 then Price Tues binary = up in 40.9% of cases
Node 7	down	If MML > -794 and MMS > 3,201.5 then Price Tues binary = down in 13.0% of cases
Node 8	down	If MML <= -794 and MMS <= -4,148.5 and MML <= -7,472 then Price Tues binary = down in 3.2% of cases
Node 9	up	If MML <= -794 and MMS <= -4,148.5 and MML > -7,472 then Price Tues binary = up in 5.6% of cases
Node 14	down	If MML > -794 and MMS > 3,201.5 and MML <= 13,579 then Price Tues binary = down in 10.6% of cases
Node 15	up	If MML > -794 and MMS > 3,201.5 and MML > 13,579 then Price Tues binary = up in 2.3% of cases

[a]The percentage cases represents proportion of the sample size at that node.
'Price Tues' is the price on Tuesday based on the second nearby futures contract.
Source: Based on data from Bloomberg.
Output taken directly from XLSTAT.

TABLE 14.5 Confusion matrix based on non-binary input changes (MML and MMS) and binary output changes (WTI prices) – training dataset 602 weeks, testing dataset 52 weeks.

Confusion matrix (training)

from\to	up	down	Total	% correct
up	233	76	309	75.405
down	61	232	293	79.181
Total	294	308	602	77.243

Confusion matrix (testing)

from\to	up	down	Total	% correct
up	14	14	28	50.000
down	2	22	24	91.667
Total	16	36	52	69.231

Source: Based on data from Bloomberg.
Output taken directly from XLSTAT.

is sufficient in predicting prices, and adding threshold information does not add any significant incremental value.

The robustness of decision trees as an analytical tool is covered in Section 14.4 about random forests.

14.2.4.1 Extending the Tree to All Trader Groups The decision tree in Section 14.2.4 uses only the MML and MMS groups as features. Table 14.6 shows the tree structure after including all trader groups, with the corresponding confusion matrix shown in Table 14.7. The full decision tree diagram is not shown in the interest of space.

The initial nodes within the tree are still split along MM features, with the SD category featuring at node 10 onwards. Overall this shows that the algorithm still chooses the MM group as the most important feature in predicting price direction.

TABLE 14.6 Tree structure based on non-binary input changes (all groups) and binary output changes (WTI prices) – training dataset 602 weeks, testing dataset 52 weeks.

Tree structure

Nodes	Objects	%	Improvement	Purity	Split variable	Values	Predicted values
Node 1	602	100.00%	50.060	51.33%			up
Node 2	278	46.18%	9.225	70.86%	MML	<= -794	down
Node 3	324	53.82%	18.483	70.37%	MML	> -794	up
Node 4	53	8.80%	3.011	56.60%	MMS	<= -4,148.5	up
Node 5	225	37.38%	4.090	77.33%	MMS	> -4,148.5	down
Node 6	246	40.86%	5.383	80.08%	MMS	<= 3,201.5	up
Node 7	78	12.96%	7.109	60.26%	MMS	> 3,201.5	down
Node 8	19	3.16%		68.42%	MML	<= -7,472	down
Node 9	34	5.65%		70.59%	MML	> -7,472	up
Node 10	17	2.82%		52.94%	SDS	<= -15,562.5	up
Node 11	208	34.55%		79.81%	SDS	> -15,562.5	down
Node 14	26	4.32%		92.31%	SDS	<= -4,014	down
Node 15	52	8.64%		55.77%	SDS	> -4,014	up

Source: Based on data from Bloomberg.
Output taken directly from XLSTAT.

TABLE 14.7 Confusion matrix based on non-binary input changes (all groups) and binary output changes (WTI prices) – training dataset 602 weeks, testing dataset 52 weeks.

Confusion matrix (training)

from\to	up	down	Total	% correct
up	259	50	309	83.819
down	90	203	293	69.283
Total	349	253	602	76.744

Confusion matrix (testing)

from\to	up	down	Total	% correct
up	17	11	28	60.714
down	12	12	24	50.000
Total	29	23	52	55.769

Source: Based on data from Bloomberg.
Output taken directly from XLSTAT.

Whilst the algorithm shows the MM group to be the most important feature, it is also important to understand that these results do not infer causality – especially when the data are set up in
a contemporaneous way (as in all the examples so far). Just because the trees mostly identify the
MM group as an important feature in predicting prices, this does not mean that MMs are driving
prices. It could easily mean that MMs are following prices.

Looking at natural gas and copper, a similar profile emerges with the MM group continuing to
be the most important feature. Table 14.8 shows the tree structure and Table 14.9 the confusion
matrix for all trader groups for natural gas.

Table 14.10 shows the tree structure and Table 14.11 the confusion matrix for all trader groups
for copper.

As mentioned above, the robustness of decision trees as an analytical tool is covered in Section 14.4 about random forests.

TABLE 14.8 Tree structure based on non-binary input changes (all groups) and binary output
changes (natural gas prices) – training dataset 602 weeks, testing dataset 52 weeks.

Tree structure

Nodes	Objects	%	Improvement	Purity	Split variable	Values	Predicted values
Node 1	602	100.00%	41.179	50.00%			up
Node 2	209	34.72%	9.320	75.12%	MMS	<= -3,631	up
Node 3	393	65.28%	12.211	63.36%	MMS	> -3,631	down

Source: Based on data from Bloomberg.
Output taken directly from XLSTAT.

TABLE 14.9 Confusion matrix based on non-binary input changes (all groups) and binary output
changes (natural gas prices) – training dataset 602 weeks, testing dataset 52 weeks.

Confusion matrix (training)

from\to	up	down	Total	% correct
down	157	144	301	52.159
Total	52	249	301	82.724
up	209	393	602	67.442

Confusion matrix (testing)

from\to	up	down	Total	% correct
up	20	10	30	66.667
down	5	17	22	77.273
Total	25	27	52	71.154

Source: Based on data from Bloomberg.
Output taken directly from XLSTAT.

TABLE 14.10 Tree structure based on non-binary input changes (all groups) and binary output changes (copper prices) – training dataset 602 weeks, testing dataset 52 weeks.

Tree structure

Nodes	Objects	%	Improvement	Purity	Split variable	Values	Predicted values
Node 1	602	100.00%	60.294	52.16%			up
Node 2	251	41.69%	17.921	74.50%	MML	<= -241.5	down
Node 3	351	58.31%	18.510	71.23%	MML	> -241.5	up
Node 4	31	5.15%	3.433	77.42%	MMS	<= -1,778.5	up
Node 5	220	36.54%	4.188	81.82%	MMS	> -1,778.5	down
Node 6	282	46.84%	5.142	79.43%	MMS	<= 1,227	up
Node 7	69	11.46%	6.652	62.32%	MMS	> 1,227	down
Node 14	63	10.47%		68.25%	SDS	<= 1,373.5	down
Node 15	6	1.00%		100.00%	SDS	> 1,373.5	up

Source: Based on data from Bloomberg.
Output taken directly from XLSTAT.

TABLE 14.11 Confusion matrix based on non-binary input changes (all groups) and binary output changes (copper prices) – training dataset 602 weeks, testing dataset 52 weeks.

Confusion matrix (training)

from\to	up	down	Total	% correct
up	254	60	314	80.892
down	65	223	288	77.431
Total	319	283	602	79.236

Confusion matrix (testing)

from\to	down	up	Total	% correct
down	6	24	30	20.000
up	16	6	22	27.273
Total	22	30	52	23.077

Source: Based on data from Bloomberg.
Output taken directly from XLSTAT.

14.3 Feature Importance

An essential attribute of decision trees, by virtue of their underlying algorithm, is their ability to identify the most important features when predicting the target variable. This is called feature importance, and in the context of Positioning Analysis refers to identifying the trader groups whose changes best explain price direction.

Feature importance can be calculated by looking at the decrease in the average Gini score, the increase in homogeneity, of all the nodes split along a given feature, weighted by the number of observations in those nodes.

Figure 14.5 is a binary decision tree to predict whether prices of copper increased or decreased over the week based on absolute changes in MML and MMS positions over that week. The decision tree initially identifies the variable MML at the first level, followed by the variable MMS at the second level.

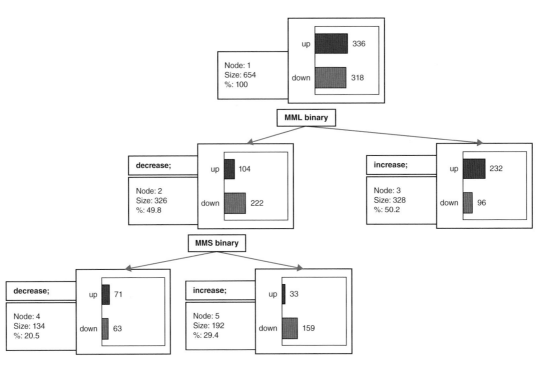

FIGURE 14.5 Decision tree based on binary input changes (MML and MMS) and binary output changes (copper prices).
Source: Based on data from Bloomberg.
Output taken directly from XLSTAT.

The Gini scores at each of the five nodes in Figure 14.5, calculated as shown in Section 14.2.2, are shown in Table 14.12.

At the first level of the tree, where the tree is split along the MML feature, the weighted average Gini score is:

$$Weighted\ Average\ Gini = \frac{(326*0.434)+(328*0.414)}{(326+328)} = 0.424$$

The decrease in Gini at this level is = 0.500 — 0.424 = 0.076. This is attributable to the MML feature.

TABLE 14.12 Gini scores.

Node number	Gini
Root Node (Node 1)	0.500
Node 2	0.434
Node 3	0.414
Node 4	0.498
Node 5	0.285

Source: Based on data from Bloomberg.
Output taken directly from XLSTAT.

At the second level, where the tree is split along the MMS feature, the weighted average Gini score is:

$$Weighted\ Average\ Gini = \frac{(134*0.498)+(192*0.285)}{(134+192)} = 0.373$$

The decrease in Gini at this level is = 0.424 — 0.373= 0.051. This is attributable to the MMS feature.

The individual feature importance is then calculated as:

$$Feature\ importance_{MML} = \frac{0.076}{0.076+0.051} = 60\%$$

$$Feature\ importance_{MML} = \frac{0.051}{0.076+0.051} = 40\%$$

14.4 Random Forests

By way of a summary: in Section 14.2, single decision trees were used to classify specific datasets. To verify the robustness, the dataset was split into a training set (602 weeks) and a testing set (52 weeks). The objective of the training set was to calibrate the model before then testing it on the testing set. Confusion matrices then report the success of the predictions in each of these datasets.

The problem with this approach is that there is the risk of overfitting, making the robustness questionable. To address overfitting issues and to increase the robustness of the decision tree approach, random forests are a satisfactory solution.

14.4.1 The Random Forest Methodology

In a random forest many different decision trees are generated. Each tree is trained on a random subset of the training dataset also using a subset of the available features.

Each of these trees is then applied to the testing data and its prediction of the target variable made. Each prediction is then averaged using a voting mechanism within the algorithm across all the trees.

For example, a random forest could be 'grown' as follows:

- 100 different subsets from the training set (with replacement) are created, each containing 100 weeks of data.[5] Each sample can include intermittent (i.e. non-consecutive) points, and because the sampling is done with replacement, a given observation may appear several times in any given sample.

---

[5] Any number for samples can be taken of any length.

- 100 different trees are then generated, each of which is trained on one of the 100 subsets. Instead of using the full set of eight features, however, each tree only uses *n* randomly selected features. Using the square root of the total number of features is widely considered to be a good value for *n*. This means that for a total set of eight features, each tree would use three randomly selected features.

- Once all the trees are trained, the forest is then applied to the testing data, with each tree in the forest making its own independent prediction. The final results are then voted upon. If, for example, 75 trees predict a price increase, and 25 predict a price decrease, the forest is then said to predict a price increase.

The usefulness of random forests, above and beyond that of decision trees, lies in the robustness of the approach and the ability to overcome overfitting. By having many different (random) trees generate independent predictions based on different subsets of the features, the variance in predictions is reduced and much of the risk in overfitting reduced. Random forests rely on the 'wisdom of crowds': individual trees (as described throughout Section 14.2) can make classification mistakes, but on average, the whole forest will make more robust and accurate predictions.

14.4.2 Random Forest Feature Importance

In the same way that feature importance is calculated for a single decision tree, the feature importance from a random forest can also be calculated. The advantage is that the results are also more robust. The feature importance from a random forest provides meaningful insight into the trader group changes that best explain price changes.

Two different measures of importance are given for each feature in the random forest. The first is based on the decrease of Gini score as described in Section 14.3. The second, called the Mean Decrease Accuracy, is based on how much the accuracy decreases when a variable is excluded.[6] The XLSTAT application uses the second method.

Figure 14.6 and Figure 14.7 show the feature importance profiles for 10 major commodities for the entire dataset between 2006 and 2018.

For crude oil (WTI), gasoline, gold, and soybean the MML group is the most important, whereas for natural gas and sugar it is the MMS group. For cotton and live cattle, the PMPUS group is the most important.

---

[6]The importance measure used in the XLSTAT application for a given variable is the mean error increase of a tree when the observed values of this variable are randomly exchanged in the OOB (out-of-bag) samples.

For each tree, the prediction error on the out-of-bag data is computed. Then the same is done after permuting each explanatory variable. The difference between the two is then averaged over all trees, and according to the choice of the user, normalised or not by the standard deviation of the differences. If the standard deviation of the differences is equal to 0 for a variable, the division is not done.

In classification, in addition to the impact of permutations on the overall error of the forest, we also measure the impact on each of the modalities of the response variable.

Source: XLSTAT help files (www.xlstat.com/).

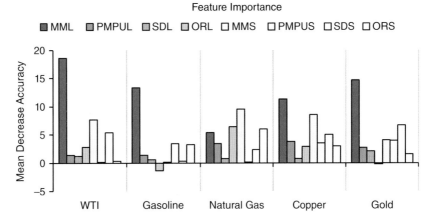

FIGURE 14.6 Feature importance (i).
This chart is not shown on the website.
Source: Based on data from Bloomberg.

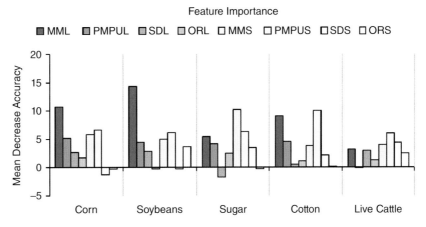

FIGURE 14.7 Feature importance (ii).
This chart is not shown on the website.
Source: Based on data from Bloomberg.

14.4.2.1 Dynamic Feature Important and Alternative Features By using a

rolling window approach, or an anchored walk forward approach, as explained in Section 8.2.4, the evolution of feature importance can be tracked over time as new data becomes available. This provides insight into shifts and changes in the market structure or in trader behaviour.

The variables included as features have so far have been focused only on changes in the directional (long and short) open interest of trader groups, but spreading data could also be included. The number of traders can also be used, either as an exclusive set of variables or in combination with the open interest variables.

More complex variables such as Concentration, Clustering, and Position Size may also be used, as defined in Section 4.1, on either an absolute basis or using rolling ranges of the data, like the Positioning Component in the OBOS framework described in Section 8.2.1. This allows for extremes in positioning to be included in the decision tree as features.

Feature importance can be a compelling way of identifying new patterns and relationships in positioning that can help improve how other positioning signals, indicators, and models are interpreted and used.

14.5 Using ML to Trade

In each of the sections in this chapter, the price (output) variable has always been contemporaneous to the positioning (input) variables as the objective of the approach has been entirely analytically driven. ML has been used to uncover relationships between changes in positioning and changes in commodity prices – specifically, as described at the outset of the chapter, which aspects of positioning are most useful in helping to understand commodity markets from a machine-learning perspective.

Having the price variables contemporaneous to the positioning variables means the model is not directly tradeable. Naturally the insights revealed in Section 14.4.2, for example, can be used to enhance and improve trading strategies based on positioning data, but the results have not been generated from a tradeable framework.

The data release schedule of COT positioning data is fully explained in Section 3.3.1, but to summarise, positioning data is released every Friday (with all CFTC related data after the market close and ICE COT data just before the market close) and refers to the previous Tuesday. Changes in positioning in this chapter run from Tuesday to Tuesday and the price changes have been set to the same schedule also.

To make the relationship tradeable, the price information in the decision tree needs to be changed from Tuesday to Tuesday to the following Monday to Monday. This is because the COT data is released on Friday, mostly after the market closes, and the earliest opportunity to trade is Monday.

Table 14.13 and Table 14.14 are like the tree structure in Table 14.8 and confusion matrix in Table 14.9, except the decision tree now predicts whether prices of natural gas increased or decreased based on the following week, running from Monday to Monday, but still based on changes in positioning from the previous week. Simply, when the positioning data is released on the Friday (for the previous Tuesday) the algorithm predicts whether prices will rise (fall) in the upcoming Monday to Monday period.

In having shifted the price data, this now makes the model 'tradeable', allowing any trades to be placed on the close on Monday night.[7]

---

[7]The trades can be placed at any time on a Monday, but the final settlement price of the day is used as this is tradeable (via futures executes at TAS (Trade at Settlement) or via S&P GSCI or BCOM excess return indices) and no estimates for slippage need to be factored into account. Whilst the model has been trained to predict prices over the full week Monday to Monday, trade can naturally be exited earlier, and the model can also be configured for shorter price periods – for example over a single day.

TABLE 14.13 Tree structure based on binary input changes (all groups) and absolute output changes (natural gas prices) – training dataset 602 weeks, testing dataset 52 weeks.

Tree structure

Nodes	Objects	%	Improvement	Purity	Split variable	Values	Predicted values
Node 1	602	100.00%	5.460	51.99%			
Node 2	127	21.10%	4.341	61.42%	PMPUL	<= -5,746.5	1
Node 3	475	78.90%	4.447	55.58%	PMPUL	> -5,746.5	1
Node 6	470	78.07%	3.489	56.17%	SDL	<= 23,064	3
Node 7	5	0.83%		100.00%	SDL	> 23,064	3
Node 12	7	1.16%		100.00%	ORL	<= -13,033	6
Node 13	463	76.91%		57.02%	ORL	> -13,033	6

Source: Based on data from Bloomberg.
Output taken directly from XLSTAT.

TABLE 14.14 Confusion matrix based on binary input changes (all groups) and absolute output changes (natural gas prices) – training dataset 602 weeks, testing dataset 52 weeks.

Confusion matrix (training)

from\to	up	down	Total	% correct
up	264	49	313	84.345
down	199	90	289	31.142
Total	463	139	602	58.804

Confusion matrix (testing)

from\to	up	down	Total	% correct
up	18	10	28	64.286
down	14	10	24	41.667
Total	32	20	52	53.846

Source: Based on data from Bloomberg.
Output taken directly from XLSTAT.

Interestingly, the tree structure in Table 14.13 shows the addition of four more nodes due to having shifted the price data. Different features throughout the tree are also seen compared to Table 14.8, which highlights the significance of the change.

The Confusion matrix in Table 14.14 shows a large deterioration in performance, due to the lag in the price data. Table 14.14 shows 58.80% of points in the training dataset are classified correctly, but falling to 53.84% for the testing dataset. Similar deteriorations are seen for other commodities and at this level the success of the model is close to being random.

Extending this single tree to a random forest framework also does not improve the results. Importantly, this suggests that ML as a trading tool based on Positioning data used in this way is unsatisfactory. The requirement to lag the price data to make the model tradeable reduces the performance of the results significantly.

It is important to understand that the performance of ML in a tradeable framework in no way renders ML an ineffective tool for analysis.

On the contrary, ML can be highly effective in identifying new patterns and relationships in the data that would be extremely challenging to identify through other channels. As mentioned above, ML can help improve how other positioning signals, indicators, and models are interpreted and used.

Reference

Mark Keenan, Michael Haigh, David Schenck, and Malavika Dinaker (2018), 'Commodity Compass – A Machine-learning Perspective on Commodity Positioning'. Société Générale (SG) Cross Asset Research – Commodities Group. www.sgmarkets.com/.

History of the COT Report

The following information has been directly extracted from the relevant websites to ensure accuracy and completeness:

www.cftc.gov/marketreports/commitmentsoftraders/cot_about.

Antecedents of the Commitments of Traders (COT) reports can be traced all the way back to 1924. In that year, the US Department of Agriculture's Grain Futures Administration (the predecessor of the USDA Commodity Exchange Authority, and in turn the predecessor of the CFTC) published its first comprehensive annual report of hedging and speculation in regulated futures markets.

Beginning as of 30 June 1962, COT data were published each month. At the time, this report for 13 agricultural commodities was proclaimed as 'another step forward in the policy of providing the public with current and basic data on futures market operations'. Those original reports then were compiled on an end-of-month basis and published on the 11th or 12th calendar day of the following month.

Over the years, the CFTC has improved the Commitments of Traders reports in several ways as part of its continuing effort to better inform the public about futures markets.

- The COT report is published more often – switching to mid-month and month-end in 1990, to every two weeks in 1992, and to weekly in 2000.

- The COT report is released more quickly – moving the publication to the sixth business day after the 'as of' date in 1990 and then to the third business day after the 'as of' date in 1992.

- The report includes more information – adding data on the numbers of traders in each category, a crop-year breakout, and concentration ratios in the early 1970s; data on option positions in 1995; and a Supplemental report in 2007 showing positions of Index Traders in selected agricultural markets.

- The report also is more widely available – moving from a subscription-based mailing list to fee-based electronic access in 1993, and, as of 1995, becoming freely available on CFTC.gov.

The COT reports provide a breakdown of each Tuesday's open interest for markets in which 20 or more traders hold positions equal to or above the reporting levels established by the CFTC. The weekly reports for Futures-Only Commitments of Traders and for Futures-and-Options-Combined Commitments of Traders are released every Friday at 3.30 p.m. Eastern time.

Reports are available in both a short and long format. The short report shows open interest separately by reportable and non-reportable positions. For reportable positions, additional data is provided for commercial and non-commercial holdings, spreading, changes from the previous report, percents of open interest by category, and numbers of traders.

The long report, in addition to the information in the short report, also groups the data by crop year, where appropriate, and shows the concentration of positions held by the largest four and eight traders. The Supplemental report is published for Futures-and-Options-Combined in selected agricultural markets and, in addition to showing all the information in the short format, shows positions of Index Traders.

Current and historical Commitments of Traders data is available on CFTC.gov, as is historical COT data going back to 1986 for Futures-Only reports, to 1995 for Option-and-Futures-Combined reports, and to 2006 for the Supplemental report.

The COT Reports

The CFTC COT report

The following information has been directly extracted from the relevant websites to ensure accuracy and completeness:

www.cftc.gov/MarketReports/CommitmentsofTraders/index.htm.

Commitments of Traders

The Commitments of Traders (COT) reports provide a breakdown of each Tuesday's open interest for markets in which 20 or more traders hold positions equal to or above the reporting levels established by the CFTC.

Please see the official Release Schedule for a calendar of release dates.

Reports are available in both a short and long format. The short report shows open interest separately by reportable and non-reportable positions. For reportable positions, additional data is provided for commercial and non-commercial holdings, spreading, changes from the previous report, percentages of open interest by category, and numbers of traders.

The long report, in addition to the information in the short report, groups the data by crop year, where appropriate, and shows the concentration of positions held by the largest four and eight traders.

Supplemental reports show aggregate futures and option positions of Non-commercial, Commercial, and Index Traders in 12 selected agricultural commodities

History of Disaggregated COT data – 20 October 2009

CFTC will make available more than three years of history of disaggregated data included in the weekly Commitments of Traders (COT) reports. History for the 22 commodity futures markets currently contained in the weekly disaggregated COT reports, first published on 4 September 2009, will be available starting Tuesday, 20 October 2009.

Machine-readable files will be located on the CFTC website, with data dating back to 13 June 2006. One type is a zipped, comma-delimited text file Historical Compressed; whilst the other type is a zipped Excel file, Historical Compressed. In addition, the three-year history will be available in a 'viewable' file on the CFTC website, by commodity group, and, within group, by commodity.

Historical Viewables: These viewable files will only be available in the 'long format'.

Please note: CFTC does not maintain a history of large-trader classifications. Therefore, current classifications are used to classify the historical positions of each reportable trader (this approach is commonly referred to as 'backcasting'; see the D-COT Explanatory Notes at Disaggregated Explanatory Notes.

Explanatory Notes

Open Interest

Open interest is the total of all futures and/or option contracts entered into and not yet offset by a transaction, by delivery, by exercise, etc. The aggregate of all long open interest is equal to the aggregate of all short open interest.

Open interest held or controlled by a trader is referred to as that trader's position. For the COT Futures-and-Options-Combined report, option open interest and traders' option positions are computed on a futures-equivalent basis using delta factors supplied by the exchanges. Long-call and short-put open interest are converted to long futures-equivalent open interest. Likewise, short-call and long-put open interest are converted to short futures-equivalent open interest. For example, a trader holding a long put position of 500 contracts with a delta factor of 0.50 is considered to be holding a short futures-equivalent position of 250 contracts. A trader's long and short futures-equivalent positions are added to the trader's long and short futures positions to give 'combined-long' and 'combined-short' positions. Open interest, as reported to the Commission and as used in the COT report, does not include open futures contracts against which notices of deliveries have been stopped by a trader or issued by the clearing organisation of an exchange.

Reportable Positions

Clearing members, futures commission merchants, and foreign brokers (collectively called 'reporting firms') file daily reports with the Commission. Those reports show the futures and option positions of traders that hold positions above specific reporting levels set by CFTC regulations. If, at the daily market close, a reporting firm has a trader with a position at or above the Commission's reporting level in any single futures month or option expiration, it reports that trader's entire position in all futures and options expiration months in that commodity, regardless of size. The aggregate of all traders' positions reported to the Commission usually represents 70 to 90 % of the total open interest in any given market. From time to time, the Commission will raise or lower the reporting levels in specific markets to strike a balance between collecting sufficient information to oversee the markets and minimising the reporting burden on the futures industry.

Commercial and Non-commercial Traders

When an individual reportable trader is identified to the Commission, the trader is classified either as 'commercial' or 'non-commercial'. All of a trader's reported futures positions in a commodity are classified as commercial if the trader uses futures contracts in that particular commodity for hedging as defined in CFTC Regulation 1.3, 17 CFR 1.3(z). A trading entity generally gets classified as a 'commercial' trader by filing a statement with the Commission, on CFTC Form 40: Statement of Reporting Trader, that it is commercially '. . . engaged in business activities hedged by the use of the futures or option markets.' To ensure that traders are classified with accuracy and consistency, Commission staff may exercise judgement in re-classifying a trader if it has additional information about the trader's use of the markets. A trader may be classified as a commercial trader in some commodities and as a non-commercial trader in other commodities. A single trading entity cannot be classified as both a commercial and non-commercial trader in the same commodity. Nonetheless, a multifunctional organisation that has more than one trading entity may have each trading entity classified separately in a commodity. For example, a financial organisation trading in financial futures may have a banking entity whose positions are classified as commercial and have a separate money-management entity whose positions are classified as non-commercial.

Non-reportable Positions

The long and short open interest shown as 'Non-reportable Positions' is derived by subtracting total long and short 'Reportable Positions' from the total open interest. Accordingly, for 'Non-reportable Positions', the number of traders involved and the commercial/non-commercial classification of each trader are unknown.

Spreading

For the futures-only report, spreading measures the extent to which each non-commercial trader holds equal long and short futures positions. For the options-and-futures-combined report, spreading measures the extent to which each non-commercial trader holds equal combined-long and combined-short positions. For example, if a non-commercial trader in Eurodollar futures holds 2,000 long contracts and 1,500 short contracts, 500 contracts will appear in the 'Long' category, and 1,500 contracts will appear in the 'Spreading' category. These figures do not include intermarket spreading, such as spreading Eurodollar futures against Treasury Note futures. Also see the 'Old and Other Futures' section below.

Changes in Commitments from Previous Reports

Changes represent the differences between the data for the current Report date and the data published in the previous report.

Percentage of Open Interest

Percentages are calculated against the total open interest for the futures-only report and against the total futures-equivalent open interest for the options-and-futures-combined report. Percentages less than 0.05 are shown as 0.0; and because of rounding, percentages may not total 100.0.

Number of Traders

To determine the total number of reportable traders in a market, a trader is counted only once whether or not the trader appears in more than one category (non-commercial traders may be long or short only and may be spreading; commercial traders may be long and short). To determine the number of traders in each category, however, a trader is counted in each category in which the trader holds a position. The sum of the numbers of traders in each category, therefore, will often exceed the number of traders in that market.

Old and Other Futures (Long Form Only)

For selected commodities where there is a well-defined marketing season or crop year, the COT data is broken down by 'old' and 'other' crop years. The 'Major Markets for Which the COT Data Is Shown by Crop Year' table (shown below) lists those commodities and the first and last futures of the marketing season or crop year. In order not to disclose positions in a single future near its expiration, on the first business day of the month of the last future in an 'old' crop year, the data for that last future is combined with the data for the next crop year and is shown as 'old' crop futures. An example is CBOT wheat, where the first month of the crop year is July and the last month of the prior crop year is May. On 3 May 2004, positions in the May 2004 futures month were aggregated with positions in the July 2004 through May 2005 futures months and shown as 'old' crop futures. Positions in all subsequent wheat futures months were shown as 'other'.

Market	First Future (new crop)	Last Future (old crop)
CBOT wheat	July	May
CBOT corn	December	September
CBOT oats	July	May
CBOT soybeans	September	August
CBOT soybean oil	October	September
CBOT soybean meal	October	September
CBOT rough rice	September	July
KCBT wheat	July	May
MGE wheat	September	July
CME lean hogs	December	October
CME frozen pork bellies	February	August
NYBT cocoa	December	September
NYBT coffee C	December	September
NYBT cotton No.2	October	July
NYBT frozen conc OJ	January	November

For the 'old' and 'other' figures, spreading is calculated for equal long and short positions within a crop year. If a non-commercial trader holds a long position in an 'old' crop-year future and an equal short position in an 'other' crop-year future, the long position will be classified as 'long-only' in the 'old' crop year and the short position will be classified as 'short-only' in the 'other' crop year. In this example, in the 'all' category, which considers each trader's positions without regard to crop year, that trader's positions will be classified as 'spreading'. For this reason, summing the 'old' and 'other' figures for long-only, for short-only, or for spreading will not necessarily equal the corresponding figure shown for 'all' futures. Any differences result from traders that spread from an 'old' crop-year future to an 'other' crop-year future.

Concentration Ratios (Long Form Only)

The report shows the percentages of open interest held by the largest four and eight reportable traders, without regard to whether they are classified as commercial or non-commercial. The concentration ratios are shown with trader positions computed on a gross long and gross short basis and on a net long or net short basis. The 'Net Position' ratios are computed after offsetting each trader's equal long and short positions. A reportable trader with relatively large, balanced long and short positions in a single market, therefore, may be among the four and eight largest traders in both the gross long and gross short categories, but will probably not be included among the four and eight largest traders on a net basis.

Supplemental Report

Based on the information contained in the report of futures and options combined in the short format, the Supplemental report shows an additional category of 'Index Traders' in selected agricultural markets. These traders are drawn from the non-commercial and commercial categories. The non-commercial category includes positions of managed funds, pension funds, and other investors that are mostly seeking exposure to a broad index of commodity prices as an asset class in an unleveraged and passively-managed manner. The commercial category includes positions for entities whose trading predominantly reflects hedging of over-the-counter transactions involving commodity indices — for example, a swap dealer holding long futures positions to hedge a short commodity index exposure opposite institutional traders, such as pension funds.

All of these traders — whether coming from the non-commercial or commercial categories — are typically replicating a commodity index by establishing long futures positions in the component markets and then rolling those positions forward from future to future using a fixed methodology. Some traders assigned to the Index Traders category are engaged in other futures activity that could not be disaggregated. As a result, the Index Traders category, which is typically made up of traders with long-only futures positions replicating an index, will include some long and short positions where traders have multidimensional trading activities, the preponderance of which is index trading. Likewise, the Index Traders category will not include some traders who are engaged in index trading, but for whom it does not represent a substantial part of their overall trading activity.

Disaggregated Commitments of Traders Report Explanatory Notes

The Commodity Futures Trading Commission (Commission) began publishing a Disaggregated Commitments of Traders (Disaggregated COT) report on 4 September 2009. The first iteration of the report covered 22 major physical commodity markets; on 4 December 2009, the remaining physical commodity markets were included.

The Disaggregated COT report increases transparency from the legacy COT reports by separating traders into the following four categories of traders: Producer/Merchant/Processor/User; Swap Dealers; Managed Money; and Other Reportables. The legacy COT report separates reportable traders only into 'commercial' and 'non-commercial' categories.

The Disaggregated COT report is being published side-by-side with the legacy COT formats at least through the end of 2019. The Commission is soliciting comment on the new report and will review whether to continue to publish both side-by-side or to replace the legacy report with the new report.

All of the COT reports provide a breakdown of each Tuesday's open interest for markets in which 20 or more traders hold positions equal to or above the reporting levels established by the CFTC. The reports are published in futures-only formats as well as futures-and-options-combined formats. The data is available in both a short format and a long format.

This initiative for providing market transparency arises from the recommendation to disaggregate the existing 'commercial' category in the Commission's September 2008 Staff Report on Commodity Swap Dealers & Index Traders. Specifically, that report recommended:

Remove Swap Dealer from Commercial Category and Create New Swap Dealer Classification for Reporting Purposes: In order to provide for increased transparency of the exchange-traded futures and options markets, the Commission has instructed the staff to develop a proposal to enhance and improve the CFTC's weekly Commitments of Traders Report by including more delineated trader classification categories beyond commercial and non-commercial, which may include at a minimum the addition of a separate category identifying the trading of swap dealers.

The Disaggregated Commitments of Traders Report

The Commission, by regulation, collects confidential daily large-trader data as part of its market surveillance programme. The data, which also support the legacy COT report, is separated into the following categories:

- 'Producer/Merchant/Processor/User';
- 'Swap Dealers';
- 'Managed Money'; and
- 'Other Reportables'.

Trader Classification

Staff use Form 40 data and, where appropriate, conversations with a trader and other data available to the Commission regarding a trader's market activities to make a judgement on each trader's appropriate classification.

Some multiservice or multifunctional organisations have centralised their futures trading. In such cases, their Form 40 may show more than one of the new categories. Division of Market Oversight staff place each reportable trader in the most appropriate category based on their predominant activity. In most cases, the choice of category is clear, but in some cases, judgement must be exercised by Commission staff as to what is a trader's predominant activity.

Some parent organisations set up separately reportable trading entities to handle their different businesses or locations. In such cases, each of these entities files a separate Form 40 and is analysed separately for determining that entity's proper Disaggregated COT classification.

A trader's classifications may change over a period of time for a number of reasons. A trader may change the different ways it uses the markets, may trade additional or fewer commodities, and may find that its client base evolves. These changes may lead to changes in classifications and categories and/or changes in the commodities to which a trader's various classifications apply. Moreover, a trader's classification may change because the Commission has received additional information about the trader.

Content of the Disaggregated Commitments of Traders Report

- **Producer/Merchant/Processor/User (PMPU)**

  A 'producer/merchant/processor/user' is an entity that predominantly engages in the production, processing, packing, or handling of a physical commodity and uses the futures markets to manage or hedge risks associated with those activities.

- **Swap Dealer (SD)**

  A 'swap dealer' is an entity that deals primarily in swaps for a commodity and uses the futures markets to manage or hedge the risk associated with those swaps transactions. The swap dealer's counterparties may be speculative traders, like hedge funds, or traditional commercial clients that are managing risk arising from their dealings in the physical commodity.

- **Money Manager (MM)**

  A 'money manager', for the purpose of this report, is a registered commodity trading advisor (CTA); a registered commodity pool operator (CPO); or an unregistered fund identified by CFTC. These traders are engaged in managing and conducting organised futures trading on behalf of clients.

- **Other Reportables**

  Every other reportable trader that is not placed into one of the other three categories is placed into the 'other reportables' category.

Spreading

The Disaggregated COT sets out open interest by long, short, and spreading for the three categories of traders – 'swap dealers,' 'managed money', and 'other reportable'. For the 'producer/merchant/processor/user' category, open interest is reported only by long or short positions. 'Spreading' is a computed amount equal to offsetting long and short positions held by a trader. The computed amount of spreading is calculated as the amount of offsetting futures in different calendar months or offsetting futures and options in the same or different calendar months. Any residual long or short position is reported in the long or short column. Intermarket spreads are not considered.

Numbers of Traders

The sum of the numbers of traders in each separate category typically exceeds the total number of reportable traders. This results from the fact that, in the 'swap dealers', 'managed money', and 'other reportables' categories, 'spreading' can be a partial activity, so the same trader can fall into either the outright 'long' or 'short' trader count, as well as into the 'spreading' count. Additionally, a reportable 'producer/merchant/processor/user' may be in both the long and the short position columns. In order to preserve the confidentiality of traders, for any given commodity where a specific category has fewer than four active traders, the size of the relevant positions will be provided, but the trader count will be suppressed (specifically, a '·' will appear for trader counts of fewer than four traders).

Historical Data

Historical data for the Disaggregated COT report are available back to 13 June 2006. Note that CFTC does not maintain a history of large-trader classifications, so recent classifications had to be used to classify the historical positions of each reportable trader. Due to shifts in trader classifications over time (as discussed above), this 'backcasting' approach diminishes the data's accuracy as it goes further back in time. Nonetheless, the data back as far as 2006 should be reasonably representative of trader classifications over that period.

Potential Limitations of the Data

Commission staff review the reasonableness of a trader's classification for many of the largest traders in the markets based upon Form 40 disclosures and other information available to the Commission. As described above, the actual placement of a trader in a particular classification based upon their predominant business activity may involve some exercise of judgement on the part of Commission staff. Some traders being classified in the 'swap dealers' category engage in some commercial activities in the physical commodity or have counterparties that do so. Likewise, some traders classified in the 'producer/merchant/processor/user' category engage in some swaps activity. Moreover, it has always been true that the staff classifies traders, not their trading activity. Staff will generally know, for example, that a trader is a 'producer/merchant/processor/user' but we cannot know with certainty that all of that trader's activity is hedging. Staff is working on improvements to the Form 40 and other methodologies in order to improve the accuracy of the trader classifications. When large reporting or classification issues are found, an announcement is made and corrections are published as quickly as possible.

Comparison of the Disaggregated Commitments of Traders Report to the Legacy Commitments of Traders Report and the Commodity Index Trader Supplement to the COT Report

The legacy COT reports divide reportable traders into the two broad categories of 'commercial' and 'non-commercial'. The 'commercial' trader category has always included producers, merchants, processors and users of the physical commodity who manage their business risks by hedging. It has also included swap dealers that may have incurred a risk in the over-the-counter (OTC) market and then offset that risk in the futures markets, regardless of whether their OTC counterparty was a commercial trader or a speculator. Those two categories of what has been reported as 'commercial' traders are separately reported in the Disaggregated COT. The 'non-commercial' category of the legacy COT included professional money managers (CTAs, CPOs, and hedge funds) as well as a wide array of other non-commercial (speculative) traders. These two categories of what has been reported as 'non-commercial' traders are separately reported as 'money managers' and 'other reportables' in the Disaggregated COT.

The commodity index trader (CIT) supplement to the COT has been published for 12 agricultural commodities since January 2007. There is some relationship between 'index traders' positions in that supplement and 'swap dealer' positions in the Disaggregated COT, but there are specific differences. The 'swap dealer' category of the Disaggregated COT includes some swap dealers that do no commodity index business and are, therefore, not in the Index Traders category of the CIT Supplemental. Also, the 'index trader' category of the CIT supplement includes pension and other investment funds that place their index investment directly into the futures markets rather than going through a swap dealer. Those traders are classified as 'managed money' or 'other reportables' in the Disaggregated COT, depending on the specific details of their business and trading.

The ICE COT Report

The ICE Futures Europe Commitments of Traders (COT) report provides a breakdown of open interest in certain of the Exchange's commodities according to the category of trader holding the position. The Exchange publishes the reports to increase the transparency of the participation in its markets.

The reports are designed to be as similar in format and content as possible to the established US Commodity Futures Trading Commission Commitments of Traders reports. ICE Futures Europe COT reports use the same format as the CFTC Long Format Disaggregated COT, as this provides the most information about traders' participation in the market (www.theice.com/publicdocs/futures/CoT_Notes.pdf).

Basis of Report

The report is generated and published on a weekly basis for the position data reported to the Exchange for the Tuesday of each week. The Exchange currently publishes its report on the Monday of the following week (subject to US Federal holidays). For each commodity reported on, two reports are produced – one containing data on futures positions in the commodity only, and another containing futures positions combined with options positions (option positions are converted to delta futures-equivalent positions).

Report Formats

The report is available in two formats:

- Each commodity reported has two pdf files generated weekly, one for the futures-only and another for the combined futures and options report.

- All commodities reported are combined into a single csv format file, with separate lines for futures and combined reports per commodity. The formatting of the csv file follows the format for the comma separated version of the CFTC COT to allow existing systems to process the information with the minimum of changes. Details of fields can be found at: www.theice.com/publicdocs/futures/CoT_Fields.pdf.

Report Contents

ICE Futures Europe requires market participants to report positions according to the reportable thresholds set out in:

www.theice.com/publicdocs/futures/ICE_Futures_Europe_Threshold.pdf.

However, in order to provide as much consistency as possible with the CFTC COT reports, the Exchange generates its COT reports to match the CFTC's own reporting thresholds for oil products as closely as possible. Traders who are to be included in the Exchange COT, therefore, must hold positions that exceed the following thresholds:

ICE Commodity Code	ICE Commodity	COT inclusion threshold	Comments
T	ICE crude oil (WTI) Crude Futures and Options	350 contracts	Directly defined by CFTC – 'Crude Oil, Sweet'
B	ICE Brent Crude Futures and Options	350 contracts	Closest CFTC equivalent 'Crude Oil, Sweet'
G	ICE Gas Oil Futures and Options	250 contracts	Closest CFTC equivalent 'No. 2 Heating Oil'
C	Cocoa Futures and Options	100 contracts	
W	White Sugar Futures and Options	100 contracts	
RC	Robusta Coffee Futures and Options	100 contracts	
T	Wheat Futures and Options	100 contracts	

The thresholds apply to individual months but trigger inclusion of all positions – as soon as a trader has a position in one month that crosses the reportable threshold, all of its positions for that commodity become reportable in the COT.

For example, Trader one has positions of 349 contracts in Sep11, Oct11, Nov11, Dec11 Brent and no other positions – they will not be included in the COT.

Trader two has positions of 10 contracts in Sep11, Oct11, Nov11 Brent and 351 contracts in Dec11 Brent – all of Trader 2's positions will be included in the COT.

Sections of the Report

Each report is divided into two main sections:

■ a section breaking down open interest by category of trader; and

■ a section showing the concentration of open interest held by the four and eight largest traders in a market regardless of categorisation (ICE Energy Contracts Only).

The Exchange will determine classifications based on all available information. The categories used by the Exchange are defined similarly to those used by the CFTC, and are as follows:

■ **Producer/Merchant/Processor/User** – Entities with exposure to the underlying physical market for the commodity which use the futures market to hedge the risks associated with such exposure. 'Commercial' participants. Examples would include oil exploration and drilling firms, specialist commodity trading firms with physical exposures, producers, exporters/importers, coffee roasters, cocoa processors, sugar refiners, food and confectionary manufacturers, millers, crushers. Utility companies who consume oil to generate power.

- **Swap Dealer** – Entities dealing primarily in 'swap' or other over-the-counter ('OTC') transactions in the commodity in question and who use the futures market to hedge this exposure. Examples would include investment banks and other complex financial institutions.

- **Managed Money** – Entities managing futures trading on behalf of clients; investment firms. Examples include hedge funds, pension funds, registered US commodity trading advisors, or commodity pool operators.

- **Other Reportables** – Every other reportable trader. Examples would include proprietary (multi-asset) trading houses, algorithmic traders, and local traders.

- **Non-reportable Positions** – This is a balancing figure and consists of the total reportable long, short, and spreading positions subtracted from the overall open interest figure for the commodity.

'Spreading' and Numbers of Traders

In accordance with CFTC practice, positions for categories other than Producer/Merchant /Processor/User are set out in the report using a 'spreading' algorithm which sets out the number of offsetting positions held in different calendar months (or the same calendar month in the case of an offsetting option position) by a trader. As an example, if Trader one (a Swap Dealer) was long 750 Nov11 Gas Oil and short 1,100 Dec11 Gas Oil, their position would be included in the COT as Long 0, Short 350, Spreading 750.

This may have the effect that the sum of the number of traders in each category may exceed the total number of traders in the market. Traders may fall into both the 'Long' or 'Short' and the 'Spreading' columns of the report and hence be in effect counted twice. Commercial participants may also be both 'Long' and 'Short'.

Information Contained in the Section

The numbers below refer to the callouts in the sample COT image shown in Figure 1 (Figure 1 is only available in the pdf, downloaded from the website (https://www.theice.com/publicdocs /futures/CoT_Notes.pdf)):

Positions – Positions reported as described above, including total open interest and non-reportable positions balancing figure.

Percentages – Percentage of total open interest in each category. Rounding issues may mean that the sum of all individual percentages may not equal 100%.

Number of traders – Number of traders in each category as described above.

'Old' and 'Other' Rows

Please note that the 'Old' and 'Other' rows are included for compatibility with the CFTC COT reports only. They are used by the CFTC for certain agricultural commodities but have no utility in ICE Futures Europe markets. The 'Old' rows will never be anything other than duplicate values of the 'All' rows; the 'Other' rows will never be anything other than zero/blank.

The ICE Futures Europe Energy Contracts reports set out the percentage of open interest held by the four and eight largest reportable traders irrespective of categorisation. The data is displayed on both a gross and net position basis. Traders with large but balanced positions (i.e. large positions on both long and short sides) will probably appear in both the long and short gross top four/eight, but not in the long and short net sections.